Garden Learning: A Study on European Botanic Gardens' Collaborative Learning Processes

Habilitation Monograph April 2014

Suzanne Kapelari

]u[

ubiquity press
London

Published by
Ubiquity Press Ltd.
6 Windmill Street
London W1T 2JB
www.ubiquitypress.com

Text © Suzanne Kapelari 2015

First published 2015

Cover design by Amber MacKay
Images used in the cover design were sourced from Pixabay and are licensed under CC0 Public Domain.
Main cover image: *StockSnap*
Background cover image: *smdesigns*

Printed in the UK by Lightning Source Ltd.
Print and digital versions typeset by Siliconchips Services Ltd.

ISBN (Paperback): 978-1-909188-63-1
ISBN (PDF): 978-1-909188-64-8
ISBN (EPub): 978-1-909188-65-5
ISBN (Kindle): 978-1-909188-66-2

DOI: http://dx.doi.org/10.5334/bas

This work is licensed under the Creative Commons Attribution 4.0 International License. To view a copy of this license, visit http://creativecommons.org/licenses/by/4.0/ or send a letter to Creative Commons, 444 Castro Street, Suite 900, Mountain View, California, 94041, USA. This license allows for copying any part of the work for personal and commercial use, providing author attribution is clearly stated.

The full text of this book has been peer-reviewed to ensure high academic standards. For full review policies, see http://www.ubiquitypress.com/

Suggested citation:
Kapelari, S 2015 *Garden Learning: A Study on European Botanic Gardens' Collaborative Learning Processes*. London: Ubiquity Press. DOI: http://dx.doi.org/10.5334/bas. License: CC-BY 4.0

This project has received funding from the European Union's Seventh Framework Programme for research, technological development and demonstration under grant agreement no 266616.

To read the online open access version of this book, either visit http://dx.doi.org/10.5334/bas or scan this QR code with your mobile device:

Contents

Abstract	v
Acknowledgement	vi
1. Introduction	1
1.1 Towards good practice in science teaching	1
1.2 Collaborative learning at botanic gardens	2
1.3 Finding a common ground	3
1.4 Overview of my work	6
1.5 Implications	7
2. Part A – Theoretical Framework	9
2.1 What is Science?	10
2.1.1 Nature of Knowledge?	11
2.1.2 The Body of Scientific Knowledge	13
2.1.3 The Science Processes and Methods	14
2.2 Selected Theories of Learning	15
2.2.1 Constructivist Learning	16
2.2.2 The Socio-Cultural Perspective of Learning	16
2.2.3 Situated Learning	18
2.2.4 Organisational Learning	22
2.2.5 Expansive Learning	24
2.3 Science Education in the 21st Century	31
2.3.1 The Concept of Scientific Literacy	31
2.3.2 Improving Science Education	43
2.3.3 Inquiry Based Science Education (IBSE)	48

    2.4 Alternative Places for Learning Science   57
        2.4.1 Learning Outside the Classroom (LOtC)   57
        2.4.2 Learning at Botanic Gardens   70
    2.5 Professional Science Teaching   75
        2.5.1 Teaching Paradigms   75
        2.5.2 Science Teaching as a Profession   79
        2.5.3 Continuous Professional Development (CPD)   86
    2.6 Design Based Research Informs Practice   97

3. Part B – Putting Theory into Practice   **101**

    3.1 The INQUIRE Project: 102
        3.1.1 The INQUIRE Idea   103
        3.1.2 The INQUIRE Framework   103
        3.1.3 The INQUIRE Network   104
        3.1.4 The INQUIRE Design   105
        3.1.5 IBST in INQUIRE   110
        3.1.5 The INQUIRE Proposal   110
        3.1.6 INQUIRE Outcomes   126
    3.2 The INQUIRE Case Study   133
        3.2.1 Rational   133
        3.2.2 Methodology   134
        3.2.3 Case Study Findings   142

4. Discussion and Conclusion   **157**

    4.1 Discussion   157
    4.2 Conclusion   167
    4.3 Future perspectives   168

5. References   **169**

6. Lists of Figures and Tables   **187**

Abstract

Current science education reform initiatives require fundamental changes in how science is taught not only inside but also outside the classroom. Thus formal and informal learning institutions are being challenged to engage in alternative ways of teaching science inside and outside the classroom.

The EU FP7 funded INQUIRE project: 'Inquiry based teacher training for a sustainable future' (EU Nr. 266616, 17 Partners; total budget € 2,3 Mio) was developed and implemented to support 14 Botanic Gardens and Natural History Museums in 11 European countries in establishing an international collaborative learning network. It also aimed to expand their understanding of inquiry based science teaching (IBST) whilst developing, implementing, assessing and revising an in-service teacher and botanic garden educators training courses on site. Partner organisations were asked to make their tacit knowledge explicit, share this knowledge and adopt positive attitudes towards both theory-based instruction and reflective practice as tools for improving their educational programmes. Cultural psychology design based research was applied to learn more about how international educational reform based projects need to be structured and implemented in order to become successful in implementing change in educational practice.

The first part of this work provides insight into the complex interplay of different theoretical aspects that informed the design, the structure and the implementation of the INQUIRE project. The second part is dedicated to a case study that gives insight into what partners learn while participating in such a collaborative expansive knowledge creation process and how this knowledge is finally embedded in organisational practice. 'Expansive Learning Theory' places an emphasis on communities as learners, on transformation and creation of culture, on horizontal movement and hybridisation and on the formation of theoretical concepts. The expansive cycle of learning proved to be a useful framework for structuring the learning processes in the INQUIRE network and shows good potential to support organisational development. It is also a useful framework for analysing how organisational learning processes take place in diverse cultural learning communities and for understanding and supporting practices where people create and develop useful and reusable resources in collaboration.

Acknowledgement

For Georg Antonia, Felix Johanna Timo

Thank you to Gail Bromley, MBE FLS for proofreading this book.

The INQUIRE Management Board: Costantino Bonomi, Gail Bromley, Justin Dillon, Elaine Regan, Asimina Vergou, Julia Willison, for all the fruitful discussions while work was in progress and their enthusiasm in maintaining the project.

The INQUIRE partners for the enthusiastic engagement in this expansive learning process.

The European Commission for funding the project and this publication Dr. Maria Korda for supporting the project as scientific project officer.

The University of Innsbruck for their support during the habilitation process.

1. Introduction

1.1 Towards good practice in science teaching

'There is little doubt that, in developing student interests and motivations towards science and technology and allowing them to become familiar with the fast-advancing developments in this area, it is essential that science education is part of the curriculum from an early age. [. . .] Science education should form a key part of the primary curriculum. But in recognising that students at this age are unable (and unmotivated) to cope with abstract ideas and tend to gain much from personal involvement activities, the 'hands-on' science education provided is easily accepted by students. Through this approach, it is easy to motivate and interest both boys and girls. This has been shown extensively by science centres across Europe, where the majority of visitors tend to be young children coming either as school groups or accompanied by their parents' (EU Commission, 2004, p. X).

Ever since the first 'Programme for International Student Assessment' (PISA) focused on science and mathematics performance in 2006, international comparative studies of educational systems have raised concerns about teaching and learning science and mathematics in schools, not only amongst policy makers but the general public. While PISA followed a long tradition of such studies which have been undertaken since the 1950s, such as the Trends in International Mathematics and Science Study (TIMSS, 1995 onwards) or The Relevance of Science Education survey (ROSE), the PISA 2006 survey confirmed a major concern which had been raised by science education experts some years beforehand. Not only did pupils' performance, knowledge and understanding of science appear to be on a much lower level than one would wish for, students also showed less interest and engagement in science or

---

How to cite this book chapter:
Kapelari, S. 2015. Introduction. In: Kapelari, S *Garden Learning: A Study on European Botanic Gardens' Collaborative Learning Processes*, Pp. 1–7. London: Ubiquity Press. DOI: http://dx.doi.org/10.5334/bas.a. License: CC-BY 4.0.

scientific careers than was expected in many countries (EU Commission 2004, Sjøberg & Schreiner, 2010; Schreiner & Schwantner 2009; Holstermann & Bögeholz, 2007).

These outcomes challenged the European Commission's goals of becoming the most competitive and dynamic knowledge based economy of the world by 2010 (EU, 2000).

Post PISA 2006, the need to deliver abundant and well-trained human resources for European research has become a matter of increasing urgency and political commitment. In addition, the essential source for a 'knowledge society' is science. Thus becoming scientifically literate is a relevant goal in the general education of all young people, not just for those opting for scientific careers. Understanding science in its rich diversity and being able to act according to this knowledge is a requisite to become a responsible and politically mature citizen.

The European Commission's growing interest in science education policy became most visible in 2007. By then, the 7th Framework Programme funding scheme 'Science and Society' was launched providing € 67m. support for raising student interest in science and careers within in and from science during the following seven years (Lena, 2010).

Two reports laid the pathway for educational projects to work on improving science education in Europe. In 2007, the European Commission published 'Science Education Now, a renewed pedagogy for the future Europe' (Rocard, 2007). The report became influential in framing the EU 7th Framework Programme 'Science and Society'. In 2008, the Nuffield Foundation published 'Science Education in Europe: Critical Reflections' (Osborne & Dillon, 2008), a report that emerged from a series of workshops involving a group of science education researchers. While the Nuffield Report focused on various aspects of science education and did not emphasise a particular approach, the Rocard Report was explicit in advocating 'Inquiry Based Science Education' (IBSE) as the remedy for Europe's problems. Thus European funding calls focused on implementing IBSE on a large scale in Europe. The distinct role of Learning Outside the Classroom (LOtC) institutions such as zoos, aquaria, botanic gardens, museums or science centres in supporting this approach was explicitly mentioned (Rocard, 2007).

1.2 Collaborative learning at botanic gardens

Between 2005 and 2013, I designed and coordinated two European Projects, the FP6 PLASCIGARDEN and the related FP7 project INQUIRE. Both projects were developed to showcase the role botanic gardens may play in supporting science education reform efforts in Europe.

For many years, botanic gardens and other LOtC institutions have collaborated with schools to provide students, teachers and families with opportunities to expand their experience and understanding of science.

'These collaborations have allowed students, and also teachers, to explore, understand, and care about a wide range of natural settings, phenomena, and cultural and historical objects. They have helped students to notice, consider, and investigate relationships between human social behaviour and environmental consequences. They have provided contexts, materials, rationales, and support for students and teachers to engage deeply in scientific inquiry processes of learning. These experiences—with an array of real-life settings, animals, professional science communities, objects, scientific instrumentation, and current research and data—have been shown to spark curiosity, generate questions, and lead to a depth of understanding and commitment in ways that are often less possible when the same material is encountered in books or on screens.' (Bevan et al., 2010, p. 11)

However many LOtC institution, and botanic gardens in particular, do not engage in larger educational reform efforts or in systematic programme evaluation (Phillips et al., 2007) and they often fail to institutionalize collaborations with schools or the educational system. The reasons for this state of affairs are manifold and are often related to the hybrid nature of these collaborations which are both formal and informal at the same time (Bevan et al., 2010). When collaborative teaching and learning programmes are put into practice, they often lack a well-developed theoretical background. This does not mean that the programmes are not successful but a purely practice-based approach stops educators from reflecting on their own practice and developing a professional stance to teaching and learning in LOtC sites.

1.3 Finding a common ground

'Cultural psychology design based research' is applied to understand more about how an imposed theoretical view such as 'implementing inquiry based science education on a large scale in Europe' is interpreted by botanic gardens and natural history museums and whether a collaborative, expansive learning environment has the potential to provide insight where projected ideas fall short through systematic examination of the participant's engagement in an intervention.

'Design-based research is premised on the notion that we can learn important things about the nature and conditions of learning by attempting to engineer and sustain educational innovation in everyday settings. Complex educational interventions can be used to surface phenomena of interest for systematic study to better promote specific educational outcomes' (Bell, 2004, p. 243).

Design based research was chosen because it has the potential to contribute to our understanding of learning in complex settings. In this regard, designing and developing an intervention is an explicitly theory driven activity. Through a retrospective analysis it is possible to map:

> '[. . .] the embodiment of particular conjectures through their design reification and to then design research studies to specifically tests the predictions that result. Such predictions pertain to both outcomes expected from the intervention and ways in which designed scaffolds are expected to function. The need to link outcomes to these expected functions across research iterations is the source of power from this analytic approach' (Sandoval & Bell, 2004, p. 200)

My theory driven approach to designing the INQUIRE intervention does not value science education research as the only source. I have additionally tried to learn from organisational behaviour studies to develop a better understanding of what makes change happen.

> 'The ultimate purpose of science education research is the improvement of science teaching and learning throughout the world.' (Abell & Lederman 2007, p. xiii)

Research in organisational behaviour studies the impact that individuals, groups, networks or structures have on behaviour within an organization. The purpose is quite similar to science education research, namely to apply such knowledge to improve an organisation's effectiveness. Educational and organisational research, however, face the same challenge as Abell and Lederman identified in their introduction to the 'Handbook of Research in Science Education' published in 2007:

> 'We must take care that the proximate causes of our research (e.g. achieving publications that count for tenure, writing conference papers so our universities will fund our travel, preparing new researchers getting grant dollars) do not derail us from achieving our ultimate purpose.' (Abell & Lederman, 2007, p. iii).

Whether and how research is still suitable for informing practice is a concern increasingly voiced by scholars in both fields:

> 'I believe it would not be inaccurate to say that the most powerful forces to have shaped educational scholarship over the last century have tended to push the field in unfortunate directions – away from close interaction with policy and practice towards excessive quantification and scientism.' (Condliffe Lagemann, 2001, p. 1)

Splitter and Seidl (2011) argue that:

> 'The generation of knowledge by academics often entails the neutralization of practical urgencies – such as the ability to identify problems for the sole pleasure of resolving them and not because they are posed by the necessities of life'. (p. 106)

Referring to the work of the French sociologist Pierre Bourdieu, Splitter and Seidl assume that:

> 'Social practice performed by individual actors is influenced not only by the actors '*individual disposition*' (such as origin, education and identity) but also by supra-individual '*objective structures*' (such as socially defined interests, beliefs assumptions and resources). Objective structures are not uniform but vary between different social spheres.' (p. 103)

Thus research and praxis are different social spheres, which exhibit different structures associated with different types of knowledge. Actors belonging to one or the other carry out their activities while facing different structural possibilities and constraints, such as being guided by different domain specific interests, beliefs and assumptions and are limited or supported by particular sets of resources. Particular conditions of one or the other field lead to a specific way of observing the world and even the language used. Splitter and Seidl (2011) cite Bourdieu to visualise a phenomenon which is most typical for science education research as it is not understood by practitioners:

> 'Instead of grasping and mobilizing the meaning of a word that is immediately compatible with the situation, we [scientists] mobilize and examine all the possible meanings of that word, outside of any reference to the situation [. . .] The scholastic view is a very peculiar point of view on the social world, on language, on any possible object of thought. (p. 105)

Science education research is often occupied by the monological paradigm of finding the universal laws or structure underpinning a phenomenon. It is predominately seeking to produce the single most coherent model of e.g. 'inquiry based science education', or 'communities of practice' and put significant efforts into examining possible meanings of terms such as 'scientific literacy' or 'pedagogical content knowledge'. By doing this, research runs the risk of overlooking the fact that knowledge is never independent of the social, historical and cultural context that gives it meaning.

An obvious theme, running through all topics addressed in the theoretical framework underpinning my work, is the discrepancy between the researcher's perception of a concept and how this one is constantly misunderstood and modified when it is used and put into practice. I suggest reconsidering the misconception that finding the perfect model is the answer to a problem and consequently helps practitioners to change their practice. I assume that we need to engage people, practitioners and researchers alike, in a dialogical process which asks them to express their everyday idea about e.g. inquiry based science teaching first and then involve them in a process of knowledge creation that is situated in the context in which it takes place. The INQUIRE project gives a practice based example of how involving mixed groups of scientists and practitioners in collaborative knowledge creation processes supports the transformation of knowledge practices pursued in botanic garden education. Improving approaches to support such a transformation of knowledge practices has been the overall goal of this work.

1.4 Overview of my work

As mentioned already, 'designed based research' is explicitly theory driven. Thus the first part of my work provides insight into the complex interplay of different theoretical aspects that informed the design, the structure and the implementation of the INQUIRE project. 'Cultural psychology design based research' in particular is grounded in Vigotskian socio-cultural theory and cultural historical activity theory and focuses on the transformation of mediated action and the cultivation of sustainable learning communities that persist over a longer period of time (Bell, 2004).

In 'Part A: Theoretical Framework', I introduce these theories, as well as 'metaphors of learning' such as learning as a situated, expansive and organisational process.

An overview to the current discussion about concepts such as 'scientific literacy', the 'nature of science, 'science inquiry' and 'Inquiry Based Science Education' gives insight into learning goals the INQUIRE projects seeks to achieve.

This section is followed by looking at concepts of teaching as a profession and the current understanding of what good professional development for teachers should look like. Finally botanic gardens as learning environments are presented and the role of teachers and educators in a LOtC setting is addressed.

In 'Part B: From Theory to Practice', I will give an overview about the INQUIRE project design and our approach to support collaborative knowledge creation. Finally, I will present a case study of two Spanish partners who worked and learned jointly as one 'activity system' in the INQUIRE project consortium. Here Cultural Historical Activity and Expansive Learning Theory are applied as a framework to interpret the significant steps of transformation that occurred during the three year project duration. A special focus is put on partner understanding of Inquiry Based Science Teaching (IBST) and their perception of competence in implementing this pedagogy into their educational programmes.

1.5 Implications

Most of the educational projects that I coordinated over the last couple of years, such as the European 6th Framework Project PLASCIGARDEN, the project 'Forschend Lernen' and the 7th Framework INQUIRE project, were designed to counteract the weaknesses of dealing with the two 'incompatible' social fields of science education research and educational praxis. This was done by supporting botanic gardens or LOtC institutions to develop either national or international 'communities of inquiry' and to establish a network of professional learners engaging in European educational reform efforts.

As project partners, botanic garden and natural history museum educators are asked to engage in collaborative knowledge creation (Moen et al., 2012) and create a domain specific understanding of how to engage with education research knowledge, generate, incorporate, evaluate, and adapt the best of the specific new ideas and practices that emerge amongst them as a group of learners and thus develop a theory of Botanic Garden learning.

This monograph is dedicated to providing a rational and theoretical basis for LOtC institutions to engage in the science education reform efforts and rely on collaborative knowledge creation processes for developing a better understanding of 'good science teaching and learning at botanic gardens' while adapting a theory-informed, critical and reflective approach to teaching and learning.

Based on this work, I believe that there is not only a need for new approaches to learning

> 'especially for understanding and supporting practices where people are creating or developing useful and reusable things in collaboration' (Moen et al., 2012, p. ix)

But also a need to recognise collaborative learning processes taking place on different levels as important assets when evaluating European funded projects.

2. Part A – Theoretical Framework

This research wishes to promote the development of professional science teaching practice inside and outside the classroom through the formation of an international learning community of botanic gardens and natural history museums.' Cultural psychology design based research' (Bell, 2004) is applied to better understand how to orchestrate innovative learning experiences amongst a network of socio-cultural diverse organisations. The research focus is put the local social world to understand

> 'how imposed theoretical views are interpreted by the participants, opening up the possibility that new theoretical insights can be gleaned about where projected theory falls short through systematic, emic examination of the participants engagement in the intervention'(ibid, p. 249)

Thus the following pages are dedicated to provide an insight into the complex 'theoretical views' that informed the INQUIRE project design and its implementation and thus account for its progression.

Let's get started with two very basic concepts, 'Science' and 'Science Learning'. Both seem to be very simple and commonly used terms. However, as soon as we look more closely at them and reflect on the science education literature, these two terms are not as easy to envisage as one thinks and are a matter of a long-lasting discourse among science educators. It is entirely possible that even each reader of this work may hold an individual perspective. The literature about attempts to define either of these two aforementioned terms is vast. However, the purpose of this paper is not to provide

---

How to cite this book chapter:
Kapelari, S. 2015. Theoretical Framework. In: Kapelari, S *Garden Learning: A Study on European Botanic Gardens' Collaborative Learning Processes*, Pp. 9–99. London: Ubiquity Press. DOI: http://dx.doi.org/10.5334/bas.b. License: CC-BY 4.0.

a synopsis of the literature on the Nature of Science or the Nature of Science Learning as that has been done elsewhere (e.g. Hohenstein & Manning, 2010, Lederman & Lederman 2012, Bransford et al., 2000) but to raise awareness about the fact that different perceptions of these concepts are omnipresent in science education.

2.1 What is Science?

When I talk about science I am mainly referring to the natural sciences, Biology in particular, and I refer to science as a particular approach to making sense of the world around us. Asking the question 'what is science?' implies there will be a definitive answer, however Science refers to a substantial breadth of human knowledge and endeavor and the boundaries of science are not clearly defined.

Science is both a body of knowledge that may be seen as a collection of isolated facts, and a process of discovery which links isolated facts into a coherent understanding of the world around us. Modern science was established as a social institution in Western Europe in the 17th Century and was accepted in the academic society in the 19th century (Thorlindsson & Vilhjalmsson 2003). There is not one interpretation of science, or one single way of applying science, or classifying a work as being scientific. The term science is an abstraction summarising multiple approaches to gaining knowledge.

With flowers, there is a great variety of different shapes and colours. Some flowers are easily recognised as being flowers and others may only be detected by a specialist's eye. However it is commonly agreed that there is a particular structure that enables us to recognise an organism as a flower and that helps us to communicate confidently and accurately about flowers. Although the term 'flower' is used commonly by the lay person, for example in a florist, it may often be used incorrectly (according to the scientific definition) for example referring to flowering heads made up of many flowers and even a whole plant with stem, leaves and flowers! It is only when we observe closely and with understanding of a flower structure that we can see the 'real flowers' and observe their different characteristics. Thus individual people's understanding and use of the term 'flower' is often very different.

In the same way, people in the science researcher's community share a common understanding of science patterns although there will also be many different perspectives when we look at domain specific aspects in more detail. As with the term 'Flower' there are macro patterns we commonly share and micro patterns we still have to define and argue about - whether they are, should or should not be included to the currently accepted concept of 'Science' (Bechtel, 1988). Discussions on these 'micro patterns', though fascinating, are not the purpose of this paper and should be a matter for science philosophers. However it is important to be aware about it because these micro patterns do influence people's perception of science inquiry and the nature of science.

Lederman and Lederman (2012) argue that to answer the question "What is science" the one valid answer delineates science into:

1. The Nature of Science Knowledge
2. The Body of Scientific Knowledge
3. The Variety of Science Process/Method

2.1.1 Nature of Knowledge?

Metaphors are central not only in young people's science learning but in scientific thoughts, discourse and practice in general. Teachers and scientist use them to explain theories and their work and they can make visual concepts a person or group hold (Lakoff & Johnson, 1980).

Ann Sfard (1998) proposed two metaphors to think about knowledge creation. The most broadly accepted one is sometimes known as "folk theory of mind and learning" and sees knowledge as a property of each individual's mind. Knowledge can be collected and accumulated in a kind of container and learning is the process the individual mind follows to fill this container. It is a matter of construction, acquisition and outcomes, which becomes visible in the process of using and applying this knowledge in new situations. This metaphor is properly known as the *acquisition metaphor* and is held in contrast to the *participation metaphor*, which sees knowledge as a process of participation in various cultural practices and shared learning activities.

In the latter the focus is more on activities (knowing) than on outcomes (knowledge). Knowledge in this metaphor is seen as an aspect of cultural practices. Knowledge is distributed not only between individuals but also over their environment. Learning is situated in these networks of distributed activities. Knowledge and knowing cannot be separated from situations where they are used or where they take place. Therefore knowledge is a matter of enculturation and learning is situated in this culture. Discourse, interaction, activity and participation supplement, or sometimes even replace the terms acquiring and accumulating knowledge (Paavola et al., 2004).

The debate between cognitive and situated perspectives of learning is nourished by these two metaphors. Sfard (1998), along with a couple of others, had already concluded at the end of the last century that both perspectives are needed and that they are not 'rivals' but complement each other (Paavola et al., 2004). Bereiter's (2002) concept of *knowledge building* argues that the emergence of the knowledge society has given rise to a view of knowledge as a thing that can be systematically produced and shared among members of a community. This infers that therefore knowledge follows a building process that includes collective work in order to produce conceptual artefacts. These artefacts may, or may not, be of practical use (eg. new technology or theories and ideas).

> 'This model makes a conceptual distinction between learning, which operates in the realm of mental states (in Popper's World 2), and knowledge building, which is generated by human minds whilst operating in a socially shared realm (Popper's World 3), which again makes use of material (World 1) objects for realisation.' (Batatia et al., 2012, p. 18)

For Paavola and colleagues (2004), scientific concepts can be seen as mediation between mind and matter.

Alongside, or even synonymously with, the discussion on metaphors of knowledge creation goes the discussion about metaphors for learning. In this respect there is no clear cut between these two metaphors. Rather

> '[. . .] the importance of these metaphors is that they present in concise form, typical and important main alternatives of understanding learning' (Paavola et al., 2004, p. 569)

Models of learning frequently combine aforementioned features in different ways and degrees. Paavola et al., 2004 conclude that although the term 'Constructivism' may become rather meaningless because it is used in many variations and interpretations, it can also be interpreted as an enhanced version of the acquisition metaphor in the sense that knowledge cannot be acquired directly but must be accumulated and constructed by the learner himself. In addition constructivism has affinities with the participation metaphor of knowledge creation, if the idea is that social and cultural practices are primarily constructed.

Engeström and Sannino (2010) argue that the 'Theory of Expansive Learning' (s. p. 31ff)

> 'does not fit into one of the two metaphors suggested by Sfard (1989). In fact, from the point of view of expansive learning both acquisition-based and participation-based approaches share much of the same conservative bias. Both have little to say about transformation and creation of culture [. . .] so the theory of expansive learning must rely on its own metaphor: expansion (p. 2).

Paavola and colleagues (2004) suggest a 'metaphor of knowledge creation' as a new and third one, while Fendwick add concepts such as participation, expansion and translation as relevant alternatives.

In terms of teaching practices our western Cartesian way of separating one from the other is keeping the discourse alive on whether teaching should focus either more dominantly on knowledge acquisition or on asking students to participate in cultural practices. Shared learning activities are still key focus for modern science education discussions.

To answer the question 'What is the nature of science knowledge' mentioned earlier, we may have to agree that generations of scientists have been gathering the knowledge we currently hold and future generations will naturally develop it further. Thus science knowledge is 'accumulated' as well as being a matter of 'participation' and 'expansion' in cultural practice (see below).

Sfard (1998) argues:

> 'After making the case for the plurality of metaphors, I have to show that this proposal is workable. Indeed, considering the fact that the two metaphors seem to be mutually exclusive, one may wonder how the suggested metaphorical crossbreeding could be possible at all' (p. 11).

2.1.2 The Body of Scientific Knowledge

The most fundamental principle in science is that scientists assume there is a world around us which does exist, which is real and can be observed and studied. Science is therefore the constructive process that humans apply to understand this world. It involves exploring natural phenomena, inventing new concepts and applying these new concepts to explain or interpret already known or new phenomena. *Knowledge* is produced and shared by a community which is united by agreed norms and social practices and is therefore socially and culturally situated. E.g. research findings are published, discussed and evaluated by peers of different nationalities. These social structures have been established over a long time already and are expanding constantly as well as successfully (Thorlindsson & Vilhjalmsson, 2003).

Scientific concepts are terms used to explain a particular phenomenon or object and they represent a knowledge content the scientific community currently shares e.g. when scientists talk about photosynthesis it is not just a term but the shared understanding of what we currently know about how plants collect an utilise sun energy. Scientists assume that by understanding single building blocks of a phenomenon and merging them together they will finally understand the bigger picture. Knowledge is accumulated and forms the scientific body of knowledge which is used to construct and reconstruct our understanding of the natural world (*acquisition metaphor*). Various concepts, laws, theories and ideas have remained unchanged for a long time now and are well represented in established specialist literature, peer reviewed journals and students textbooks. Scientists rely on this accumulated body of knowledge and work hard to establish the truth. However, it needs to be recognised that what is accepted knowledge today may change in the future. New or different perspectives and even contradicting knowledge could arise. This does not mean that anything produced by scientists is not trustworthy; a scientific concept that has been termed theory or law is the best understanding that we currently have. It has been tested and challenged, and questioned and tested again and to date it has not been proved wrong. However, there is always room for building on our knowledge and understanding, even for those commonly accepted theories or physical laws. There may still be aspects which have not been considered or a lack of technology that can offer an alternative perspective. There may also be an exceptional case not yet discovered.

2.1.3 The Science Processes and Methods

Lederman and Lederman (2012) summarized the characteristics of scientific inquiry as such: Scientific Inquiry extends beyond the mere development of process skills such as observing, inferring, classifying predicting measuring, questioning, interpreting and analysing data. Scientific inquiry includes the traditional science processes but also refers to the combining of these processes with scientific knowledge, scientific reasoning and critical thinking to develop scientific knowledge. The critical thinking aspect is particularly crucial in science. A skilled performance in scientific thinking cannot be separated from scientific knowledge eg. predicting or interpreting observations are very greatly depending on the context. Thus it makes it a huge challenge not only for students but for science teachers or science educators to engage in authentic inquiry. The contemporary view advocated for science inquiry is that the question guides the approach and the approach varies widely within and across scientific disciplines and fields. Thus no one single fixed set or sequence of steps is available which can be expected to cover all types of scientific investigations. Experimental design is often advocated as "the scientific method" but it is not representative of scientific investigations as a whole. Scientists rely on theory and create models to mimic the real world because this enables them to test predictions and explain puzzling observations. Thus science involves the invention of explanations which requires creativity in the sense of e.g. developing an experimental design or interpreting data.

One has to admit that scientists do not look at data without prejudice because observation is always filtered by existing preconceptions. Scientific knowledge is subjective. Therefore critical reasoning is applied. A scientific process does not only involve observations of the world only but scientists are required to use all their senses and ask causal questions. It includes recording accurate descriptions of what has been done and what has been observed as well as consideration of alternative ideas. Generating logical predictions along with planning and conducting reproducible experiments or observations are essential.

Data is collected to decide between competing explanations not to confirm already existing ones. Finally reasonable conclusions are provided and newly developed knowledge is disseminated. It is presented to the scientific community to be discussed, peer reviewed, challenged and questioned. Science therefore includes teamwork, as well as being a social process; not one single person can be blamed or acclaimed for what we know, or do not know or what we believe is correct or incorrect.

Although there is this scientific idea of gathering objective knowledge, scientists have to admit that not every single member or even whole groups of the scientific community may follow similar goals. There are always people who do not scrutinise competing explanations, but prefer to find or produce evidence for their own explanations. We find others who claim the stage of theory for a knowledge that has not been tested properly or is still subject of contradicting views. These people draw conclusions from weak evidence and try to hide this fact as it often helps them to further their careers or it improves their financial situation - however, that is human nature. It is important for those working in science research to address these issues openly and to support those teaching and learning science to be aware about it.

The concept of scientific literacy which will be addressed later is asking learners to develop knowledge and skills to distinguish between good and bad science. However, this is making high demands on lay persons and may not be realistic.

2.2 Selected Theories of Learning

Educational psychologist assume that learning theories and ideas relevant to education can provide important information for practitioners and thus need to be considered when designing, implementing and improving educational programs. However, general philosophical theories such as behaviourism, cognitivism, constructivism, humanism or socialism often fail to provide detailed guidance in organizing instructions (Weibell, 2012).

> 'In the past decades learning theory has turned away from being an oversimplified general theory, and has evolved into a complex theory with several parameters that need to be specified for different real-world conditions. The idea that all kinds of learning processes in any situation can be accounted for by one limited general set of laws or mechanisms, has been replaced by a view on learning that acknowledges the importance of the *content* of learning, as well as the nature of the learning *situation*. Domain specificity and situatedness are now generally recognized as major parameters of any theory of learning. Context has become a hot issue in modern educational science. (Van Oers, 1998, p. 473).

Our understanding of science learning in particular changed after the so called "cognitive revolution" in psychology in the 1960s. Education and in particular mathematics and science education, has gained new insights from psychology, brain research and the social sciences. In the following section I will refer to a few movements which are influential not only in my work but in science education in general; these are 'constructivist learning', socio-cultural perspective of learning', 'situated learning', 'expansive learning' and the 'knowledge creation approach to learning'. In addition I consider theories of 'organisational learning' fruitful to understand transformation of knowledge practices in this context.

2.2.1 Constructivist Learning

'Constructivist Learning' although as a concept rather meaningless because it is used in many variations and interpretations basically puts the focus on the individual that "constructs" knowledge him or herself while building upon already existing knowledge and ideas. In the constructivist context knowledge is a well-defined entity that can be considered independently of individual humans. A corpus of content knowledge has been acquired and passed on from generation to generation. Thus knowledge does not belong to any particular individual. It is more or less independent of the context in which it is used (e.g. scientific knowledge). Transfer of knowledge is expected to occur.

However it is the purpose of constructivist education to support the individual becoming creative and innovative through analysis, conceptualizations, and to synthesis prior knowledge and experience to create new knowledge. 'Social Constructivism' recognises that the learner's version of the truth is influenced by his or her background, culture or embedded worldview (see below).

2.2.2 The Socio-Cultural Perspective of Learning

A sociocultural approach to learning and development has the potential to recognize the essential relationship between learning processes and their cultural, historical and institutional setting. When we look at implementing 'Inquiry Based Science Learning' in botanic gardens, natural history museums or schools later, it will become evident that there are differences when this takes place in different countries e.g. Spain or in Austria, as well as differences brought about by the different role a teacher or an educator plays in these settings etc. Processes instead of forms of mental functioning are of concern to a socio-cultural background.

Wertsch (1991) cites Shweder 1990 when he argues:

> 'Cultural traditions and social practices regulate, express, transform, and permute the human psyche, resulting less in psychic unity for humankind than in ethnic divergences in mind, self and emotion' (p. 7),

Russian philosophers such as Vygotsky's, Leont'ev, Luria and others ideas are fundamental to the current understanding of sociocultural situatedness although Vygotsky's did not deal explicitly which the major topics currently applied in sociocultural studies. However, basic themes that run through Vygotsky's writing are fundamental to the sociocultural approaches to thinking and learning. Their power derives from ways in which they are intertwined. These are:

- attempts to understand the nature of mental processes by analysing static procedures of development only, will often be misleading.
- higher mental functioning in the individual derives from social life
- human action on both the social and individual planes is mediated by tools and signs (Wertsch,1999).

A fundamental assumption of sociocultural approaches to learning is that actions, rather than the human being or the environment considered in isolation, provide the entry point into the analysis.

> "When action is given analytic priority, human beings are viewed as coming into contact with, and creating their surrounding as well as themselves through the action in which they engage" (ibid, p. 8)

Habermas argues that many types of categories of action can be distinguished which are based on the relationship between the actor or learner and the environment. He takes Popper's three world theory to categorize three type of environment in which activity takes place

- facilitated by physical objects or physical states
- facilitated by states of consciousness, mental states, behavioural disposition of act
- facilitated by "objective contents of thought" (e.g. scientific or poetic thoughts, works of art) (Wertsch, 1989)

Although language is often assumed as being the most important mediating action applied, these two other environments should not be neglected. Actions taking place between the actor and the world of physical objects may be summarised as producing or working with any kind of physical representations of understanding (Wertsch, 1989) such as hand-on tools, lesson plans, portfolios, posters etc.

Wertsch (ibid) particularly stresses the point that:

> 'the most central claim I wish to pursue is that human action employs "mediational means" such as tools and language and that this means shape the action in essential ways. According to this view it is possible as well as useful to make analytic distinction between action and meditational means but the relationship between action and medi-

> tational means is so fundamental that it is more appropriate when referring to the agent involved to speak of "individual(s)-acting-with-meditational-means" than to speak simply of "individual(s)". Thus, the answer to the question of who is carrying out the action will invariably identify the individuals in the concrete situation and the mediational means employed (p. 12)

This is in contrast with approaches that treat the individual as a passive recipient of information from the environment or approaches that focus on the individual and treat the environment as secondary, serving merely as a device to trigger certain developmental processes. The actor is assumed to reach a desired state by choosing means that have promise of being successful in the given situation and applying them in a suitable manner. This is based on a decision among alternative courses of action, with a view to the realisation of an end, guided by maxims and based on an interpretation of the situation (Wertsch, 1989).

A sociocultural approach to mediated action need not involve explicit comparison; the main criterion is that the analysis is linked in some way with specific cultural, historical or institutional factors. However the notion of "situatedness" implies a contrast with other possibilities. It is an accepted opinion that universality exists. Universalistic and sociocultural approaches are not assumed to be out-and-out contradictions, however educational research tends to often overemphasise universalistic approaches.

> 'Choosing to focus on either universal or sociocultural situatedness, one makes certain essential assumptions about which phenomena are interesting and deserve attention. The existence of these assumptions and their implications are not often appreciated however and the result has been endless misunderstanding and bogus argument. . . . It is a choice between two different research agendas, both of which need to be addresses and both, where possible, integrated (Wertsch, 1989, p. 7)'

Sociocultural approaches are well supported by a couple of philosophers and cultural psychologists; Locke, Decartes, Vigotsky, Leont'ev, Bakhitin, Piaget or Berry, Cole, Shweder or Toulmin are often cited in this context (Wertsch, 1989).

2.2.3 Situated Learning

The situated learning` movement is assumed to be . . .

> 'a radical critique of cognitivist theories of learning [because this theory is] emphasising the rational aspect of learning within communities of practice in contrast to the individualist assumption of conventional theories'(Handley et al., 2006, p. 641).

'Situated Learning' emphasises the idea that much of what is learned is specific to the situation in which it is learned. Hence learning is not something that takes place in the isolated individual only while acquiring new ideas, concepts and knowledge but is produced and reproduced in the social interaction of individuals when participating in a society. This participation is intrinsically tied to the context in which it takes place and implies both the aspect of knowing, as well as 'being and becoming' a member of a certain community. Most of all, participation in practice is assumed to be a necessary condition for learning. Modes of participation and becoming or being a member of the community are important (Anderson et al., 1996, Yakhelf, 2010).

In 1991, Jean Lave and Etienne Wenger published their book, 'Situated Learning: Legitimate Peripheral Participation' and introduced an epistemological principle of learning which was termed 'Community of Practice (CoP) and Situated Learning'.

The authors explained their theory of learning through an apprenticeship model by which newcomers to a community learn from other participants, during which time they are allowed to take over more and more tasks in the community and gradually progress to become 'masters' and enjoy full participation. This earlier perspective implied that

> 'legitimate peripheral participation in a community inevitably leads to full socialisation, thus resembling earlier socialisation theories following Vygotsky'. (Handley et al., 2006, p. 643)

Members of a CoP are expected to develop a mode of belonging and an identity in practice.

However, later both authors admitted that various forms of participation are both possible and fruitful and that becoming a full participant might not be aspired by all members of such a community.

The concept of Communities of Practice has been similarly taken across social, educational and management science and is currently one of the most articulated and developed concepts within broad social theories of learning (Barton & Tusting, 2005).

However as it happens frequently in education:

> 'the concept of communities of practice has been taken up and used by people working in many different areas. It has had an immediate appeal and perceived usefulness across a range of situations. Like any useful concept people have used it in a variety of ways, some have kept close to the original formulations and some developed it. Some have found it to be exactly what they want and others have criticised it and identified its limitations, proposing alternatives. Some have taken the whole theoretical apparatus of situated learning. Other have taken just the phrase and adapted it to their own uses combining it with concepts from other fields

and incorporating it into other theories. For some it has become a central concept which a whole theory revolves around; for other it has been more peripheral and has been incorporated into other theories. This is probably the fate of any useful concept'. (Barton & Tusting, 2005, p. 2)

Etienne Wenger, cited by Booth and colleagues (2004) put it like this:

> 'It takes time for CoPs to emerge, flourish and to become productive. More important, they cannot be mandated or managed in a heavy-handed way. CoPs, then, are an investment in the organization's future, not a quick fix to be applied for the sake of short-term gain. Most important, many will exist whether or not management chooses to encourage and support them; they are a natural part of organizational life. And that means they require a minimal investment on the part of the organization.'

Therefore these communities are characterised and define themselves along the following dimension (Booth et al., 2004, Amin & Roberts, 2006).

- *Members show a mutual engagement:* they interact with each other in many ways. This engagement binds members together in a social entity.
- *Members are joined by an enterprise:* they have a common endeavour which is understood and continuously renegotiated by its members
- *The community shares a repertoire of common resources* such as language, style, routines, sensibilities, artefacts; resources that members have developed over time and by means of which they express their identities as members of the group
- *The community negotiates meaning in practice*

However, it is important to emphasise that CoP cannot be prescribed or installed to facilitate learning processes. They need to develop naturally and can be guided or supported by people interested in their development. For Wenger (1998) CoPs are important places of negotiation, learning, meaning, and identity.

Wenger (2002) does not restrict the concept of CoP to the school context only but believed that in a CoP, social learning occurs as soon as people who have a common interest in some subject or problem collaborate over an extended period of time to share ideas, find solutions and build innovation.

Based on this notion he argues that CoPs move through various stages over time which can be characterised by different levels of interaction among the members.

Wenger (1998) argues that the existence of a CoP may not be evident to its members because

> 'a community of practice' need not be reified as such in the discourse of its participants' (p. 125).

Nevertheless, he argues, a community of practice does display a number of characteristics including those listed below (Amin & Roberts, 2006)

Key characteristics of a Community of Practice compiled from Wenger (1998, p. 125/6).

- Sustained mutual relationships — harmonious or conflicting
- Shared ways of engaging in activities
- The rapid flow of information and propagation of innovation
- Absence of introductory preambles, as if conversations and interactions were merely the continuation of an on-going process
- Very quick setup of any problem to be discussed
- Substantial overlap in participants' descriptions of who belongs to the CoP
- Knowing what others know, what they can do, and how they can contribute to an enterprise
- Mutually defining identities
- The ability to assess the appropriateness of actions and products
- Specific tools, representations, and other artefacts
- Local lore, shared stories, inside jokes, knowing laughter
- Jargon and shortcuts to communication as well as the ease of producing new ones
- Certain styles recognised as displaying membership of the CoP
- A shared discourse reflecting a certain perspective on the world

Amin and Roberts (2006) argue that:

'Since the study by Lave and Wenger (1991) there has been an explosion of research on CoPs, and broader practice-based approaches, to learning and knowledge generation in a variety of diverse settings. Much of this literature, whether it reveals the existence of CoPs or reports on the application of the framework to particular learning and knowledge generation contexts, works with definitions that are far from the original conceptualisation of CoPs [...]

Alongside the increasing popularity of communities of practice research, the approach has begun to attract criticism concerning, for instance, the neglect of power, its failure to take into account pre-existing conditions such as habitus and social codes, as well as its widespread application within organisational studies beyond its original focus on situated learning, and the term 'community' itself, which is problematic, embodies positive connotations and is open to multiple interpretations' (p. 4)

For Yakhelf (2010) learning a practice is not only to become a member of a community but also to be able to reflect upon what is lived, experienced and imagined.

> 'The link between knowing in practice (being a practitioner) and knowing a practice (or the result of the process of being a competent practitioner) is reflexivity. Knowing in practice requires participating competently in the knowledge embedded in that practice. For knowing a practice entails disembodying knowledge through an act reflexive knowledge' (p. 41).

Although originally used to describe a mode of social learning, it is now clear that CoPs are seen as having an impact far beyond their original field. They explain learning taking place in a wide range of educational areas as well as in business management or even politics.

According to Barton and Tusting (2005) the CoP based 'Theory of Situated Learning':

- appears to resolve some pervasive concerns of social sciences about learning
- represents a theory of learning which acknowledges networks and groups which are informal and not the same as formal structures
- allows for groups which are distributed in some ways and not necessarily in face to face contact
- the overall apparatus is a significant rethink of learning theory of value to anyone wanting to take learning beyond the individual
- is attractive as a middle-level theory between structure and agency which is applicable to and close to actual life and which resonates with detailed ethnographic account of how learning happens.
- Has been proved as a theory and has value in practice.

Part of its appeal may be nurtured by the idea that CoPs are seemingly natural formations which enhance learning. This is important for those aiming to implement change.

The Concept of CoP takes learning out of the formal classroom and addresses the variety of groups and locations where learning takes place such as teacher professional development offers or learning through educational projects and collaboration, in the workplace or even in everyday life.

2.2.4 Organisational Learning

As mentioned earlier many scholars have dealt with finding ways to deal with the area of conflict between the learning as an individual task or as a team work. One approach is the so called 'integrationist perspective' by developing a theory of 'organisational learning' (Starkey et al., 2004).

According to this perspective Dyck and colleagues (2005) argue that 'organisational learning begins with cognitive processes of individuals and is enhanced and preserved by organisational processes (p. 388)

If learning is valued as a situated process in a social context the individual learner cannot be the only centre of attention. The social group, subgroup or organisation in which this learning takes place has to be recognises as an entity for learning. It is necessary to understand the process through which individual learning advances organisational learning and to address the role individual knowledge and memory plays in the process through which individual learning becomes embedded in the organisations memory and in its structures.

'Organisational memory and knowledge' is the capability all members of an organisation have developed collectively over time. Its application depends on historically evolved collective understanding and experience. To draw distinctions in the process of carrying out their work in a particular concrete context, members of the organisation enact sets of generalisations (Kim, 2004).

How learning is expected to take place, what is valued as important and what is assumed to be 'good teaching' at Botanic Gardens, Zoos or Natural History Museums is not only a matter of each individual educator education and understanding. It is influenced by organisational traditions, knowledge and experience accumulated over time. This may or may not be recognized or valued explicitly.

Organisational knowledge can be embedded in a variety of repositories such as educational programmes, including individuals, routines, and trans-active memory systems. A collective understanding of organisational knowledge is seen as a key to understanding organisations' growth. This knowledge enables the organisation to use its resources accordingly. It is a distinctive way of thinking and acting in the world (Kim, 2004).

Thus from this perspective organisational learning is defined as a change in the organisation's knowledge that occurs as a function of experience. Organisational knowledge herein includes declarative knowledge, such as facts, and procedural knowledge, such as skills and routines which are shared in a particular community. Organisational knowledge may be measured either by the cognition of organisational members or by taking a behavioural approach. The latter focuses on knowledge embedded in performance such as accuracy or speed etc. or in practices or routines. Changes to those are accepted as changes in knowledge. Thus organizational learning can be defined as a change in the range of potential behaviours. However, it needs to be acknowledged that organisations may acquire knowledge without a change in behaviour (Argote, 2013).

When assessing knowledge by measuring changes in practice or performance, tacit as well as explicit knowledge is captured. This may circumvent the limitation of current approaches to measure learning by assessing changes in cognitions through questionnaires and interviews (Hodgkinson & Sparrow, 2002).

In this work I focus on knowledge embedded in practice and view changes as indicative that organizational learning occurred (Argote, 2013).

At a practical level, the ability to learn and adapt is critical to the performance and long term success of organizations. Because organizational learning occurs over time, studying organizational learning requires time and series of longitudinal data. However, we need to be aware, that behavioural approaches to analysing learning need to be sensitive to other factors that might affect change in behaviour (Argote, 2013).

> 'If we view a group as a mini-organisation whose members contribute to the groups shared mental models, then the model can represent group learning as well as organisational learning. A group can then be viewed as a collective individual, with its own set of models, which contributes to the organisation's shared mental model and learning. This is consistent with the notion that groups themselves are influenced by organisational structure and type of management style and therefore can be treated as if they were "extended individuals" (Kim, 2004, p. 41).

Organisational/sub-group learning occurs in a context which includes the organisation and the external environment in which the organisation or sub-group is embedded. Therefore as mentioned above a socio cultural approach to learning needs to be taken into account because this assumes that action is mediated and that it cannot be separated from the milieu in which it is carried out (Weber, 2008).

2.2.5 Expansive Learning

Activity Theory

Activity theory is a

> 'Philosophy and cross-disciplinary framework for studying different forms of human activity [. . . hence it is] a philosophical framework for studying different forms of human praxis as developmental process. Both individual and social levels are interlinked at the same time' (Kunit, as cited in Jonassen, 2000)
>
> 'Activity theorists argue that conscious learning and activity (performance) are completely interactive and interdependent. Activity cannot occur without conscious (the mind as a whole) and consciousness cannot occur outside of the context of activity' (Jonassen, 2000, pp. 97–98)

Initiated by Vygotsky and his Russian colleagues the principles of "Activity Theory" evolved from Vigotsky's (1978) triangular model visualising the relationship between the stimulus (S) and the response (R) which is transcended by a complex mediating act (X).

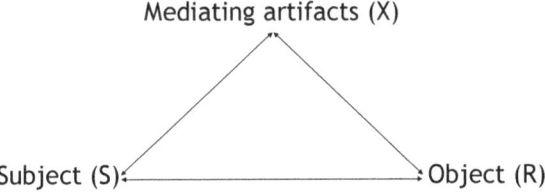

Figure 1: Common reformulation of Vygotsky's mediated act (Engeström, 2001).

Thus Vygotsky was first to insert "mediating acts" which are called "cultural artefacts" into human action.

> 'The individual could no longer be understood without his or her cultural means; and the society could no longer be understood without the agency of individuals who use and produce artefacts . . . . Objects became cultural entities and the object-orientedness of action became the key to understanding human psyche (Engeström 2001, p. 143)

The "cultural –historical approach" to Activity Theory, termed 'Second Generation Activity Theory' by Engeström (2001) included Leontev' s idea that the "difference between the individual action and a collective activity" needs to be considered with Il'enkov adding "internal contractions as the driving force of change and development". Western researchers included other influential domains, such as rules, the community and the division of labour, which provided "Activity Theory" with the potential of a great diversity of applications (Engeström, 2001).

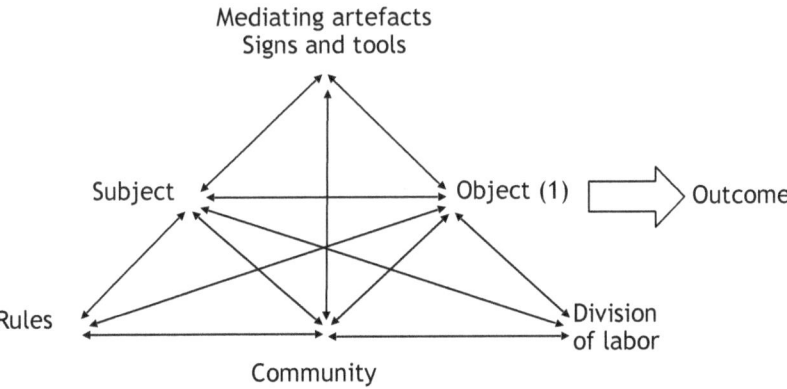

Figure 2: The structure of a human activity system (Engeström, 1987, p. 78).

Michael Cole (1988) pointed out that this second generation activity theory was insensitive towards cultural diversity and should be seriously challenged.

However the 'Third Generation of Activity Theory' needed to develop conceptual tools to understand dialogue, multiple perspectives and networks of interacting activity systems.

According to Engeström (2001), aspects such as "dialogically", the notion of Activity Networks, Actor Network Theory, the concept of Boundary Crossing and the concept of Third Space have shaped further discussion. These developments opened the doors for the formation of the 'Third Generation of Cultural Historical Theory; which was published in 2001 and which is most appropriate in my context.

> 'the object (e.g. lesson plan) moves from an initial state of un-reflected situationally given "raw material" to a collective meaningful object constructed by the activity system (partner institution) and finally to a potentially shared or jointly constructed object (e.g. best lesson plan published by partners at the end of the INQUIRE project duration). Thus the object is a moving target, not reducible to short-term goals (p. 136)

In relation to the case study presented in the second part of this work the current shape of Activity Theory may therefore be summarises by 5 principles (Engeström, 2001):

1. The prime unit of analysis is a collective, artefact-mediated and object-oriented activity system (INQUIRE partner organisation) seen in its network relations to other activity systems (INQUIRE consortium). Goal directed individual and group actions (course design, lesson plans, portfolio of evidence, posters presented at meetings etc.) are relatively independent but subordinated units of analysis, understandable only when interpreted against the background of the entire activity system (INQUIRE project).
2. An activity system is always a community of multiple points of view, traditions and interest. The division of labour creates different positions for

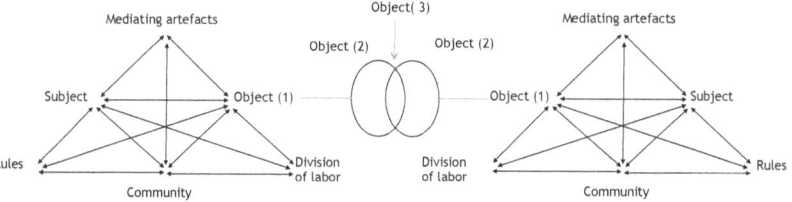

Figure 3: Two interacting activity systems as minimal model for the third generation of activity theory (Engeström, 2001 p. 136, cited by Kapelari, 2015).

the participants (INQUIRE-Management Board, hierarchy in partner institutions). The participants bring with them their own diverse histories and the activity system itself carries multiple layers and strands of history encapsulated in its artefacts, rules and conversations. The network multiplies this 'muti-voicedness' and is a source of both problems and innovation, demanding actions of translation and negotiation.
3. Activity systems get transformed and shaped over the length of time: The History of the entire activity system (INQUIRE project) needs to be studied both as a 'local history of the activity and its objects' and as a 'history of the theoretical ideas and tools that shape the activity'.
4. Activity systems are open systems. Contradictions accumulate structural tensions within and between activity systems. When one activity system adopts new elements from outside this may clash with already existing ones, generating disturbance and conflict, but also innovative attempts to change the particular activity.
5. There is a possibility of expansive transformation in activity systems; however they move through relatively long cycles of qualitative transformation. As the contradictions of an activity system are aggravated, some individual participants begin to question and deviate from established norms. An expansive transformation is accomplished when the object and motive of the activity are reconceptualised to embrace radically wider horizon.

Expansive Learning and Knowledge Creation

'Expansive Learning Theory' adds another set of 'somewhat philosophical' perspectives which need to be considered in the context of this work.

> 'Expansive learning refers to processes in which an activity system, for example a work organization, resolves its pressing internal contradictions by constructing and implementing a qualitatively new way of functioning for itself'. (Engeström, 2007, p. 24)

Engeström argues that 'Expansive Learning' is – in reference to Lave and Wenger's original legitimate-peripheral-participation framework – not a one way movement from incompetence to competence but includes horizontal movement while learners construct new concepts or objects for their activity. Thus expansive learning

- is concerned with learning of new forms of activities as they are created rather than the mastery of already known and well-defined existing knowledge and skills.

- is mainly concerned with collective learning rather than individual learning and
- although it acknowledges vertical learning Engeström (2000) suggests that 'we focus on constructing a complementary perspective, namely that of horizontal or sideway learning and development (p. 533)'

Contradictions originating within an activity system or between two or more activity systems are supposed to trigger change. It is assumed that human collective activity systems move through a cycle of change, which includes 7 steps:

1. Questioning/primary contradiction
2. Historical analysis and/or actual empirical analysis
3. Modelling the new solution
4. Examining the new model
5. Implementing the new model
6. Reflection on the process and realignment with neighbours
7. Consolidating the new practice

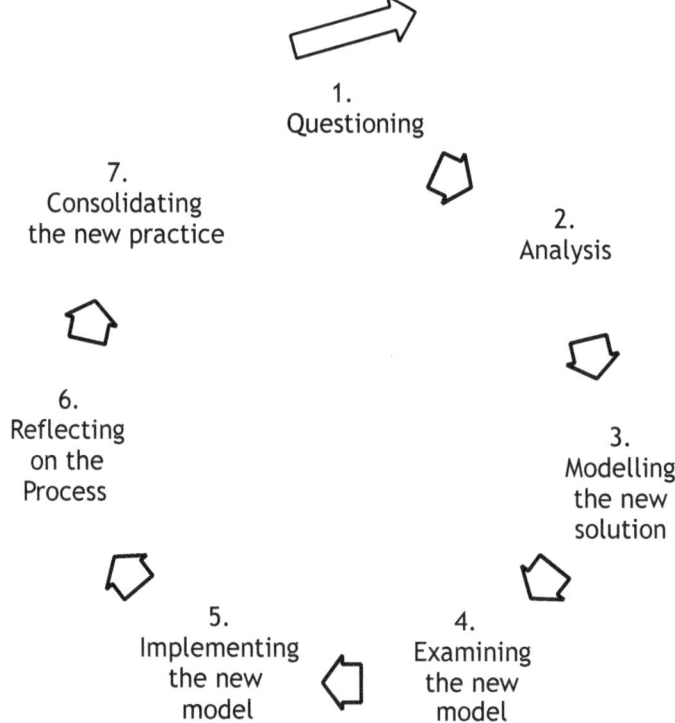

Figure 4: The expansive learning cycle (Engeström, 2007, cited by Kapelari, 2015).

'Ascending from the abstract to the concrete' is achieved through specific epistemic or learning actions. Together these actions form an expansive cycle or spiral. The process of expansive learning should be understood as construction and resolution of successively evolving contradictions in the activity system (Engeström & Sannino, 2010, p. 5).

Models of learning as a cyclic process are manifold in research literature and often show, beside differences, many similarities. E g. John Dewey´s 'Instructional Model of Learning' includes defining the problem, noting conditions associated with the problem, formulating a hypothesis for solving the problem, elaborating the value of various solutions, and finally testing the ideas to see which provide the best solution for the problem.

Bybee and colleagues (2006, p. 5) cite Dewey`s article 'Democracy and Education' published about a 100 years ago, as such

> 'Dewey further describes the relationship between experience and thinking. He summarizes the general features of the reflective experience: (i) perplexity, confusion, doubt, due to the fact that one is implicated in an incomplete situation whose full character is not yet determined; (ii) a conjectural anticipation—a tentative interpretation of the given elements, attributing to them a tendency to affect certain consequences; (iii) a careful survey (examination, inspection, exploration, analysis) of all attainable consideration which will define and clarify the problem in hand; (iv) a consequent elaboration of the tentative hypothesis to make it more precise and more consistent; (v) taking one stand upon the project hypothesis as a plan of action which is applied to the existing state of affairs: doing something overtly to bring about the anticipated result, thereby testing the hypothesis' (p. 150).

Engeströms 'Model of Expansive Learning' however enables us to theorise group, community and work based learning and adds new perspectives. It describes the capacity of learners working collaboratively to interpret and expand the definition of the object of an activity and to respond to it in a way that is most appropriate to the situation/cultural context in which the object is applied. It emphasises knowledge that is embedded in practice and values both conceptual artefacts (ideas, opinions etc.) and material practices (e.g. lesson plans).

Expansive learning not only values 'the process of vertical improvement along some uniform scales of competences' but recognises a horizontal movement, the exchange and hybridisation between different cultural contexts and standards of competences` (Engeström & Sannino, 2010, p. 2).

In their article 'Models of Innovative Knowledge Communities and three Metaphors of learning' Paavola and colleagues (2004) discuss Nonaka and Takeuchi´s 'Model of Knowledge Creation', Engeström's 'Model of Expansive

Learning' (s.p. 35) and Bereiter's 'Model of Knowledge building' (mentioned above) and argue

> 'The models we have reviewed emphasize that previous conceptions of learning have been inadequate for dealing with innovative, expansive or progressive aspects of knowledge advancement in a profound way. Neither acquisition nor the participation approach has been sufficient, at least not in ideal typical forms (p. 569)

They argue that

> 'The main focus of the acquisition perspective has been on the acquisition of knowledge that is more or less ready-made or on clear-cut developmental rules or phases, rather than on the creation of something "expansively" new. The participation perspective typically has focused on examining how knowledge and practices are passed from one generation to another in traditional cultures or in cultures without substantial and deliberate changes or cultural transformations (see, e.g., Lave and Wenger, 1991). The focus has been on how newcomers become old-timers by participating in cultural practices, not on the radical advancement of knowledge or practices '(p. 569).

Although these arguments indicate a rather limited view on 'knowledge acquisition' and 'knowledge participation' and authors attenuate these claims while continuing, these arguments reveal a commonly recognised weak point in education practice in general and in science education practice in particular, which still mainly focuses on accumulating facts, predetermined outcomes and following a traditional path.

In the context of my work the metaphor of 'knowledge creation' is rooted in Engeströms model of expansive learning is most appropriate because:

> 'knowledge-creation models conceptualize learning and knowledge advancement as collaborative processes for developing shared objects of activity. Learning is not conceptualized through processes occurring in individuals' minds, or through processes of participation in social practices. Learning is understood as a collaborative effort directed toward developing some mediated artifacts, broadly defined as including knowledge, ideas, practices, and material or conceptual artifacts. The interaction among different forms of knowledge or between knowledge and other activities is emphasized as a requirement for this kind of innovativeness in learning and knowledge creation [...]. A broader perspective is needed because it is important to understand those [cultural] practices through which innovative knowledge communities function. The focus is not on the certainty of knowledge but how knowledge is used and how it is developed. The models

of innovative knowledge communities are important just because they analyze processes of knowledge creation in a detailed and concrete way. Such analysis requires that both social and epistemological perspectives be taken into account.' (Paavola et al., 2004, pp. 569–570).

2.3 Science Education in the 21st Century

In the 20th century, the main goal for science education in Austria was to deliver a certain amount of content knowledge, which was often considered to be solid reproducible facts. Those able to accumulate and reproduce this knowledge were considered to be well prepared for a scientific carrier.

21rst century science education is no longer valued only by those wishing to go into scientific or scientific related careers but by all members of an educated society. Supporting every child to become *"scientifically literate"* is now more than a buzzword amongst science educators and curriculum planners and science education authorities in Europe although it may not be on the agenda of all science teachers yet and can manifest itself in in different ways.

The term "scientific literacy" is used to show that science knowledge is regarded an object of economic, political and cultural value, as important as 'basic skills' such as reading, writing or mathematics. Scientific literacy is considered to be important to have and useful for anybody who wishes to lead a successful life and become a major and active citizen of a modern society, able to question scientific outcomes, to value them for personal decisions and to act according to these decisions.

Since the PISA assessment gained influential coverage in both the media and political discussions, the concept of *'Scientific literacy for all students'* is becoming more and more popular in Austria as well as other countries.

2.3.1 *The Concept of Scientific Literacy*

Given the length of history for the rhetoric of science education one would presume that there would be a clear definition of *scientific literacy* already. As with the terms 'Nature of Science' or 'Inquiry Bases Science Education', this is unfortunately not the case.

The term "Scientific Literacy" first appeared in the educational literature of the US in papers authored by Paul Hurd and Richard McCudy in 1958 and since that time the various definitions have been discussed in great detail, with emphasis placed on one or another aspect that are shared across many definitions (Hodson, 2007).

The European science education community, that joined the discussion a couple of years later, frequently cites the OECD PISA Framework when it refers to scientific literacy as a global goal for science education.

In 1999 the OECD pointed out that:

> 'An important life skill for young people is the capacity to draw appropriate and guarded conclusions from evidence and information given to them, to criticise claims made by others on the basis of the evidence put forward, and to distinguish opinion from evidence-based statements.' (OECD, 1999, p. 59)

In 2006 PISA OECD defines *Scientific Literacy* as the capacity to

- use scientific knowledge,
- identify questions and
- draw evidence based conclusions in order to understand and help making decisions about the natural world and the changes made to it through human activities.

It is important to emphasise that both scientific knowledge (in the sense of knowledge about science) and the process by which this knowledge is developed are essential for scientific literacy. They are bound together in this understanding of the term (OECD, 2007).

Besides a well-developed understanding of fundamental scientific concepts, the limitation of scientific knowledge and the nature of science as human activity, the PISA definition also implicitly includes students' abilities to read, write and understand scientific language as well as being able to analyse, extract meaning, interpret and evaluate scientific texts.

> 'It is the scientific language that shapes our ideas, provides the means for constructing scientific understanding and explanations, enables us to communicate the purposes, procedures, findings and explanations of our inquiry and allows us to relate our work to existing knowledge and understanding' (Hodson, 2007, p. 2).

'Drawing evidence based conclusions' stands for a whole set of abilities that scientifically literate people are expected to have such as:

- being able to identify questions which can be answered by science.
- knowing how and whether this scientific knowledge can be applied
- being able to select and evaluate information and data, cautiously and consciously (PISA 2006)

The PISA scientific literacy definition does not mention 'intellectual independence and autonomy' explicitly although it is very likely that these aspects are covered (Hodson, 2007).

Intellectual independence for non-scientists has been a goal of science education for decades (Norris, 1997) and is one INQUIRE learning goal I will address in the second part of this work.

- 'To be intellectually independent is to assess on one one´s own the soundness of the justification proposed for a knowledge claim'. Depending on the source, either based on personal science content knowledge or on the basis of good reasons or evidence for believing that somebody else has good reasons for his or her believes, the justification requires more or less understanding of the scientific content (Aikenhead, 1990, p. 132 cited in Norris, 1997)
- [...] 'understand and help make decisions' includes valuing the understanding of scientific knowledge as a goal which needs to be achieved and which can be applied in the context of human values related to social, political and economic dimensions. 'Science is in many respects the systematic application of some highly regarded human values – integrity, diligence, fairness, curiosity, openness to new ideas, scepticism, and imagination. Studying science will instil these values. (AAAS 1989, cited in Hodson 2007, p. 11)
- [...] 'the natural world and the changes made to it through human activities' refers to physical settings, living things and the relationship among them. Decisions about the natural world include those associated with issues which address oneself and/or the family, the community and the world as such (PISA 2006).

Science education plays an important role in providing the context and supporting students to develop these abilities. Science is concerned with developing structured and reproducible approaches for testing ideas and offers theories based on evidence. While including creativity and imagination the critical and rational perspective is not neglected and the combination of both is the approach science takes to advance our understanding of the natural world (OECD, 1999).

The OEDC framework for testing students' knowledge and skills PISA defines Scientific Literacy as an individual's:

- Scientific knowledge and use of that knowledge to identify questions, acquire new knowledge, explain scientific phenomena and draw evidence-based conclusions about science-related issues
- Understanding of the characteristic features of science as a form of human knowledge and enquiry
- Awareness of how science and technology shape our material, intellectual and cultural environments
- Willingness to engage in science-related issues, and with the ideas of science, as a reflective citizen (OECD, 2013, p. 100).

Thus Scientific Literacy has a significant metacognitive dimension. Students need to know what they know, and when the knowledge can and should be utilized as well as how to recognize deficiencies in their own knowledge and how to compensate for them (Hodson, 2007).

Science Literacy is therefore more rooted in learning about science and doing science than in learning science facts only.

Why is it important to become scientifically literate?

PISA 2006 points out that Scientific Literacy does not presume a dichotomy where people are either scientifically literate or scientifically illiterate. It is a continuum, which progresses from less developed to more developed.

A cultural approach to Scientific Literacy includes a societal and an individual dimension. The individual is asked to engage in a life-long learning process. It is assumed that good science teaching has the potential to provoke this perpetual process. Thus in our knowledge society the scientifically literate individual is expected to gain a range of profits.

A public understanding of science is assumed to be important for a society as a whole, because Scientific Literacy . . ..

- increases the competitiveness and economic strength of a society (s. p. 50ff)
- increases the number of recruits for science jobs (students at universities, researchers, people working in the industry and technology sector etc. (s. p. 50ff)
- provides greater financial support for science research, industry and technology
- leads to more realistic public expectations as to what science can do (awareness of the characteristics of science enquiry)
- helps counter opposition from religious groups
- counteracts anti-science behaviour
- supports the acceptance of science/scientists
- reduces public suspicion about science based innovations (e.g. GMO)
- supports scientists as expert witnesses for both sides in legal disputes
- values what science does for the economy (e.g. jobs, money to earn). Scientific literacy is therefore regarded as a form of human capital that sustains and develops the economic well-being of a nation
- enriches the cultural health and the intellectual life of a nation
- enhances democracy and responsible citizenship

Any individual member of society who works towards becoming scientifically literate may result in the ability to;

- make informed decisions affecting one's health, life style, security, economic well being

- live up to the demand of advanced science skills; people are expected to develop their learning skills and learn to progress within their jobs
- value science as helpful for learning, reasoning, thinking creatively, making decisions, solving problems
- value the intellectual, aesthetic, moral and ethical benefits of science
- develop one's own ethical standards and codes for responsible behaviour
- take responsibility for decisions about one's own health and the environment

It is assumed that Scientific Literacy supports people to become and stay responsible and active citizen in the community.

Hodson (2007) argues that a curriculum aiming for supporting students to become scientifically literate should give insight into what science is and what scientists do. This includes various elements such as:

- exploring the nature of science
- exploring various views of science
- engaging in scientific inquiry
- making the case for the history of science

However, the concept of scientific literacy has been reconceptualised by educators and policy makers to a large extent. This diffusion of the concept can be interpreted as a result of economic, political and cultural logic which have been applied. Each of these logics has an influence on the particular mix of what is considered more or less important whenever learning goals are defined and implemented in curricula, instructional material and in assessment. Eneaney (2003) argues that:

> 'the public discourse about scientific literacy is driven by economic and political logics while curricular implementation is grounded in world culture (p. 218)

Dillon (2009) argues:

> The longevity of the term scientific literacy relies on its ability to be seen as an umbrella for radical different philosophies of science education. However, the evidence suggests that when attempts are made to effect curriculum change to promote 'scientific literacy' the unreconciled philosophical clashes hinders progress (Dillon, 2009).

However, discussions revolving around the concept of scientific literacy raise the question whether the tension between 'those three logics' or the 'unreconciled philosophical clashes' should be blamed only or whether we need to reconsider the key question: 'what does it mean to be educated in this days and age?' We may need to question our assumption about 'global education as the ultimate goal for all children'. Global knowledge, global skills and global values such as those considered important in the 'scientific literacy' debate;

> '[...] cannot resolve the crisis of meaning in our societies because they are not asking the important questions about what we stand for and which knowledge we should teach children [...] Values of diversity, tolerance, empathy, participation, or being a 'global citizen' all avoid asking difficult questions about which ideas and cultural practices are better than others'. (Standish, 2012)

The latter questions are those practitioners need to answer on a daily basis. They need to decide what they want students to know at the end of the day. As we will see later the process of descending from an abstract understanding of a concept such as scientific literacy, inquiry, nature of science as they are discussed among scholars, to the concrete teaching and learning in an everyday science classroom consequently leads to individual or organisational interpretations and reconstructions of the concept. The question is whether it is possible or even desirable to train practitioners to adopt values and practices that have been developed by others without engaging in expanding a particular understanding that may resemble their own values, their socio cultural context, their attitudes, knowledge and skills.

Scientific Literacy and Environmental Education

The PISA in Focus 2012, Environmental Education report argues that today's students are growing up in a precarious natural environment. 'Climate Change' and the loss of biodiversity threaten ecosystems. The lack of clean water, the immense production of waste and polluted grounds jeopardise the health of millions of people every day.

Since individual actions have an impact on the environment it is assumed that scientific literacy' includes 'Environmental Literacy' because the actions of individuals have an impact on the environment.

Scientifically literate people are supposed to be equipped with knowledge about environmental issues and therefore tend to seek more information. Thus they are considered to be better prepared to make informed decisions about their daily life and how they lead it.

The EU PISA in focus report shows that, across the OECD 19% of 15-year olds perform at the highest level of proficiency in environmental science (Level A) PISA scale). At this level students can constantly identify, explain and apply scientific knowledge related to a variety of environmental topics. They can

> '[...] link different information sources and explanation and use evidence from those sources to justify decisions about environmental

issues. They clearly and consistently demonstrate advanced thinking a reasoning in the science relevant to the environment and use the understanding to develop arguments in support of recommendations and decisions in both the social and the global situation (OECD, 2012, p. 2)

A large proportion of students are under-equipped to meet environmental challenges. Across the OECD countries the average of 16% of the students performs below the baseline level of proficiency.

However the interdisciplinary field of environmental education (EE) has been in existence for c. 40 years. It has received considerably more attention in recent years as contested issues about the environment, such as environmental pollution, environmental protection, climate change and sustainable living become common topics in public, media and political debates.

Attempts to characterise the concept of Environmental Education as well as that of Sustainability Education, however, have come up with a multiplicity of interpretations.

The United Nation Conference on Environmental Development (UNCED) referred to education as being critical to promoting sustainable development and for improving the capacity of people to address environmental and development issues;

> 'There is a need to increase people's sensitivity to, and involvement in, finding solutions for environment and development problems. Education can give people the environmental and ethical awareness, values and attitudes, skills and behaviour needed for sustainable development. To do this, education needs to explain not only the physical and biological environment, but the socio-economic environment and human development' (UNCED, 1992, para 36.3.).

Thus as an interdisciplinary field Environmental Education aims to:

- Foster clear awareness of, and concern about, economic, social, political, and ecological interdependences in urban and rural areas.
- Provide every person with the opportunity to acquire the knowledge, values, attitudes, commitment, and skills needed to protect and improve the environment.
- Create new patterns of behaviour towards the environment in individuals, groups and societies as a whole.

Regula Kyburz-Graber (2013) summaries a strand of environmental education research which developed as a reaction to social requests concerning environmental problems:

- promoting individual behavioural change through improving strategies and research

- enhancing environmental awareness through environmental literacy, usually closely linked to natural literacy
- enhancing humans relationship to nature and ecological awareness through experiencing nature
- promoting action competence through action oriented learning
- promoting ethical reflection and awareness of cultural context and diversity
- becoming a critical thinker through transformative and critical education

Bailin and colleagues (2010) argue, in respect to education for critical thinking, that:

> 'Becoming proficient at critical thinking itself involves among other things the acquisition of certain sorts of knowledge. For example the knowledge of certain critical concepts which enable one to make distinctions is central to critical thinking' (p. 272).

Environmental science is taught in schools in almost all OECD countries. Most students learn about it in subjects such as 'natural sciences', 'biology' and 'geography'.

It is generally agreed by researchers that learning about the environment outside the classroom has a great potential to support students learning (Rickinson et al., 2004). According to school heads questioned in the course of the 2006 PISA study most 15 year old students attend schools that provide at least one 'Out of the Classroom' (LOtC) learning activity offer. Outdoor education and trips to museums are the most common activities.77% of students in OECD countries attend schools that offer outdoor education and 75% offer schools visits to museums, 65% offer school visits to science centres.

School plays an important role in providing information about air pollution, energy, extinctions of plants, etc. Thus most often students learn about environmental matters in school. High performing students also refer to media and the internet to improve their knowledge (Grafendorfer & Neureiter, 2009).

Zint (2012, p. 9) summarises potentially successful practices and assumes that instructional practices cannot foster changes in behaviours if they:

- lack clearly defined behavioural outcomes and objectives,
- focus on general environmental knowledge or attitudes (vs. ones related to desired behaviours),
- are imposed from the top down (i.e. not designed to meet audiences' needs),
- passive (i.e. information transmission focused, lacking participant involvement), and
- are short (i.e. a few hours) in duration.

However they do foster changes in behaviours if they:

- have behavioural outcome and objectives,
- are designed based on behaviour theories/models [see (Heimlich & Ardoin, 2008) for a review of relevant theories/models],

- consider participants' needs, context and background,
- incorporate experiential learning (e.g. field trips, in service learning), and
- are longer (i.e. 1–2 years) in duration.

Based on science education research findings Zint (2011) suggests to apply the following instructional practices and cites authors accordingly (p. 10)

- (long term) place-based hands-on science inquiry (Bodzin, 2008; Endreny, 2010; Patterson & Harbor, 2005),
- outdoor learning experience (Bodzin, 2008),
- demonstrations/models that make invisible parts of watershed systems visible (Covitt et al., 2009),
- instructional technology (e.g. Web-based GIS maps and google Earth) Bodzin, 2008)

Scientific Literacy and Plant Science

Within the last few decades a phenomenon became more and more visible in civilized countries. As more people are living in urban or suburban environments, daily interactions with plants fewer than at any time in human history. This urbanization is therefore fostering a profound and continuing disconnection with nature where plants are becoming 'alien species' for young children and future generations (Richards & Lee, 2002). There is however an urgent need to raise student and other people´s interest in plants. Biodiversity loss, climate change, feeding our world's population, increasing limitation of drinking water resources and the need for comprehensive health care are only a few of the biggest challenges for our population in the 21st century. None of these problems will be solved without profound knowledge about plants, how they live and what can do for us. Learning about plants should therefore be a central pillar within science education that focuses on developing scientifically literate mature citizens.

Becoming scientifically literate in Austria

According to the national curriculum, the goal of science education in Austria is to develop scientific competences (BiFI, 2011). Grafendorfer & Neureiter (2009) published a study based on the Austrian specific data collected via the PISA 2006 assessment. They looked closely at how Austrian students experience science learning in class. Four categories of science teaching approaches were assessed:

Approach 1: Students engage in discussions, are asked for their opinions and ideas and to explain these

Approach 2: Students conduct experiments in the laboratory by following given instructions. They watch teachers demonstrating these experiments and they are asked to draw conclusions from them.
Approach 3: Students are exposed to inquiry based learning
Approach 4: Science knowledge is related to an everyday context.

Results showed that Austrian 15-16 year olds rarely experience inquiry based (IB) learning in class. Interestingly, only 5% of high level performing students (PISA Level 5 and above) state that they are often asked to do investigations and draw their own conclusions (the IB approach) whereas students that stated that they often experienced IB in class, often showed a low level proficiency (PISA, level 1 and below) - c37% of the Austrian students who stated this were registered at this low PISA level.

Discussion related and context related science teaching approaches are most commonly experienced by Austrian 15-to 16 year olds in science classes. While the Austrian emphasis on discussion related methods is higher, doing experiments, inquiry bases learning and context related learning is below OECD average.

Austrian head-teachers report on various activities that support student engagement in science. The most popular is taking part in fieldtrips and excursions; these are supported by 90% of all participating schools. 70% of all Austrians schools provide opportunities for students to learn about environmental issues via fieldtrips into nature as well as visits to museums and science centres.

Austrian 15-16 year olds mainly learn about scientific topics in school. 30% of the Austrians students declare that they gain additional knowledge about the topics 'nuclear power' and 'climate change' from the media. 50% also learn about 'health and diet' at home. 50% of this age group spent 2-6 hours/week on science classes in school. 17% do not have any science classes. Learning about science via free choice activities appears to not be very popular with Austrian teenagers; 15-16 year olds never or rarely read about scientific topics in books (93%) nor do they watch science programs on TV (87%). Only 4% attend science groups regularly or often.

Looking at the Austrian curriculum, science education has a social responsibility to support students in a world where knowledge and technology are rapidly changing. This should be done to support students to acquire the knowledge and competences, alongside discussion techniques in order to develop and become mature critical thinking citizens. The general educational goals, regarding the domain of nature and technology in the Austrian curriculum for 10-18 year olds (AHS, NMS, HS) are:

- to develop knowledge about interdependencies in nature which is considered essential to establish a conscious way of managing and using the environment by means of modern technology

- to develop an understanding for scientific phenomenon and ways of looking at questions and problems in mathematics, science and technology is regarded the foundation for inclusion in a modern technologically minded society.

Education in science should therefore convey basic knowledge, decision-making authority and the capacity to act. Students should be qualified to deal proficiently with the moral concepts and ethical questions connected with science and technology as well as with humans and their environment. Formalizations, modelling, abstractions and a concept of space should be conveyed as essential requirements for analysing and finding solutions to problems. (BMUKK, 2000).

Austrian curricula mirror the internationally discussed concept of scientific literacy, although the focus is primarily on what to convey more than on what to achieve. No particular focus is put on understanding the Nature of Science (NOS) in the way that the PISA concept of scientific literacy does.

The term *'scientific literacy'* is frequently translated in German as 'Naturwissenschafts-kompetenz' (Grafendorfer & Neureiter, 2009) or 'Naturwissenschaftliche Grundbildung' meaning 'basic scientific literacy' (Reinhold, 1997, Rost et al., 2005). The latter implies that people may reach different levels of scientific literacy. It is assumed that there are further stages of scientific literacy to reach after school, which might be achieved through a life-long learning process. However benchmarks for whether or not somebody has achieved this 'basic scientific literacy' are ill-defined. Although the PISA definition of scientific literacy described above is assumed to be broader than the processes included in most science curricula of participating OEDC nations, Austrian experts assume that the compliance with the Austrian Curriculum is comprehensive (Eder, 2009).

Economy based needs for improving science and technology education in Austria

A cultural approach values scientific literacy as being important for each individual human. Political, social and economic perspectives are often raised in addition to justify the need for improving science education in Europe.

Enhancing the knowledge level of a society is assumed to improve the competitiveness and the innovation potential of the whole nation.

Holzinger and Reidl (2012) published the study, 'The Humanresourcen Barometer' recently and show that human capital, which is the knowledge, skills and competences associated with each individual person, forms the basis of economic success not only for a company but the whole country. It also increases competitiveness as well as the potential for a nation's social development. An increasing in competitiveness has an effect on the job market, resulting in an increasing demand for higher qualified employees. Providing enough work-force for knowledge based economy challenges the education and employment market, particularly when one takes the demographics into account.

The Innovation Union Scoreboard (IUS, 2013) gives a comparative assessment of the innovation performance of the EU 27 member states and the relative strengths and weaknesses of their research and innovation systems. The overall ambition of the Innovation Union Scoreboard is *'to inform policy discussions at the national and EU level by tracking progress in innovation performance inside and outside the EU over time'*. The measurement focuses on the Summary Innovation Index (SII) which includes 'Enablers' (human resources, open, excellent attractive research systems, finance and support), 'firm activities' (firm investments, linkage and entrepreneurship, intellectual assets) and 'outputs' (innovators and economic effects).

Based on this index, EU states are put into four performance groups:

- Innovation Leaders, which is currently led by Sweden, followed by Germany, Denmark and Finland, who are well above the EU27 average.
- Innovation Followers, the group that Austria and the UK belong to, which are less than 20% but more than 10% above the EU average.
- Moderate Innovators, those less than 10% below but more than 50% below the EU27 average and
- Modest innovators are below 50% that of the EU 27. Bulgaria, Romania, Poland and Lithuania are at the bottom end.

Austria has recently been demonstrating a dynamic catching up process, putting the country into the 'Innovation Followers' group. Austria has to admit however that it has improved in some aspects but has not yet reached its goals to become an 'Innovation Leader'. The 'Humanressourcen Barometer' is looking at the Austria's development in great detail. Based on the findings of the Austrian Human Resources Development between 1999 and 2010 the following issues will need to be addressed in the future;

- The ageing of the human resource for in science and technology
- The demand by Austrian innovation strategies for a higher number of highly qualified human capital, which will be difficult to supply
- The lack of equal opportunities for women in science and technology which is currently leading to a decrease in the human capital in science and technology
- The tertiary education sector failing to supply the demand for highly qualified human resources in science and technology
- The fact that the demand for a higher human resource for science and technology is currently met through a high percentage of non-natives.

- The proportion of non-employed or inactive human resources in science and technology is very low in Austria leaving no scope to supply future demands with people who are already well educated.

Figures show clearly that Austria is improving in its efforts to raising the number of higher educated people in general. The years 2002–2011 show a 65% increase in students finishing their studies at university and 138% more graduating at colleges. These changes can be explained by the fact that an increasing number of colleges (Fachhochschulen) have been founded in Austria in the last 20 years and the by the implementation of 'bachelor' programmes.

Looking at these numbers in more detail, we recognise certain aspects that need to be considered for the delivery of science education and science education reform efforts in Austria.

Between 2002 and 2011 we see an increase of 40% of students signing up at universities in Austria. Science and Technology courses show about the same increase in student numbers (40% and 52% respectively). At colleges, technology and science is even more popular, with an increase of 81%-85% in student numbers.

This contradicts the European Commission's perception that the interest of young people in science and technology related careers is decreasing.

However, in relation to other academic subjects, the number of young people interested in science and technology studies is still low; in addition we still see a large discrepancy between the number of female and male students in science and technology related subjects. Most female students study pedagogy related studies the lowest numbers are seen in technology related studies. Male Students prefer to study the social sciences followed by technology and science related subjects (Holzinger & Reidl, 2012).

Taking the human resource development in our country into consideration, the Austrian science education systems obviously needs develop new strategies of how to counteract the current trend that young people, females in particular, tend to follow in their career choice.

2.3.2 Improving Science Education

Science Education has traditionally been assigned the role of transmitting knowledge. However, over the past 50 years, there have been dynamic changes in our conceptualisation of science learning and of science learning environments, integrating concepts such as 'situated learning' or the 'socio-cultural perspective of learning' (see. above).

These changes have important implications for how we interpret the role of inquiry in school science education programmes as well as curriculum development, teaching practices and assessment techniques (Duschl & Grandy, 2008).

Whereas traditionally science education mainly focused on the acquisition of a body of content knowledge and conceptual understanding, there is now an acknowledgement within science education that learners' should understand the nature of science knowledge and the nature of science processes/methods as discussed earlier.

This has a significant impact on student science learning itself. In addition to alternative concepts, students come to science instruction with naïve theories and/ or misconceptions about the Nature of Science (NOS). These beliefs about science impact student understanding of the content knowledge itself (Lederman, 2007).

Seeking for improvement of science teaching in Europe

Next to others an EU expert group lead by Michel Rocard launched the Report 'Science Education Now a Renewed Pedagogy for the Future of Europe' in 2007 addressing the issue that there is a decline in the interests of young people for careers in Science.

Experts claim (ibid p. 7–11) that;

- science education is far from attracting crowds and in many countries the trend is worsening.
- the origin of this situation can be found, among other causes, in the way how science is taught.
- many on-going initiatives in Europe actively contribute to the renewal of science education. Nevertheless, they are often small-scale and do not actively take advantage of European support measures for dissemination and integration.

Accordingly the Rocard Report (2007) aims for bringing about a 'radical change in young people's interest in science and to identify the necessary pre-conditions' (p. 5).

Expert findings (p. 13–14.) suggest that;

- A reversal of school's science teaching pedagogy from mainly deductive to inquiry-based methods provides the means to increase interest in science.
- Renewed school's science-teaching pedagogy based on IBSE provides increased opportunities for cooperation between various actors in the formal and informal arenas.
- Teachers are key players in the renewal of science education. Among other methods, being part of a network allows them to improve the quality of their teaching and supports their motivation.

IBSE is assumed to increase young people's interest and attainment levels while at the same time stimulating teacher's motivation in teaching science. Two best practice models, the POLLEN and the Sinus Transfer project funded in FP6 and through German grants, are considered to have proven capable of increasing children´s interest and attainments in science. 'With some adaption', the authors argue, 'these initiatives could be implemented effectively on a large scale that would have the desired impact' (ibid, p. 14–15).

Although IBSE is a teaching approach to find favour with education policies and European funding schemes it is still not well defined and meanings associated with 'inquiry' are manifold (Capps & Crawford, 2013).

At almost the same time, a report to the Nuffield Foundation edited by Jonathan Osborne and Justin Dillon (2008) raised concerns about Science Education in Europe and offered critical reflections and several recommendations.

According to this report, the seven recommendations given that require addressing in the near future are:

1. To educate all students both about the major explanations of the material world that science offers and about the way science works. Science courses whose basic aims is to provide a foundational education for future scientists and engineers should be optional
2. More attempts are required to innovative curricula and ways of organising the teaching of science in order to address the issue of low students motivation.
3. EU countries need to invest in improving the human and physical resources available to schools for informing students both about careers in science and careers derived from science
4. EU countries' should ensure that teachers of the highest quality are provided for students in primary and lower secondary school and the emphasis on science education before 14 should be on engaging students with science and scientific phenomena (extended investigative work and hands-on experimentation is recommended)
5. Developing and extending the ways in which science is taught is essential for improving student engagement. Transforming teacher practice across the EU is a long term project and will require significant and sustainable investment in continuing professional development (CPD)
6. EU governments should invest significantly in research and development in the assessment in science education
7. Good quality teachers, with up to date knowledge and skills are the foundation of any system of formal science education. Systems to ensure the recruitment, retention and CPD of such individuals must be a policy priority in Europe.

Thus the authors put teachers, teachers CPD and development in science teaching at the centre of progress and stressed the fact that young children in primary and low secondary school in particular should get the best teachers. They focus on science being taught to all children, providing a response to the goal of all students becoming scientifically literate. It does, however emphasis the point that it is not a general aim that all student become scientists (Osborne & Dillon, 2008).

The Austrian teacher training system has recently followed this advice and a new teacher training law has been published asking all teachers from primary school upwards to attend a five year academic education process provided by at universities and pedagogical colleges. It will be important in the future that these training institutions put emphasis on science and technology education for teachers and require a fundamental and well devolved understanding of how to teach science content as well as science pedagogy to young children in particular.

Classroom practice in Europe

The recent OECD Teaching and Learning Survey, TALIS 2008, was carried out to fill the gaps in international data about teaching practices as well as the working conditions for teachers and the learning environments in lower secondary school. It surveyed 7,000 teachers and 4,000 school principals in 24 participating countries (Vieluf et al., 2012).

Three dimensions of classroom teaching practices were identified in TALIS 2008. These dimensions are 'structuring', 'student orientation' and 'enhanced activities'.

- 'Structuring' activities describe teaching practices which clarify the structure of a unit or lesson and its ultimate goals, as well as test whether all students have understood the content and performed their task
- 'Student orientation' activity concerns group work and adaptive instruction but also students participation in classroom planning

Both dimensions ask for practices that involve close interaction of the teacher with the whole class, small groups or individual students.

- 'Enhanced activity' does not include the latter but instead summarises practices that give students the chance to work independently over a longer period of time.

Key findings show that only a minority of teachers has a profile that demonstrates a comparatively diverse use of classroom teaching practices. Teaching practices are influenced by pedagogical traditions and national cultures, resulting in qualitative differences in the frequency of diverse teaching activities applied.

Professional development in Europe

According to TALIS 2008 findings the main driving-forces for advancement in teaching practice are;

- developing a larger repertoire of classroom teaching practices
- taking collective responsibility and
- working co-operatively to improve instructions.

Professional learning communities are assumed to be an alternative and even more successful way for the professional development of teachers in the long run. They provide the space for learners to discuss and exchange knowledge as well as make use of the social capital individual members provide (Hofman & Dijkstra, 2010).

TALIS 2008 investigate whether teachers participate in professional learning communities to develop their practice. Here the concept of a professional learning community is rooted in the socio-constructivist idea and in models of learning organisations mentioned earlier. Professional learning communities include 5 characteristics namely:

- co-operation among teachers (such as team teaching)
- holding a shared vision,
- having a clear focus on learning,
- practicing reflective inquiry and
- engaging in the de-privatisation of practice (e.g. work cooperatively to share their teaching methodology, issues and successes)

Exploring whether all these five dimensions of a Community of Practice (CoP) are being implemented, findings reveal that teachers in Europe hardly ever participate in professional learning communities. Large differences can be observed in the implementation of certain aspects that characterise communities of practice. Findings also revealed that 55% of the teachers participating in the TALIS survey wanted more professional development because they felt they needed more help around the topic of classroom management and working with special needs students. The larger the repertoire of teaching practices, the more tools teachers hold in their 'toolbox' (Vieluf et al., 2012). Professional development is a key to ensure that teachers have this full 'toolbox'. In the long run, teacher networks may provide an alternative and even more successful way to professional development of teachers. The network provides the space for learners to discuss and exchange knowledge, as well as makes use of the social capital individual members provide (Hofman & Dijkstra, 2010).

2.3.3 Inquiry Based Science Education (IBSE)

At the beginning of the 20th century, 'Inquiry Based Science Learning`(IBSL) environments were already assumed to be fruitful ways to put cognitive theory and social-constructivist ideas into practice, as well as provide space for situated learning in a more 'authentic' science context (s.p. 23ff).

Educational theorists and psychologist such as Dewey, Schwab, Ausuble, Bruner and others have repeatedly asked for school science to become less didactic and trans-missive and less focussed on accumulating facts and procedures. Good science teaching was already presumed to be more effective if it explicitly included learning about the nature of scientific knowledge as well as inquiry-based activities.

However, implementing change in any educational system is a particularly slow process. Hence there is no wonder that the same ideas appear to be still extremely progressive today.

As the nature of scientific knowledge is situated, practiced and collaboratively generated a 'renewed' European science pedagogy is asking for the inclusion of more activities such as experimentation, trial and error, hypothesis testing, presenting, communicating and debating into everyday science teaching (Rocard, 2007). Lunetta and colleagues (2007) assume that there is a widespread agreement among scientists, policymakers, researchers, science teacher educators and presumably science classroom teachers, that students should experience inquiry in the science classroom or at LOtC institutions more often. It is assumed that the teaching of inquiry based learning will support student ability to meet 21st century science education goals (s.p. 38ff)

What is Inquiry Based Science Education?

The inquiry based education movement has been strong in the United States of America for a couple of decades now and the National Science Education Standards have required the implementation of inquiry based learning in US science classrooms since 1996 already. Because of this science education research literature frequently refers to the US National Science Research Councils definitions for science inquiry in the classroom. Here 'inquiry' is defined as a science knowledge gaining process and is characterised by 'the diverse ways in which scientists study the natural world and propose explanations based on evidence from their work" (NRC, 1996, p. 23).

Referring to the NRC 1996 definition, Anderson (2002) argues that the term 'inquiry' is used:

1. to describe the many processes that professional scientists apply. The US National Science Education Standards stress the point that these non-linear, sometimes messy pathways, should not be confused with the formulaic method.

2. to describe the active learning process that students engage in modelled after the inquiry process of professional scientists. Harlen (2013, p. 12) assumes that using skills employed by scientists means to:
   - progressively develop ideas
   - make observations,
   - raise questions
   - examine books or other source of information,
   - plan investigations,
   - use tools to gather, analyse and interpret data,
   - use sufficient and relevant data for testing hypothesis
   - be rigorous and honest in collecting data
   - keep careful records throughout the investigations
   - repeat data collection
   - draw conclusions
   - review what is already known in the light of evidence,
   - propose answers, explanations and predictions
   - communicate results and share ideas.

In short, this process is described as:

> 'inquiry' is content in and of itself: a process about which students should learn and in which they participate. The standards clearly spell out though, that inquiry is more than a process, more than something students should do. It is a vehicle for learning science content. The second definition of inquiry in the standards refers to specifically designed experiences and activities that lead to knowledge and understanding of scientific ideas and content'. (Asay & Orgill, 2009, p. 58)

Daphne Minner and colleagues (2010) add a third point to Anderson's definition arguing that the term inquiry also applies to;

3. the pedagogical approach that teachers employ when designing or using curricula that allow for extended investigations.

A variety of terms are used in Europe to talk about inquiry-based approaches in science learning. Inquiry Based Science Learning (IBSL), Inquiry Based Science Education (IBSE) or Inquiry Based Science Teaching (IBST) are often used synonymously in various contexts. The situation becomes even worse whenever the term is translated. In German for example IBSE is translated as "*Forschendes Lernen*" which neither offers a reference to "*Bildung*" (education) nor to inquiry 'based' which means '*sich orientieren an*' oder '*aufbauend auf die Naturwissenschaften*' (science based).

In everyday German '*forschen*' is mainly used in the context of research, which may lead to confusing '*Forschendes Lernen*' with 'what scientists really do'. So in the German context I prefer to use the term *'Forschungsorientiertes naturwissenschaftliches Lernen'*. This literally refers to 'inquiry based science learning'.

Inquiry Based Science Teaching

In this monograph I will refer to the NRC´s definition of IBSE presented above and will use the term Inquiry Based Science Teaching (IBST) to make explicit that I am talking about a variety of pedagogical approaches that teachers or LOtC educators employ to supports inquiry based science learning either in class or outside the classroom. These various approaches to inquiry instructions makes it difficult to get a clear picture about what students actually gain from IBST based learning environments and whether the learning lives up to proposed expectations (Minner et al., 2010). So far there is evidence that good IBST provides opportunities for students to:

- Learn meaningfully (Kubicek, 2005)
- Learn about the nature of science and develop scientific ways of thinking (Bianchini & Colburn, 2000, Caps & Crawford, 2013)
- Develop a better understanding of content knowledge (Minner et al., 2010)
- Develop the ability to evaluate scientific data and models (NRC, 2001)
- Overcome pre-existing misconceptions (NRC, 2001)
- Are often motivated to learn about science (Palmer, 2009)
- Develop positive attitudes towards science (Brown, 1996)

Minner, Levy, and Century (2010) argue that inquiry teaching has essential features which should be applied and which are described by the NRC (1996; and 2000, p. 25) as following:

- Learners are engaged by scientifically oriented questions
- Learners design and conduct investigations
- Learners give priority to evidence, which allows them to develop and evaluate explanations that address scientifically oriented questions
- Learners formulate explanations from evidence to address scientifically oriented questions
- Learners evaluate their explanations in light of alternative explanations, particularly those reflecting scientific understanding
- Learners communicate and justify their proposed explanation

However, the US National Science Education Standards make a distinction between full and partial inquiry. In full inquiry all of the essential features are present, whereas in partial inquiry only some of the essential features mentioned above can be observed. Research has shown that a full inquiry process is almost never applied (Asay & Orgill, 2009) and

[...] that there was no statistically significant association between amount of inquiry saturation and increased student science conceptual learning. However, subsequent model refinement indicated that the amount of active thinking, and emphasis on drawing conclusions from data, were in some instances significant predictors of the increased likelihood of student understanding of science content (Minner et al., 2010, p. 493)

These findings raise the question whether active thinking and decision making needs to be embedded in a full inquiry cycle or might be equally effective when applied outside the investigative context.

[Research on] this kind of work could significantly help practitioners with limited time and resources determine when to increase the emphasis on active thinking or responsibility for learning (decision-making) in their science teaching. (Minner et al., 2010, pp. 493–494)

Inquiry Based Science Learning

Barron and Darling-Hammond (2010) use the term 'inquiry based learning' to describe a 'family of approaches', which include project-based learning, design based learning and problem based learning. Asay and Orgill (2009) provide multiple research-based evidences that teachers are equally uncertain about the term 'inquiry'. Some describe inquiry as discovery learning ('Entdeckendes Lernen'), project based learning, hands-on learning, authentic problem solving, classroom discussions, and debates while others equate inquiry learning with an increased level of student direction allowing students to ask their own questions, to determine which data to collect or to design procedures.

For others, inquiry learning is sometimes seen as an unstructured and unguided student centred approach to learning (Mayer, 2004; Kirschner et al., 2006). Morrison (2013) explored elementary teachers conceptions about inquiry and found that teachers frequently hold ideas about inquiry, such as it is all about 'finding things out' or 'exploring and experimenting with things around us'.

Recent findings indicate that the majority of teachers surveyed (n = 26!) held limited views of inquiry based instruction and these views were reflected in their teaching practice. Most commonly, teacher's focus on the basic abilities required for inquiry instead of the essential features or important understanding about inquiry (Capps & Crawford, 2013).

Different views on inquiry learning are based on different views of 'science inquiry', 'science learning' or 'attitudes towards students and their ability to learn science'. It is also widely accepted that teacher beliefs about teaching, learning and the nature of science can influence their practice (Hogan & Berkowitz, 2000). Elementary teachers in particular have limited understanding of the subject matter and also often have weak pedagogical content knowledge that they can apply to support inquiry based learning (Appleton, 2007).

In addition, there is disagreement about the various ways that these learning processes can be facilitated and the degree of structure that needs to be provided by the teacher. Minner, Levy and Century (2010, p. 476) found that 'classroom inquiry shows varying degrees of direction or instruction given by the teachers and these distinctions are often poorly articulated by scholars and practitioner alike'.

However, the amount of direction and decision-making applied by the teacher versus the student is known to be particularly influential to students learning. The scope between open and guided inquiry, and the role scaffolding plays in students learning outcomes have been frequently discussed in literature. (Hmelo-Silver et al., 2007; Wichmann & Leutner, 2009; Kirschner et al., 2006; Mayr, 2004)

The term 'scaffolding' is used to define a particular way of providing help to the learner. This support is tailored to the learners needs in achieving his or her goals at any one moment. Scaffolding should also build on itself at the pace of the student. The best scaffolding provides help in a way that contributes to learning; effective scaffolding provides prompts and hints that help learners to figure issues out themselves. It supports student's active construction of knowledge (Wichmann & Leutner, 2009).

> ,Precisely the lack of shared understanding of defining features of various instructional approaches has hindered significant advancement in the research community on determining effects of distinct pedagogical practices' (Minner et al., 2010, p. 476)

New curriculum initiatives, focused on inquiry using complex instructional strategies, were found to promote significant increase in learning among students more often. These effects, however, were not always sustained as curriculum reforms were scaled up and used by teachers who did not have the same degree of understanding or skill in implementation (Barron & Darling-Hammond, 2010).

When is Inquiry Based Science Teaching effective?

Research has shown that different formats of instruction are suitable to different learning outcomes and some formats seem to be more effective than others.
Good IBS teaching is assumed to include formats such as:

- students are expected to come up with high quality performance/presentations and teachers provide guidance and feedback about the process and the quality of student's work (Barron et al., 1998)
- outcomes are evaluated and learning is repeatedly assessed; self and teacher assessment (Harlen, 2013)

- students are asked to think about possible solutions of a problem first e.g. formulate hypothesis (Schwartz & Martin, 2004)
- iterative cycles of reflection and action are applied and opportunities to learn from experience and feedback are provided
- learning activities include teamwork and collaboration as well as small and large group discussions (Barron & Darling-Hammond, 2010)
- Emphasis is put on active thinking and on drawing conclusions from data to increase student understanding of science content (Minner et al., 2010)

Classroom research indicates that well designed carefully thought out materials and connected classroom practices are needed to capitalise on inquiry approaches. Without careful planning, students may miss opportunities to connect their work with the key concepts underlying a discipline (Petrosino, 1998).

Authentic problems and projects afford unique opportunities for learning but authenticity in and of itself does not guarantee learning (Barron et al., 1998, Thomas, 2000). Thus providing students with rich resources and an interesting problem are not enough. Students need help to understand the problem, as well as support in how to apply science knowledge, how to evaluate their experimental or other inquiry based designs, how to explain failures, and how to engage in revision. In addition they need to be explicitly prompted to use information resources. Teachers are expected to scaffold, not to impose participation structures and classroom norms that encourage accountability. By scaffolding teachers admonish students to use evidence, take a collaborative stance and reflect critically on their findings (OECD, 2012).

When designing co-operative group work teachers should pay careful attention to various aspects of the work processes and to the interaction among students. Slavin (1991) argues that it is not enough to simply tell students to work together. They must have a reason to take one another's experience, opinions, findings and arguments seriously. Therefore teachers should consider setting group tasks with structures promoting individual accountability.

In addition the teacher plays a critical role in establishing and modelling practice for productive learning conversations. In doing this successfully he/she supports students to improve their social and behavioural skills, self-concept, academic outcomes and their ability to concentrate on the task. Observing group interaction carefully can provide substantial amount of information about the degree to which work is productive. Johnson and Johnson summarised 40 years of work on co-operative learning and came up with basic elements that are important across a range of different models and approaches. These are positive interdependence, individual accountability, structures that promote face to face interaction, social skills and group processing (Barron & Darling-Hammond 2010).

Teachers need to apply well designed formative and summative assessment to not only support students learning but to become more proficient in designing an inquiry base learning environment themselves (OECD, 2012). Collaborative and inquiry approaches to learning require that we consider classroom activities, curriculum and assessment as a system in which each interdependent aspect is essential to provide a learning environment that will promote robust learning. Indeed, teacher's ability to assess both formatively and summatively has enormous implications for what is taught and how effectively this is done. Research suggests that thoughtfully structured performance assessment can support improvements in the quality of the teaching (Barron & Darling- Hammond, 2010).

Formative assessment is assumed to create fundamental changes in teacher's abilities to teach effectively.

> 'As [teachers] use assessment and learning dynamically, they increase their capacity to derive deeper understanding of their student's response; this then served to structure increased learning opportunities" (Darling Hammond, Ancess & Falk 1995, as cited in Barron & Darling- Hammond, 2010, p. 210).

Thus formative assessment not only helps the student to monitor their learning process but assessment outcomes provide teachers with evidence to critically reflect on their own performance.

> 'All assessment of students' achievements involves the generation, interpretation, communication and use of data for some purpose. In just this simple statement there is room for an enormous range of different kinds of activity, but each will involve a) students being engaged in some activity, b) the collection of data from that activity by some agent, c) the judgement of the data by comparing them with some standard and d) some means of describing and communicating the judgement. There are several forms that each of the components of assessment can take (Harlen, 2013).

Currently, science education research does not provide a straight-forward operating procedure in IBST that has proven to be consistently effective (Minner et al., 2010).

However, the following basic feature are frequently named as important characteristic;

Science inquiry is always based on natural phenomena and is expected to give answers to scientific questions only. E.g. scientists may not be able to answer a question such as 'why is the sky blue?' but can answer 'how does it happen that the sky appears blue?'

A scientific question, either one triggered by student curiosity or by the teacher is commonly seen as a starting point for classroom/LotC inquiry.

A particular observation or demonstration can be used to promote these questions. The 'quality' of the question is strongly related to the number of learning opportunities the particular learning environment offers (Crawford, 2000).

To articulate possible answers to the question, based on pre-existing knowledge, is the next step assumed to be crucial for developing a deeper understanding of the phenomenon. Existing beliefs are considered important in a conceptual development process. While possible explanations or hypothesis are formulated pre-existing concepts are made explicit. A hypothesis will also lay the foundations for the following data collection process.

Data could be collected via an experimental design, observation, literature research, interviewing experts, exploring a LOtC site and taking notes etc. Different phenomena or questions require different approaches to collecting evidence.

Collected data needs to be analysed and conclusions need to be drawn from this data. This one and the following steps are assumed to be most important in a successful inquiry process.

Next the outcomes are presented and discussed in groups of any chosen size. Finally the knowledge gained is challenged by the students and the teachers in the light of their own or expert knowledge. Expert knowledge can be available in person (e.g. at a LOtC site) or via a thorough literature research. Final conclusions are expected to be consistent with currently broadly accepted scientific understanding (Asay & Orgill, 2009, Minner et al., 2010, Capps & Crawford, 2013).

In short the presence of a scientific content, various types of science related student engagement and components of instruction, which emphasise student responsibility for learning and decision making (e.g. to decide which question to investigate, to identify where and when help is needed in developing the design, to decide on how to organise data, draw and discuss conclusions, to decide on how to communicate results) is essential (Minner et al., 2010). In addition, learners should be asked to critically evaluate what they read and are expected to express themselves well both verbally and in writing. Knowledge generated by students that is usable and integrated in everyday experience should be favoured over compartmentalized and contextualised knowledge of facts and procedures. Collaboration and conversation amongst students is critical because it allows the learner to benefit from the power of articulation. Articulation is most effective when scaffolded. When learners externalise and articulate their developing knowledge they learn more effectively. The best learning takes place when learners articulate their unformed and developing understanding and continue to articulate it throughout the learning process. Articulation and learning are a mutually reinforcing feedback loop. While thinking out loud learners learn more rapidly and deeply than by studying quietly. Articulation makes reflection (thinking about the process of learning) and metacognition (thinking about knowledge) possible and reflection has been proved to deepen understanding (Sawyer, 2006, 2008).

Last but not least the concept of the nature of science needs to be made explicit throughout the whole inquiry process. Although it is commonly expected of students, they do not necessarily understand the nature of science whilst doing science. The rational of why science is done in a particular way needs to be addressed (Sadler et al., 2010). Last but not least learners should be asked to apply and understand mathematics in various aspects of science inquiry (Capps & Crawford, 2013).

IBSE challenges teacher's professionalism

To assist teachers in their implementation of inquiry based learning various models have been developed, discussed, favoured and dismissed within the last two centuries of IBSE history. Following these discussions it becomes increasing obvious how both critical and challenging it is for teachers to plan and enact inquiry based instructions. According to Roehring and Luft (2004) four factors have a crucial impact on teacher's performance;

Factor 1) Science content and pedagogical knowledge:
Science teachers who implement inquiry based instruction need to understand the prominent concepts in their discipline. Knowledge that is fragmented or compartmentalized does not help teachers to craft instructions that best represent inquiry. Teachers need a deep and highly structured content knowledge base. In biology, teaching this becomes particularly challenging because prominent concepts of the discipline are constantly evolving and developing. In addition teachers need to understand the principles of IBST in very detail to become effective in scaffolding student learning.

Factor 2) Individual views of the Nature of Science:
Supporting young people to understand the Nature of Science is a central aim in modern science education. However teachers hold a wide variety of beliefs about the nature of science and need to reflect on their personal understanding first in order to later scaffold 'authentic' science learning experiences effectively. Thus teachers need to reflect on ccommon assumptions and need to address them explicitly when a particular scientific approach is applied.

Factor 3) Individual views of teaching science
Teachers often hold very personal views of teaching, their students confidence to achieve tasks, subject matter and student learning etc. These beliefs about teaching and learning have a strong impact on teacher classroom practice (Fang, 1996). Research has shown that teachers that hold a more positivist view of science tend to hold a trans-missive view of teaching, whereas those holding a more contemporary view of science knowledge are more likely to espouse a constructivist view of learning (Pope & Gilbert, 1983)

Factor 4) Changing roles in learning
In inquiry based practices teachers and students have to fulfil different roles compared to traditional classroom practices. These changes need to be made explicit for those enacting them – students and teachers alike. E.g. students need to feel responsible for their own learning and teachers need to be confident that their students are capable of doing that.

None of these factors were found, in isolation, to be predictive of the quality of the implementation of inquiry based instructions, because the interplay of these factors makes the difference. Factors work collectively, in different degrees, to influence instructions. Holding a contemporary view of the nature of science is necessary, but not sufficient, to implement inquiry based lessons. However, novice teachers with a contemporary view of science are more likely to implement inquiry lessons in their curriculum. Teachers who hold student centred beliefs are also more likely to implement Inquiry in their classroom. Content knowledge alone does not guarantee the implementation of inquiry based lessons, however, strong content knowledge combined with a student centred belief and a contemporary view of the nature of science increases the likelihood that inquiry is implemented in the classroom (Roehring & Luft, 2004)

Inquiry based science teaching has been a buzz-word in Europe since the Rocard Report was published by the European Commission in 2007. However,

> 'there is still no consensus as to what it [inquiry based teaching] actually is and what it looks like in the classroom (Anderson, 2002)'. If the academic community has not reached consensus, how can we expect teachers to understand what inquiry is and how to teach science in this way?' (Capps & Crawford, 2013, p. 523).

So far science education research does not provide one straight forward operating procedure that has proved to be the most effective way to support student learning. It is still teacher's responsibility to find out whether their IBST approach is efficient in achieving desired learning outcomes. However, we will see later that this uncertainty has a great potential to challenge practitioners and science education researchers to 'cross boundaries' and to initiate expansive and collaborative learning processes which finally will 'renew science pedagogy in Europe'.

2.4 Alternative Places for Learning Science

2.4.1 Learning Outside the Classroom (LOtC)

All learning takes place in settings that have particular sets of cultural and social norms and expectations and that these settings influence learning and transfer in powerful ways (National Research Council 2000)

More than any other species, human beings are designed to be flexible learners and, from infancy, are active agents in acquiring knowledge and skills (Donovan & Bransford, 2005). In doing so, learning is not restricted to formal education institutions like schools, colleges or universities, but also occurs beyond the classroom (Bentley, 1998).

Visiting institutions such as science museums, science centres, botanic gardens, zoos or aquaria in a school based context offers learners a wide range of learning options and the opportunity to explore what is interesting for each individual learner. These places provide authentic experiences using real objects and, particularly in zoos, aquaria and botanical gardens - living organisms (Wellington, 1998, Falk & Dierking, 2000).

In the international context, the use of places other than the classroom for teaching and learning is termed "Learning Outside the Classroom" (LOtC). Institutions providing learning experiences for school classes or student groups are therefore included under the title banner of 'LOtC institutions' (LOtC) in this work. The Council for Learning Outside the Classroom website (http://www.lotc.org.uk/) provides a comprehensive summary of sites which can be used for learning outside the classroom. From a qualitative perspective, however, one has to admit that all these various learning environments offer very different opportunities for learning and the quality of the learning experience in each individual LOtC setting may differ, in the same way that it differs with learning science in any classroom.

An Ambivalent Attitude towards Learning

According to the 'Science Center World Congress', over 310 million people actively participate in engagement programmes organized by over 2500 science centres in more than 90 countries annually (Hein, 2012). These institutions include a variety of places such as traditional museums, natural history museums, historic houses and outdoor centres (e.g. national parks), and heritage and botanic gardens. While new places for learning are emerging constantly, traditional institutions such as Museums, Botanic Gardens or Zoos have dramatically progressed by embracing an educational role.

In 1992 the American Association of Museums proposed:

> 'a new definition of museums as institutions of public service and education, a term that includes exploration, study, observation, critical thinking, contemplation and dialogue' (AAM, 1992, cited in Hein, 2012, p. 178)

While some authors claim that a 'paradigm shift' has taken place, changing museums, zoos and botanic gardens from old fashioned, inward looking institutes with collection of objects into educational institutions committed to serve divergent audiences, others, including those working alongside Botanic Gardens are more cautious.

Hein (2012) argues that:

> 'the concept of museums as institutions in the service of the public is as old as the museums themselves. Conversely, during this same period and continuing today there are museum professionals who consider education to be a secondary function of museums with collection and preservation of cultural objects being their primary concern. . . . And others have always incorporated a vision of progressivism into their practice, both pedagogically ant politically' (p. 179).

Taking the history and the current status of botanic gardens into consideration, the tension between those persons viewing such institutions as primarily educational and those seeing the role as preservers and collectors of living species is not likely to disappear in the near future.

> 'However since there is still evidence that education is still not recognized as equal to curatorial activity in many museums (including botanic gardens). I doubt that we will see a true paradigm shift in any time soon (Hein, 2012, p. 179).

It's not only the case that the LOtC institutions themselves place education and learning as a secondary activity. Many teachers still conduct visits to LOtC's as 'add on's' rather than as 'add in's' to their teaching agenda, treating them merely as a 'nice day out', even though research has shown that best learning results can be achieved when LOtC learning is integrated with the everyday school curriculum (Cox Petersen, 2003).

The Potential of LOtC Learning

Research shows increasingly clear data that learning outside the classroom (LOtC) is associated with several positive outcomes for students such as more engagement in learning and higher levels of academic achievement. (Dillon & Osborne, 2007; Dillon, 2007; Rickinson et al., 2004). The "Committee on Learning Science in Informal Environments" comprised of 14 experts from the fields of science, educational psychology, media and informal education conducted a broad review of the literature that is related to learning science in informal settings and published their outcomes in 2009 (Bell et al., 2009). The committee found abundant evidence that across all venues individuals of all ages learn science. LOtC sites are good in that they provide the space for life-long learning experiences with science, have the potential to support systematic learning and reliable knowledge about the natural world as well as the development of important skills for learning science. They are rich with real world phenomena and are therefore places where people can pursue and develop science interests, engage in science inquiry and reflect on their experiences through articulating their views in conversation with others. Structured, non-school, science programs which include sustained self-organized activities for science enthusiasts can feed or stimulate interest in science in both adults and children and may positively influence academic achievement for students. These programmes may also expand the participant's knowledge of future science career options (Bell et al., 2009).

Rickinson and colleagues (2004) concluded that:

> 'Fieldwork can have a positive impact on long-term memory due to the memorable nature of the fieldwork setting . . . it can lead to individual growth and improvements in social skills. More importantly, there can be reinforcement between the affective and the cognitive, with each influencing the other and providing a bridge to higher order learning. . . . There is significant evidence that social development and greater community involvement can result from engagement in school grounds projects. Students develop more positive relationships with each other, with their teachers and with the wider community through participating in school grounds improvements' (p. 24).

Phillips and colleagues (2007) survey, with 475 science oriented LOtC institutions in the United States of America, confirms these assumptions. Authors conclude that LOtCs do have a great potential to support K 12 (pupils between 5–18 years) science education.

Many practitioners, researchers and educational policy makers already recognise the potential of learning experiences provided in a LOtC setting. The 2007 European Rocard report 'Science Education Now – A renewed pedagogy for Europe 'explicitly mentioned LOtCs as potential partners for implementing inquiry based science education on a large scale in Europe. The UK government recently introduced a new education Manifesto, 'Learning Outside the Classroom', which acknowledges the wealth of research on the impact and benefits on children's learning using 'out of classroom' approaches. (LOTCM, 2007). The National Educational Standards in the USA calls attention to the potential science museums have to foster student interest in science and to support student understanding of science. The Austrian Science Center Network was founded in 2006 and currently joins more than 130 partners contributing actively to the community by developing, offering or using interactive science centre activities. (for more information see: http://www.science-center-net.at/index.php?id=238)

In Austria, 90 % of the schools which participated in the PISA 2006 assessment use excursions and LOtC visits to support student engagement in science.

Additionally, 70% of schools ask their students to learn about environmental issues not only in class but in nature reserves, museums and science and technology centres (Grafendorfer & Neureiter, 2009).

The LOtC Science Learning Environment:

According to Bell, Lewenstein, Shouse, and Feder (2009) science oriented LOtC sites have the potential to create learning environments, which provide the quality and the space for fruitful science learning. Visiting these places one expects that students will be able to:

- experience the excitement, interest and motivation to learn about phenomena in the natural world
- generate, understand, remember and use concepts, explanations, arguments models and facts related to science
- manipulate, test, explore, predict, question, observe and make sense of the natural and physical world
- reflect on science as' a way of knowing', on processes, concepts and institutions for science and on their own processes in learning about phenomena
- participate in scientific activities and learning practices with others, using scientific language and tools
- think about themselves as science learners and develop an identity as someone who knows about, uses and sometimes contributes to science.

'Thus learning at science oriented LOtC sites is distinct from, but overlaps with, the science specific knowledge, skills, attitudes and dispositions that are ideally developed in schools' (ibid, p. 4).

However, learning environments created in science oriented LOtC institutions are very diverse in nature and this diversity is enhanced when educational managers, school liaison officers, communication assistants, guides, explainers, wardens, museum teachers, botanic garden educators, rangers etc. are asked to support and facilitate the learning processes taking place in workshops or in any other kind of on-site engagement with visitors. In this paper I will refer to these people as "educators" going forward.

Peacock and Pratt (2011) summarised a number of additional factors that impact on the quality of these environments, namely:

- The physical layout, structure, design and collections on display in the garden or the building. This can either distract (e.g. museum shop, narrow paths, etc.) or support learners (e.g. glasshouses, carnivorous plants, good group gathering places, availability of seminar rooms, outdoor setting etc.) to focus on explicit learning objectives.

- The socio-cultural background of all participants (e.g. teachers, students, educators participating in a workshop etc.). Also their perception of this particular learning environment, their related experiences (personal history) as well their perceived significance of the learning goals and the artefacts presented in this context (e.g. 'exciting versus boring plants')
- The learning activities afforded and the constraints of physical arrangements, social groupings, accessibility and localised distractions.
- Tension between the conflicting agendas of all the stakeholders responsible for running the site e.g. funding bodies, University boards, interpretation and exhibition designers, scientists, visitor services and educators as well as the approaches to learning in such a context by teachers, students or any visitors.

The field trip learning environment

The term 'learning environment' is usually applied in educational literature to any setting in which learning takes place. This term is even more appropriate in the context of learning at botanic gardens, zoos, national parks or outdoor centres, because the word 'environment' has a specific contextual meaning in such sites and is used regularly in their educational programmes. Learning in and about a 'living or natural environment', as well as 'environmental education' are often key priorities.

Thus a context related learning environment is created whenever teachers take their students on field trips to outdoor LOtC settings where they may or may not ask locally based educators for support.

In their review of literature, DeWitt and Storksdieck (2008) argue that a substantial body of research has been accumulated on fieldtrips over the past 30 years which has provided evidence that, from the perspective of cognitive and conceptual learning outcomes. . . .

> '. . . under certain favorable circumstances, fieldtrips may lead to somewhat better learning outcomes than school based instructions' (p. 181).

Anderson, Lucas, Ginns, and Dierking (2000) report on a great deal of research that has been done to assess the cognitive effects of class visits to outdoor settings. E.g. educational programs associated with parks have proven to enhanced environmental stewardship, environmental attitudes, knowledge about the natural world, and positive attitudes toward the parks.

Sellemann and Bogner (2013) recently reported evidence that learning about climate change at a botanic garden has a significant increase of 'knowledge scores' in a post visit test and that this score showed no decrease in a retention test, which was taken 4–6 weeks after the event. While some research results suggest that school based instructions might provide 'more learning per unit' additional outcomes, such as process skills or awareness of life- long learning community infrastructures, have been reported.

Besides increased cognitive learning, field trips provide positive affective and social experiences. Gains in motivation or interest, sparked curiosity or improved attitudes towards the topic are visible.

> 'Learning on and from a field trip, hence, is no longer seen as simply an extension or improvement of classroom teaching, but as a valuable supplement and addition to classroom instruction, as well as an excellent way to prepare students for future learning' (DeWitt & Storksdieck, 2008, p. 181).

Field trip learning can be a valuable supplement and addition to classroom instructions as well as an excellent way to prepare students for future learning (Storksdieck et al., 2006). The effect of field trip learning is unique for its long-term impact. Various scholars have emphasized that individual learning may appear or come to maturity a long time after the experience has ended. Even 16 months after the visit, students were still able to recall names of exhibits, remember activities they did and were able to refer to guide explanations. (Bamberger & Tal, 2008). Bertsch, Unterbruner and Kapelari (2008) showed that the cognitive knowledge gained by primary students in a field trip based 'school - botanic garden' project did not decrease during the 6 months following the close of the project.

However, students appear more likely to remember social and personally relevant aspects of a field trip; however they unfortunately also retain less favourable memories of fieldtrips such as those trips that seemed overly structured and left little room for their personal agenda (DeWitt & Storksdieck, 2008).

Factors which impact fieldtrip learning

Field trips have the potential to live up to the expectations for science learning as mentioned above, but are very much influenced by a complex set of individual, situational, social and historical factors which may limit, as well as enhance, science learning. These dependencies have to be reflected on and made visible in order to understand how a field trip learning environment can contribute most effectively to a learner's development. The field trip setting as such might not be a guarantor for success. DeWitt and Storcksdieck (2008) argue that:

> 'Fortunately for many concerned with the outcomes of field trips, research indicates that both cognitive and affective learning can occur as a result of class visits to out-of-school settings and surrounding experiences, but such learning is fundamentally influenced by a number of

factors, including the structure of the field trip itself, setting novelty, prior knowledge of the students, the social context of the visit, teacher agendas and actions on the field trip, and the presence or absence and quality of preparation and follow-up experiences' (p. 182).

Learner's individual perception of the environment:
Peacock and Pratt (2011) state that it is possible to distinguish different ways in which individual people comprehend terms or ideas, and how they respond to a particular environment. The latter may range from those who strongly identify with it to those who strongly reject it. With regard to botanic gardens in particular, the term 'natural environment' can be perceived in very different ways. Whilst an ecologist or environmentalists would never use the term in a botanic garden context, visitors often refer to botanic gardens as being 'a natural environment' because it is an open space full of living organisms.

The physical quality of a field trip learning environment is based on people's ability to make sense of the environment because the learning experience is highly situated within this physical environment. Sense making influences the transferability of knowledge and subsequent learning, as well as its long-term impact (Bamberger & Tal, 2008).

Relating science content to personal experiences is assumed to foster lifelong learning (Eylon, 2000). The physical setting of a botanic garden or any other outdoor learning space facilitates this process by taking real objects from real life and presenting them in a scientific context. Over and above the novelty of the fieldtrip setting has an influence on students' conceptual and possibly affective learning. Irrespective of whether the novelty of the environment is either very strong (because students never have been at the botanic garden before) or altogether absent (because students visit the place on a regular basis) new perspectives might be mitigated through giving a particular orientation to the trip prior or during the visit (DeWitt & Storksdieck, 2008).

Pre-existing knowledge
Interviews with children after their visits revealed that an important determinant of what students learn during engagement with artefacts is the knowledge they bring with them, often from their personal lives rather than from previous experiences in school (Peacock & Bowker, 2009; Österlind, 2005; DeWitt & Storksdieck, 2008; Blum et al., 2013).

This impact of prior knowledge on conceptual learning is well documented in the formal as well as in the LOtC or informal learning environment (Krüger, 2007; Falk & Storksdieck, 2005; Bell et al., 2009).

In addition student's individual interest in the topics they are engaged with as well as their own and their teacher's motivations and agendas shapes the learning on the field trip (Bell et al., 2009; DeWitt & Storksdieck 2008).

Social interaction
Social interaction includes both the interaction within and outside the small group a learner is working with. Sharing discoveries and experiences with others is assumed to support learning. Working in small student groups whilst on site allows students to ask more questions, do more hands-on work or just generally become more involved in the programme of activity (Price & Hein, 1991). The characteristics of the small group (e.g. gender balance, expertise and interest of members etc.) an individual learner is working with, may additionally shape the learning (Bell et al., 2009; DeWitt & Storksdieck, 2008).

According to studies done by Cox-Petersen and colleagues (2003) and Tal and colleagues (2005) a considerable amount of interaction is taking place, not only amongst the students themselves but also between the museum educator and the students. Less interaction is observed between teachers and their students. Österlind (2005) argues that pupils may not learn from each other and conversations between pupils about the content of the activity are sparse. In terms of conceptual development, the interaction between the pupil and the teacher respectively the educator or the pupil and the textbook (e.g. museums guide, or additional written information) seems to be more fruitful.

Based on their review of literature and the meta-analysis done by others such as Rickinson Dillon, Teamey, Morris, Choi, Sanders, and Benefield (2004) as well as Peacock and Pratt (2011) argue that field trip learning environments include factors which are not apparent in classrooms. In a fieldtrip setting Vygotsky's theory of mediated action (educator/teacher – child – object, see p. 31) has a different quality to that achieved in classroom learning. The field trip environment potentially allows children to interact with a wider range of adults (including scientists or museum educators) as well as a wider range of physical and mental 'objects' (e.g. living organisms, hands-on exhibits, group discussions etc.).

The fieldtrip structure
Although the impact of the program structure is assumed to be an important factor for learning from school field trips, the degree of structure has been debated in literature.

Some authors argue that guided tours or specific attention focusing devices (e.g. compulsory tasks, worksheets, textbooks etc.) may increase cognitive learning, others that overbearing structures diminish interest in the learning outcomes or positive attitudes toward the visit (Österlind, 2005; DeWitt & Storcksdieck, 2008). Because of this, highly structured field trips are often criticised for adopting a class-room style and task oriented approaches, which focus pupils on the process of 'schooling' (Peacock & Pratt, 2011, Adams et al., 2008).

For example, the values of worksheets, which are still popular with LOtC school-visit programmes are seriously questioned by Griffin and Symington (1997). Authors argue that worksheets require children to behave like school pupils with the associated goals that this entails, such as accuracy and completion of tasks. In this way, they seriously narrow the student's focus to only fill in or tick those boxes the worksheet requires. Carli (2013) reported a case study carried out at the University of Innsbruck Botanic Gardens in the course of the INQUIRE project. Interview outcomes revealed that when students used a worksheet for their insect observations in the garden they predominately answered the question: 'Why do you observe these insects?' with ' because we have been told to do so'. Scarcely any child responded appropriately to the initial purpose of the activity which was to find out 'why insects visit flowers'. Peacock and Pratt (2009) argue that their own studies reveal similar results.

However, both teachers and students feel that learning can be supported with well thought-out worksheets and that they can be highly productive in promoting discovery- and an inquiry style field trip experience (Kisiel, 2003). Therefore, they should not be dismissed out of hand, but those responsible for developing them, need to be aware that worksheets applied in a fieldtrip setting should:

- encourage observation
- allow time for observation
- refer to objects rather than labels
- be unambiguous about where information might be found
- encourage talk amongst group members (DeWitt & Storksdieck 2008, p. 186)

The use of worksheets is a norm presumably based on an educator's individual experience, either through their own education or during their teacher training sessions either on or off site. So the institutional history, as well as the cultural history, of educators who choose particular LOtC learning environments may need to be reflected on, particularly because they may be perceptually 'similar' to school learning.

Different cultures of learning
The situation mentioned above highlights another factor that should be considered in field trip learning environments – the tension between the two cultures of learning; this may or may not be obvious for either the teachers or the museum/ botanic garden educators.

Field trip learning environments bring together two different cultures of learning – the formal, classroom based learning and the out of school learning, sometimes referred to as 'informal learning' (Bell et al., 2009). Phillips, Finkelstein, and Wever-Frerichs (2007) argue that this fusion may blur the quality of learning outside the classroom. As long as 15 years ago, Griffin and Symington (1997) were already arguing for a move from task oriented to learner oriented strategies for field trips. According to Tal, Bamberger, and Morag (2005) 100% of school visits to museums in Israel are guided by a site-based educator. At

Innsbruck Botanic Gardens a maximum of 10 out of 150 school classes visit the garden annually without booking any activity programme offered by garden educators. When designing and organising fieldtrips or LOtC visits, it is the priority of both teacher and educator alike to explicitly understand the quality of learning outside the classroom if they want to support their students to get the most out of it.

The teacher's role
Teachers are the key decision makers in planning and implementing field trips and they play an important role both directly and indirectly in their students' appreciation of LOtC sites as places for learning.

From a socio-cultural perspective, teachers knowledge about, as well as their personal attitude towards LOtC learning is a product of historical, cultural and social backgrounds. These naturally influence the decision of whether a teacher takes his or her students on field trips or not and, if he or she does, how these field trips are structured, organised and what final learning outcomes are set.

Often not only teachers but head-teachers and even parents attempt to impose the same rules, goals, processes and cultural norms, which are operative in a classroom on off-site settings. These include notions of what constitutes school work, curriculum pressures and concerns about the effective management of students' time and behaviour. Rebar (2012) argues that a teacher's individual field trip experience as a student as well as their recent experience as a field trip leader, serve as models for later excursions. So teachers pre-visit agendas directly influence their own behaviour and expectations about the LOtC learning experience (Falk et al., 1998). According to Bamberger and Tal (2008), teachers in Israel often conduct field trips because the Israeli Ministry of Education acknowledges and appreciates LOtC learning experiences. They fund a large number of such institutions and money is allocated according to the number of student visits and the educational programmes offered. As a result Israeli teachers who organise field trips believe that LOtC learning is a highly valuable educational experience for their students, stimulating interest and motivation in science and developing scientific and social skills (Michie, 1998; Anderson & Zhang, 2003; Bamberger & Tal, 2008).

Falk, Moussouri, and Coulson (1998) discovered 6 key reasons why visitors to go to a museum, which are:

- the place is recognized as a leisure/recreational/cultural destination
- the educational aspects related to the aesthetic, informational, or cultural content of the museum is considered important
- it is a familiar, repeated activity that takes place at certain phases in one's life (e.g. parents taking their children because they experienced museum visits as children themselves)

- the visit is seen as a social event, as a "day out" for the whole family/ friends/ the class which provides the chance for individuals to enjoy themselves separately and together
- fun and enjoyment of going there in one's free time and/or see new and interesting things in a relaxing and aesthetically pleasing setting.
- practical external factors such as weather, proximity to the museum, time availability, crowd conditions, and the entrance fee contribute to many visitors' decision-making process.

Kisiel's (2005) study revealed several similarities between visitor motives and teacher motives when organising field trips. The expectation of combining learning and entertainment seems to be important not only for visitors but teacher alike. He also assumes that there are more motivations which appear in different combinations when planning a field trip. These are that the topic addressed via the field trip is connected to the curriculum, different and new learning experiences are provided, life-long learning is encouraged and interest and motivation is enhanced. Tal, Bamberger, and Morag (2005) add to this list arguing that teachers organise field trips because they have the desire to change the learning environment, to provide social experiences and general enrichment as well as to provide concrete experiences with abstract and complex phenomena. However, the most often mentioned motivation for a teacher to make a particular fieldtrip is that the topics addressed during the visit are 'connected with the curriculum'.

Anderson and Zhang (2003) found that teachers take students to museums as a way to teach subject matter that cannot be covered effectively in the classroom. Therefore the field trip is considered to complement and supplement classroom teaching, although what this connection looks like in reality is not well defined. Although research has provided convincing evidence that pre- and post-processing activities performed in school enhance field trip learning outcomes and provide the link to classroom science practice, there is considerable evidence that such activities do not take place very often (Anderson et al., 2000; Cox-Petersen et al., 2003; Anderson & Zhang, 2003; Tal & Bamberger, 2008). Very little preparation is done for museum excursions, and even then, most of the preparation is technical and focuses on schedules and instructions regarding clothing and food (Griffin & Symington, 1997).

Conflicting issues arise when teachers are motivated to connect the field trip activities to their science teaching curriculum. Time constraints are often named as preventing teachers from employing pre- and post-visit strategies. In addition, teachers often do not define their goals for the field trip and they hardly ever perceive the museum activity as an engaging socio-cultural learning experience (Cox Petersen et al., 2003; Kisiel, 2003). Teachers struggle with logistical issues, various student needs and pressure for accountability that limit their ability, and willingness, to provide proper preparation and post-visit activities (Griffin, 2004). Most of the studies that have been reported about meaningful preparation or follow-up activities described research settings, in which the researchers were involved in preparing the activity with the teachers or the museum staff (Anderson et al., 2000; Bertsch et al., 2008). In addition, it would be preferable that teachers plan follow–up trips to the same museum. These further visits are considered important for understanding that an exhibit in a given context does not have to change for children to gain new and meaningful insight. Follow-up visits build on, and lead to new, learning experiences that result in new knowledge. (Wilde & Urhahne, 2008)

The LOtC educator's role
Whereas the role of the teachers in LOtC learning has already been studied extensively, little is known about the role educators play in this process.

> 'Research on the effective use of field trips and museums as school resources has been predominantly conducted from the perspective of teachers and students, despite the fact that there are museum staff, both paid and unpaid, who have responsibilities to design, organize, and implement educational experiences for visiting school groups and who have been there since the inception of museums Furthermore, such individuals have a significant role in shaping the nature of the educational experiences afforded by their museums' (Tran, 2007, p. 178).

The educators who develop and implement the visit programme are part of the memories many students retained post field trip and it is assumed that a short, educator–led lesson, as a part of the exploration through a museum gallery or other LOtC site has a positive effect on the content knowledge that students gain from their visit (Tran, 2008).
As with teachers, educators hold different perspectives and motivations when it comes to teaching and learning and these are again based on their socio-cultural setting and history. While teachers and educators share a motivation to combine learning and entertainment and to promote science learning through field trip activities, educators put considerably more emphasis on providing memorable events and offering positive experiences, irrespective of the teacher's intent or desire to primarily connect the field trip to their curriculum and curriculum standards. Educator goals are predominantly affective and developed to nurture interest in science, plants or nature as well as in engendering a desire for the student /teacher to return to their LOtC site for future educational offers. This is deemed more important than content acquisition (Tran, 2008).
Educators assume that, after many short but positive experiences, students develop an understanding of scientific phenomena. When developing a personal interest in learning about science they assume that learners will come back to LOtC institutions throughout their lifetime (Adams et al., 2008)

Expectations about what teachers and educators anticipate from each other when being merged as a team to facilitate student field trip learning experiences are rarely made explicit before or even during the visit. Tran´s (2008) qualitative study revealed roles that educators dedicate to accompanying visit teachers which are quite similar to those I have experienced myself when working with school classes at the Botanic Garden in Innsbruck. The function of the classroom teacher include being a timekeeper (e.g. arriving on time, keeping an eye on the time during the day, informing the educator early enough when the tour has to come to an end etc.), managing the students behaviour, contributing to the general progression of the lesson and being a person who offers educators a certain amount of flexibility in developing the experiences for the lesson. In many cases however, the accompanying teachers step back from their duty to facilitate student learning; they rarely interact with their students and hand over this role to the site educator in charge.

2.4.2 Learning at Botanic Gardens

Learning about plants

What is Botany?
Plant Science, synonymously called Botany or plant biology, is a discipline of biology which focusses on gaining knowledge about plants. It covers a wide range of scientific disciplines including research on structure and morphology, growth, reproduction, metabolism, development, diseases, geographical distribution, chemical properties and evolutionary relations among taxonomic groups of plants etc. Currently the system of plants includes about 400 000 plant species and it is estimated that many more have not been found or named yet. Botany includes a look back on the long history of important philosophers and natural scientist working in this field. Theophrastus 371–287 BC may have been the first we would call a botanist. As a student of Aristotle, he invented and described many principles of botany. Many important botanists- philosophers, doctors, clerics and natural scientists followed Theophrastus and their work and publications formed the foundation of our current knowledge about plants; this work continues today. Botany is an important current field within modern biological science, dealing with questions essential to human existence. In public however, botany is often seen as a rather old fashioned, phased-out model of science and its relevance for a modern society is vastly underestimated (Simpson, 2006).

Why study plants?
Plants are the basis of nearly all life on earth. They are the only organism able to transfer sun light into chemical energy (carbohydrates) which can be used by most other organisms as their only source of food energy. Therefore pants

are called primary producers and are located at the base of most food chains. In addition plants produce structural compounds such as certain amino acids and others substances essential to metabolism in many heterotroph organisms. Without plants humans, and most animals as well as a couple of microorganisms and fungi would not exist.

The appearance of photosynthesis on earth fundamentally changed our planet. The atmosphere gained oxygen. Oxygen dependent respiration occurred. This may have been a necessary precursor to the evolution of multicellular organisms such as animals and humans.

The oxygen rich atmosphere permitted the establishment of an upper ozone layer which protects life from excess UV radiation and allows organisms to inhabit more exposed niches.

The survival of plants is essential for maintaining the health of the ecosystems and they are particularly important for humans in numerous direct ways. Directly, or indirectly via the food chain, plants are our only food source. Fossil fuels, wood and charcoal are plant based energy resources. We need plants to build houses, produce paper, fibre, medicine and many more items.

Plant science is as diverse as plant use and as important. Some of the fields of plant science are very practically oriented, such as agriculture and horticulture focusing on plants as food or energy crops or on cultivating ornamental plants. Forestry is concerned with the cultivation and harvesting trees for lumber and pulp.

Pharmacognosy deals with natural drugs, many of which originate from plants. Basic research in plant science has as its goal understanding the nature of plants in great detail; how they grow and adapt to their environment, how changes in their diversity may affect the ecosystem, how they are related to each other and how they interact with their environment are only a view aspects investigated by botanists. This knowledge may or may not be of first hand practical use but has the potential to be extremely useful in the future (Simpson, 2006).

What do we know about learning about plants?
Although plant knowledge seems to be essential for understanding life on earth, plants remain a mystery to many learners, teachers and pupils alike. They do not eat, they rarely move, they do not have eyes or fur and they do not communicate with people - or at least not in any way we yet understand. Within the last few decades a phenomenon has become more and more obvious in civilized countries; although plants are the basis for all life on earth, they seem to have disappeared from textbooks as well as from young people's minds (Wandersee & Schussler, 2001).

A study investigated plant and animal photographs in elementary science textbooks and showed that animal pictures are far more numerous than those of plants. It is also three times more likely that the animal picture carries a specific name than a plant picture does. Plants are commonly identified not by their name, but by a specific plant part or life-form. (Link-Perez et al., 2010). Maple is simply called 'a tree', tulips are colourful flowers and elder is just a bush. Asked to categorize plants, pupils of all ages focus on distinguishing life-forms or use ethno-botanical criteria e.g. whether a plant is either usable/edible or non-usable/non-edible for humans. Hardly any students show knowledge about scientific strategies that enable us to put plants into families or orders (Krüger & Burmester, 2005). Although environmental sciences are still well attended courses at universities, students who choose botany as a scientific career are rare. In addition, students arrive at university with less direct experiences of plants than in former times (Uno, 2009). The Marbach-Ad (2004) study, focusing on first year college students, showed that a general interest in biology (4.7/5) and in humans (4.2/5) were key reasons why students decided to major in biology, while an interest in plants (2.1/5) was at the bottom of the list. Same results are common in studies such as PISA or ROSE.

Science education authorities are increasingly worried about the lack of interest in science in general and in chemistry and physics in particular in pupils and students. A lack of interest in mathematics and technical sciences by young people is also a matter of international concern. A large amount of funding is now provided for European educational activities that encourage student interest in these particular fields of science (Lena, 2010). Nevertheless, the obvious lack of student interest in botany is still underrepresented in public discussions.

Wandersee and Schussler (2001) coined the term 'Plant blindness' and define it *as failing to see, take notice of, or focus attention upon plants in one´s everyday life* (Wandersee & Clary 2006, p. 1.). Some authors find an explanation for this phenomenon in human psychology and argue that humans automatically 'put animals first' because they themselves belong to the Animal Kingdom (Hoekstra, 2000). In addition, human brains are designed to recognize things that are different to the surroundings, in particular when they are moving (Tunnicliffe, 1996) which may explain why humans 'see' more animals than plants. A few studies show that whenever people do notice plants and find them interesting they appreciate them in a different way to animals (Tunnicliffe & Reiss, 2000, Wandersee & Schussler, 2001). As animals may be more instantly appealing, an appreciation of plants often benefits from the guidance and shared enthusiasm of a third party (Strgar, 2007).

History of botanic gardens
There are currently 1775 botanic gardens and arboreta in 148 countries around the world. Although it is not easy to define precisely what a botanical garden is, all of them share a scientific basis.

In about 800 AD Charlemagne issued the well-known plan 'Capitulare de villis Imperialibis' which recommended that 89 specific plants should be included in estate and monastery gardens throughout his empire. Contemporary to this, Abbot Haito of Reichenau created an ideal monastery garden in St. Gall in

Switzerland which included a physic garden, a kitchen garden and an orchard and showed a layout quite often copied in historical Botanic Gardens. However, monastery gardens were only used for cultivating plants for use and not for research. The main focus of Botanic Gardens is the study of plants, which may be the reason why the history of Botanic Gardens may not be traced back as far as monastery gardens. The history of Botanic Gardens therefore is presumably rooted in the foundation of physic gardens in Italy in the 16th and 17th centuries. Gardens at that time were solely established for the academic study of medicinal plants. Medicinal gardens spread to universities and apothecaries all over Europe. The arrival of the 'age of exploration' and the beginning of international trade caused botanic gardens to experience a change in their strategic direction. More and more, the gardens promoted and encouraged botanical exploration in the tropics. Some established gardens also helped to found new gardens, which were created almost solely to receive and cultivate tropical commercial crops such as cloves, tea, coffee, breadfruit, cinchona, palm oil and cocoa. At universities, not only were tropical plant collections steadily increasing, but much more focus was put on cultivating new species from newly explored territories.

The Botanic Garden at Innsbruck University was established in 1798. After the Bavarians shut down the University of Innsbruck in 1810, the garden was reestablished in 1826. Shortly after that time, the Botanic Garden attracted more attention, not only on the national but also on the international level. The then head of the garden, A. Kerner, became world famous for his collection of Alpine plants in 1876 and was praised for his idea that each botanic garden should focus on cultivating plants from a specific area and should aim for maximum performance in that aspect. At the beginning of the 20th century, after the relocation of the Institute of Botany and the Botanic Garden from down-town Innsbruck to its current location, the aspects of research and the training of students in botany gained interest.

However, during the second half of the 20th century, their importance in the field of science research diminished, not just in Innsbruck Botanic Gardens but in many other botanic gardens as well. The garden 'role' as a hub for the collection and propagation of diverse species and as places for scientific study was relegated to a backwater. Many gardens therefore became municipal and civic 'pleasure gardens', rarely conducting scientific programmes. During this period of botanic garden history, the only real scientific activity undertaken by gardens was the accurate labeling of collections and the exchanging of seeds on a worldwide basis. Fortunately, in the last 30 years, botanic gardens have seen a revival as scientific institutions due to the emergence of the conservation movement. Conservation is now seen by many gardens as their rasion d'etre (BGCI, 2002).

Botanic garden education
When the first botanical gardens were founded in Italy in the 16th century Pisa, (founded1543/44) and Padua (founded 1545), these sites were already gardens

dedicated to teaching and learning. They were used to train medical doctors and pharmacists and became centres of plant research. Later, their educational function included the training of botany students and horticulturalists, who respectively examined the plants either from the scientific point of view or with the intention of cultivation and trade in particular plants for commercial reasons. Botanical gardens founded in the 18th centuries, such as Kew Gardens (founded 1759) and many others in both Europe and the tropics, supported not only plant collections but herbaria, fruit and seed collections and extensive libraries with plant literature and paintings. An extensive network was established between gardens to share both their knowledge and living specimens. These networks are still in use today. Nowadays while the distribution of crop plants, as well as plant research has diminished, public education has become more important

Public science education at botanic gardens
Unlike zoos, botanic gardens were slow to consider education of school children as an important agenda. Only a few gardens like Brooklyn Botanic Gardens (New York), New York Botanical Garden or Kirstenbosch Botanic Garden (Cape Town) are able to look back on more than 70 years history of teacher training, children´s gardening or teacher employment. Nowadays the situation is rapidly improving. For quite a few years now, botanic gardens consider the education of school children as one of the important aspects of their remit (Sanders, 2007). A study conducted by BGCI (2007) showed that a little more than a fourth of the gardens examined (n = 120) that consider education necessary to achieve the protection of plant diversity do not have a budget dedicated to educational purposes, and there are only a few gardens that have large education departments. An average of two full time employees work in education sections in botanic gardens and for the most part only one of these has a pedagogical qualification. Only a third of the part-time educational stuff has relevant qualifications (Vergou, 2010, Kneebone & Willison, 2006). The BGCI report provides evidence that Botanic Gardens are increasingly engaging in public education, but unfortunately they failed to ask for evidence of any effects the educational provision has on learning (Vergou, 2010). Although research is increasingly clear that out-of-school learning is associated with several positive outcomes (see p. 70ff) education programmes developed and applied at botanic gardens are based mainly on practical approaches to teaching and learning. They hardly ever take education research knowledge into account. Apparently botanic gardens, as well as other Learning Outside the Classroom institutions (LOtC) do not focus on evaluation of their programs in any great detail. Action research, or science education research based on theory and evidence, is not commonly established in these settings. A survey with 475 LOtCs in the United States of America uncovered some recurring patterns around LOtCs and their support for schools and named a lack of outcome measures as one of them (Philips et al., 2007).

Although educational activities at botanic gardens are very popular with teachers and students, they are sparsely documented in science education research literature. Studies about the effectiveness of teaching and learning programmes offered by botanic gardens are rare (Sanders, 2007). As a result, botanic gardens have difficulties sharing their understanding of teaching and learning with each other and the broader educational community.

2.5 Professional Science Teaching

2.5.1 Teaching Paradigms

When we think about professional development we assume that teaching is a profession that one can be trained in and that it develops in the course of a teacher's life. This is a paradigm of teaching that might not be shared by all people and, in particular, may not be shared by botanic garden and museum educators.

Kuhn (1970) introduced the word 'paradigm' to refer to the set of practices which define a scientific discipline. Thus paradigm describes a conceptual world-view, how something is conceptualized or viewed and including a whole package of beliefs, values, attitudes and practices.

Geoffrey Squires (1999) names seven paradigms to explore the number of different views on teaching and their practical consequences.

- Teaching as a common-sense activity
- Teaching as an art
- Teaching as a craft
- Teaching as an applied science
- Teaching as a system
- Teaching as reflective practice
- Teaching as a competence

Another paradigm which has been nurtured by science centres, museums and galleries in the last few decades is:

- Teaching as an entertainment

Squires (1999) argues that the problem is to explain not how one paradigm displaces another but how a number of conflicting or competing paradigms somehow coexist. In teaching in particular, this is one reason why dual systems of teacher education have evolved in various countries. Although individual people may hold different perspectives on teaching and may put emphasis on one or the other paradigm, each of these have a substantial literature attached to it and do have their strengths and limitations. In addition individuals may not only hold one, but a set of paradigms they regard as useful to describe 'teaching' and put an emphasis on one or the other depending on the situation applied them e.g. when referring to different aspects of a teacher's life such as teacher education, teacher practice, teacher? recruitment etc.

Teaching as a common-sense activity (Squires, 1999)

Actually, there is evidence that humans do have a natural competence to teach which can be observed even with small children. Humans are able to teach others without being trained beforehand (Papousek & Papousek, 2002). So this seems to be a fundamental human skill that develops very early during childhood.

This fundamental skill may explain why teaching is so often seen as an activity that can be done by anybody without any prior training. At universities, as well as at other tertiary education sites, it is very common that people who have been trained in a science subject are expected to be efficient at teaching science. A study with 120 Botanic gardens showed that hardly any staff who worked in education held an educational degree (Vergou, 2010) Similarly, university tutors are rarely being asked to provide evidence for teaching skills when employed as professors or senior lecturers.

Squires (1999) assumes that the common sense paradigm is based on two different features

- Firstly, everybody has experience in being taught for a couple of years in life – by observing teachers during childhood and adolescence people believe they have developed an understanding of what teaching is. When it comes to teaching, many people have some idea about it already.
- Secondly, the things we do in teaching are not very different to things we do in everyday life such as organizing resources, planning events, explaining things to other people, asking and answering questions etc. So what needs to be learned is how to lecture or assess and how to manage a room full of children. It is often assumed that this can be done through a process of trial and error or by being an apprentice to a more experienced teacher.

Common-sense knowledge relies on simplified representations of the world. When teaching is regarded as a matter of common sense, it is assumed that most people can do it as most people have some common sense and experiences with teaching. Common-sense does not reflect generalisation or universality – it focuses on the situation at hand and is passed on through examples, cases and stories. It is anecdotal and therefore one cannot agree or disagree with an argument because one cannot agree or disagree with a story. Anecdotal knowledge tends to become a normative charge and an implicit expectation about concurrence and assent. This makes it more difficult for the practitioner to stand back from the practice of the group and bring his or her analytical power in. However, common sense is also associated with the notion of a cumulative experience and the idea that people acquire it over time. It is the know-how or know-why that is valued, rather than knowledge and it is assumed that experiences are instructive. A teacher cannot be awarded a higher commendation than being classified as an 'experienced' teacher (Herzog & VonFelten, 2001). Implicit thinking is often misleading because it is based on experience that draws a connection between things that is 'comfortable' not necessarily because it is right.

Teaching as an art (Squires, 1999)

Regarding teaching as an art seems old fashioned and still quite popular. Venville and Dawson published a book named "The art of teaching science: for middle and secondary school" in 2012. Although editors do not take the expression literally, the paradigm is still vivid in people's heads.

Attempts to improve the national teacher training system in Austria have called for selection criteria, or processes, to establish who should be accepted for participating in initial teacher training courses. Although this process does not explicitly argue that teachers are 'born not made'– which would imply that training does not make a difference – there is a strong sense that selection, or self-selection, may be as important as training.

The art paradigm offers an argument for those that are simply not being able to come up with solid criteria for what makes a 'good' teacher. As with the arts a judgement is assumed to be a matter of taste or perspective. The general statement is accepted that one can be a good teacher for one student and a bad one for the other.

Teaching is a matter of one's personal style and as with contemporary art – it is difficult or impossible, to tell whether something is good art = good teaching or no art = bad teaching.

Teaching as a craft (Squires, 1999)

While teaching as common-sense argues that training is not necessary and teaching as an art assumes that it is impossible to decide whether the teaching is indeed good or bad, the paradigm of teaching as a craft does call for training. One can demonstrate a craft, imitate its practice, refine it and master it. The craft paradigm sees teacher training from the 'master and apprentice' perspective. Those who see themselves as being successful in working in this craft support novice teachers by sharing their experience and thoughts, developing and providing teaching resources and lesson plans based on their own experience, as well as supporting newcomers to acquire skills they themselves have already developed. Teaching skills are acquired by observation and detailed analysis. Programmes to train people are developed and are assumed to be successful in advancing the expertise of young teachers. Logically, craft knowledge is specific to a person who has reached the master status and is often related to specific cases or situations. It may not develop into more than individual responses to local situations.

Teaching as an applied science (Squires, 1999)

In its distinct form the applied science paradigm assumes that a teacher's work involves the application of scientific principles and evidence to practical tasks. It assumes that a teacher relies on research to inform his or her practice. Research is expected to provide the knowledge needed to develop and improve teaching. It is presumed that research investigates and discovers fundamental patterns and consistencies that provide teachers with the evidence needed to intervene in events with a higher degree of confidence. The applied science paradigm requires teachers to consider research knowledge as relevant to their professional work and to engage in practitioner research themselves to inform their work.

Teaching as a system (Squires, 1999)

The paradigm teaching as a system is comparative to the terms often used to address education as whole. On a regional, national or even international level, we refer to the education system as one that sets up rules, curricula, teacher education and employment schemes, educational standards and beliefs. System theory visualizes systems as self-regulated structures composed of regularly interacting or interrelating groups of activity. The system sets standards about what teaching is and how it should look and limits the range of choices the individual teacher has. System thinking is often expressed when people complain about overcrowded curricula, limited time for teaching outdoors or the limited provision of resources.

Teaching as reflective practice (Squires, 1999)

Since the time of John Dewey, thinking about one's own practice has been termed 'reflective thinking' and has received continual attention in teacher training. The reflective practice paradigm assumes that teaching and learning about teaching are demanding tasks because they centre on complex, interrelated sets of thoughts and actions. In teaching, there is not necessarily one way of doing something, instead a range of actions can be applied to a given task. The teacher is required to search for a balance between perhaps contrary positions or to select from two or more options by considering alternatives. Teaching as reflective practice is assumed to solve classroom problems by asking teachers to disengage temporarily from the immediacy of practice and think about what they are doing and what they are thinking about it.

Teaching as a profession (Squires, 1999)

Professionalism is justified by a social framework, which is characterise by research knowledge and/or practice based standards. This quality is considered important for their representatives being or becoming experts in their field. The social group develops levels of professionalism such as e.g. the new Teachers´ Standards which came in force in the UK in 2012. These standards are assumed to set out the characteristics of excellent teachers (Coates, 2011). They set benchmarks for the basic elements of high quality teaching such as subject content knowledge, classroom performance, teaching/learning outcomes, the environment and the ethos to be created in the classroom etc. Teaching as a profession assumes that standards can be established, reached and assessed. It is expected that these standards are reliable structures that can guarantee good quality performance of those called experts in the field (in this case, master teachers).

Teaching as entertainment

Teaching as entertainment calls for learning environments that are challenging and motivating and by doing this requires learners to participate in these educational activities voluntarily. Learning is expected to be engaging, enjoyable, fun and entertaining. It stimulates all senses, is emotional and affective. Teaching as entertainment is distinguished from the type of teaching that takes place in school or at university because it provides free choice and self-directed learning spaces. Although teaching as entertainment still intends that learning should take place it is expected that it happens on the way, without any particular effort. The focus is not on a particular learning outcome or product that has been determined at the start; the emphasis is put on a joyful learning experience. TV programs, digital game-based learning, learning outside the classroom and science events such as 'researcher nights' are good examples for this paradigm.

2.5.2 Science Teaching as a Profession

Even though being a teacher at school is regarded as a 'profession' and requires a teaching degree acquired through, and certified by, the formal education system, professional standards for teachers are vague in Austria compared with those in the UK for example.

Teaching, however, does not necessarily require official training. University teachers hardly ever hold a teaching degree. The metaphors of 'Teaching as common sense' and 'Teaching as Art' seem to still be quite commonly accepted and lead to the assumption that knowledgeable people master teaching intuitively. If not, it is assumed that a sequence of trial and error steps will improve proficiency in practice. Educators in LOtC Site often follow the same tradition.

However the most important determinant for student achievement is teacher competency and this is not solely based on subject content knowledge (McKinsey and Company, 2007; Sammons et al., 2007). Science Teaching as a profession includes a spectrum of meanings, practices and ideologies which emerge out of the work and the commitments of policy makers, teachers/educators, school boards, trainers, scientists and the public and is highly related to a particular socio-cultural context. A body of research literature already provides insight and nurtures the discussion about how teacher knowledge is constructed, organised and used, or what makes a 'good teacher' (e.g. Fraser et al., 2012, Darling-Hammond et al., 2009; Darling-Hammond & Bransford, 2005, Loughran et al., 2006; Shulman, 1998a; Pollard et al., 2008; Coates et al., 2012). Different perspectives and emphasis are put on various aspects. There is no one single set of knowledge or reality associated with any model of 'the Professional Science Teacher'.

Shulman (1998a) names 'six commonplaces' shared by all professions in general which have been renamed for more clarity (*first terms* used are the original ones): Professionals are assumed to root their work in:

- *Service to society* = 'social values': implying ethical and moral commitments
- *A body of scholarly knowledge* = 'research': forms the basis of the entitlement to practice. This knowledge is gathered in two research fields: Science education research and science research. Both research outcomes and paradigms are considered fundamental
- *Engagement in practical action* = 'practice': the need to enact knowledge in practice
- *Uncertainty* = flexibility: caused by the different needs of clients and the non-routine nature of problems, hence the need to develop judgement in applying knowledge
- *The importance of experience* = experience: the need to learn by reflecting on one's practice and its outcomes
- The development of a professional community (of teachers /science teachers) that aggregates and shares knowledge and develops professional standards.

The John Bransford and colleagues (2005) framework for understanding teaching and learning adds the teacher perspective to Shulmans 'general' aspects as a vision of professional practice that includes:

- Knowledge of learners and their development in a social context
- Knowledge of the subject /science matter and the curriculum goals
- And knowledge of teaching (Pedagogical Content Knowledge) (Shulman 1998a) in terms of subject/science matter, diverse learners assessment and classroom/group management

Schulman emphasises the enhancement of teacher and educator 'Pedagogical Content Knowledge' (PCK) as well as requiring them to refer to the body of scholarly knowledge e.g. 'science education research literature' to inform their practice.

The teacher competencies framework

Cross cultural views of teaching and learning require discussing, developing and implementing frameworks for 'teacher competencies' related to the

	Subject matter knowledge
Knowledge and understanding	Pedagogical Content Knowledge (PCK), implying deep knowledge about content and structure of subject matter: • knowledge of tasks, learning contexts and objectives • knowledge of students' prior knowledge and recurrent, subject-specific learning difficulties • strategic knowledge of instructional methods and curricular materials
	Pedagogical knowledge (knowledge of teaching and learning processes)
	Curricular knowledge (knowledge of subject curricula – e.g. the planned and guided learning of subject-specific contents)
	Educational sciences foundations (intercultural, historical, philosophical, psychological, sociological knowledge)
	Contextual, institutional, organizational aspects of educational policies
	Issues of inclusion and diversity
	Effective use of technologies in learning
	Developmental psychology
	Group processes and dynamics, learning theories, motivational issues
	Evaluation and assessment processes and methods
Skills	Planning, managing and coordinating teaching
	Using teaching materials and technologies
	Managing students and groups
	Monitoring, adapting and assessing teaching/learning objectives and processes
	Collecting, analysing, interpreting evidence and data (school learning outcomes, external assessments results) for professional decisions and teaching/learning improvement
	Using, developing and creating research knowledge to inform practices
	Collaborating with colleagues, parents and social services
	Negotiation skills (social and political interactions with multiple educational stakeholders, actors and contexts)
	Reflective, metacognitive, interpersonal skills for learning individually and in professional communities
	Adapting to educational contexts characterised by multi-level dynamics with cross-influences (from the macro-level of government policies to the meso-level of school contexts, and the micro-level of classroom and student dynamics)

(Continued)

		Subject matter knowledge
Dispositions: Beliefs, attitudes, values, commitment		Epistemological awareness (issues concerning features and historical development of subject area and its status, as related to other subject areas) Teaching skills through content Transferable skills
		Dispositions to change, flexibility, ongoing learning and professional improvement, including study and research
		Commitment to promoting the learning of all students
		Dispositions to promote students' democratic attitudes and practices, as European citizens (including appreciation of diversity and multi-culturality)
		Critical attitudes to one's own teaching (examining, discussing, questioning practices)
		Dispositions to team-working, collaboration and networking
		Sense of self-efficacy

Table 1: Aspects of teacher competence (EU Expert Group, 2013, p. 45).

particular national context in which they should be applied (EU Expert Group, 2013). Based on research, the EU Expert Group (2013) has compiled a list of competencies to be used as a reference for fruitful discussion as well as a starting point for further developments in the international arena of educational policy and practice.

Pedagogical Content Knowledge (PCK)

Pedagogical Content Knowledge (PCK) is my particular research field and is as Loughran, Berry, and Mulhall (2006) put it:

> '[. . .] to the heart of what it means to be an expert professional: one who chooses to use a particular teaching procedure, at a particular time for a particular reason, because through experience (and possibly through engagement with education research literature and professional development activities) that teacher has come to know how teaching in that way enhances student learning of the concept under consideration' (p. 9).

In contrast to practical knowledge such as classroom teaching, PCK builds on the profession's collective wisdom. Hence it is more formal and not as personal or as situated in classroom events as practical knowledge. Although directly linked to classroom practice, the concept of PCK may describe ideas or approaches that enable teachers to develop an expertise that is more adaptive to a larger range of classroom settings.

'PCK is a heuristic for teacher knowledge that can be helpful in understanding the complexity of what teachers know about teaching and how it changes over broad spans of time' (Schneider & Plasman, 2011 p. 533)

When Shulman published his ideas of PCK in 1987 his definition of the concept was rather vague.

'[Pedagogical content Knowledge] represents the blending of content and pedagogy into an understanding of how particular topics, problems or issues are organized, represented and adapted to the diverse interests and abilities of learners, and presented for instruction. Pedagogical content knowledge is the category most likely to distinguish the understanding of the content specialist from that of the pedagogue '(p. 8).

The science education research community still struggles to agree on a definitive understanding of PCK. In the German speaking science education research community, Shulmans idea of PCK was taken up as 'Fachdididaktisches Wissen' which 'comprises declarative knowledge about subject specific student requirements and strategies for communication as well as procedural knowledge in terms of PCK skills (Schmelzinger et al., 2010, p. 190).

The authors cited above note that the equalisation of the Anglo-American concept of PCK (which is based on the US American curriculum traditions) with the concept of 'Fachdidaktisches Wissen' (based on German curriculum traditions) may be vulnerable.

However it seems to be legitimate to use the term PCK synonymously with 'Fachdidaktisches Wissen' because currently it is the most appropriate we have.

While Shulman explained PCK as an amalgam of content and pedagogical knowledge and exclusive to teachers' professional knowledge, research literature refers to PCK either as a discrete domain of teachers professional knowledge or as dependent on content knowledge, pedagogical knowledge and context knowledge and therefore not separable. This area of conflict nurtures multiple conceptions of PCK. The Austrian teacher education tradition refers to 'fachdidaktisches Wissen' as one of four domains in teacher education which also include, 'content knowledge', 'pedagogical knowledge' and 'practical – school based- knowledge'.

Pedagogical Science Content Knowledge (PSCK)

Pedagogical Science Content Knowledge (PSCK) intrinsically ties subject matter, including knowledge about the 'Nature of Science' and the 'Nature of Scientific Processes and Methods', to pedagogical and context knowledge. While

Components of science teacher PCK	Categories for each component of PCK
Orientations to teaching science	Teachers' ideas about... • purposes and goals for *teaching* science • the nature of *science* • the nature of teaching and learning science for *students*
Student thinking about science	Teachers' ideas about... • students' *initial* science ideas and experiences (including misconceptions) • *development* of science ideas (including process and sequence) • how students *express* science ideas (including demonstration of understanding, questions, and responses) • *challenging* science ideas for students • appropriate *level* of science understanding
Instructional strategies in science	Teachers' ideas about... • *inquiry* strategies (e.g., questions and including how to use, how science is developed, and how student thinking is supported) • science *phenomena* strategies (e.g., demonstrations or predict-observe-explain and including how to use, how science presented, how student thinking is supported) • *discourse* strategies in science (e.g., argument, writing, presenting, or conferencing and including how to use, how science portrayed, and how student thinking is supported) • general *student-centred* strategies for science (vs. teacher-centred) including how to use and when, how science is represented, and match to student needs and thinking
Science *curriculum*	Teachers' ideas about... • *scope* of science (importance of science topics and what science is worth knowing or teaching) • *sequence* of science (organizing science content for learning) • curricular *resources* available for science • using *standards* to guide planning and teaching science
Assessment of students' science learning	Teachers' ideas about... • *strategies* for assessing student thinking in science • how or when to *use* science assessments

Table 2: Science teacher pedagogical content knowledge (PCK), aspects and categories; Schneider and Plasman (2011) pp. 538–539.

considered to be domain specific, PSCK asks science teachers to have a rich conceptual understanding of their particular subject content as well as of subject related processes. They also need to have an understanding of epistemologies which need to be combined with expertise in developing, using and adapting teaching procedures, strategies and approaches to their individual learners needs in a particular learning environment (Shulman, 1989a).

In short: 'It is what teachers know about their subject matter and how to make it accessible to students (Schneider & Plasman, 2011, p. 534)

Neither the knowledge of pedagogy nor a deep knowledge of science can stand-alone. Lacking either will challenge teachers' abilities and skills as a professional. According to Schneider and Plasmans' (2011) literature review (n = 91 relevant research articles), PCK for science teaching Includes five components which are 'Orientation to Teaching Science', 'Students Thinking About Science', 'Instructional Strategies in Science', 'Science Curriculum' and 'Assessment of Students Science Learning`. It is obvious that PCK components such as knowing about student alternative conceptions, important big ideas related to the context, conceptual hooks or triggers of learning are not well understood when rich understanding of the subject content is lacking (Loughran et al., 2006).

While PSCK is sometimes considered an academic construct the ideas are deeply rooted in the belief that teaching requires more than just delivering science knowledge to students and student learning is more than just receiving this knowledge.

In the context of this work, PCK is specifically addressed in terms of instructional strategies in science and the knowledge about this component necessary to implement inquiry based science teaching in school and at LOtC institutions.

Science educational research literature informs practice

Professionalism, in terms of wider comprehension, is also justified by professional actions, which are in line with domain specific (research) knowledge. The quality of an action is related to this domain specific knowledge. To own this professional knowledge is considered important for representatives when classified an expert in the field. In terms of professional science teaching, one has to consider that there are a minimum of four research areas that feed into this profession. These are 'science research', 'science education research', research on school related pedagogy' and 'practice based research in schools and educational settings'. The first one follows a different research paradigm than the second and the third. Practice based research may follow another set of paradigms.

Accepting all research fields as equally important for working as a professional, science teachers is particularly challenging. Whenever 'encultured' either explicitly or implicitly in science research paradigms, science teachers educational history may prevent or hinder them from accepting other epistemological approaches. In addition, the body of research knowledge is continuously developing in all fields which make it almost impossible to keep up to date even with one single research area. Research literature on science education is extensive and the outcomes of research seem to speak more to researchers themselves than to practitioners, who are on the whole not the producers of this knowledge but who are expected to be the end users. Frequently, it is also mentioned that research and practice are different in context. Research knowledge if often defined by its creation and the questions which need to be answered (Fraser et al., 2012). Thoughtful analysis of practical experience however is not meaningful until it is placed in a framework that enables professional teachers to relate it to other research findings and theorize about it. Science educational research does however have the potential to complement, contextualize and enhance the practical understanding, particularly for practicing teachers when researchers take the time to probe, analyse and evaluate practice based teaching from a variety if perspectives (Pollard et al., 2008).

2.5.3 *Continuous Professional Development (CPD)*

In workplace setting in general 'Professional Development' refers to:

> 'the acquisition of skills and knowledge both for personal development and for career advancement. Professional development encompasses all types of facilitated learning opportunities, ranging from college degrees to formal coursework, conferences and informal learning opportunities situated in practice.' (http://en.wikipedia.org/wiki/Professional_development)

The metaphor of 'Teaching as a Craft' presents teachers as being adaptive experts who relish challenges and are continually looking for ways to educate themselves. According to their attitude to professional development, they continuously adopt new ways of thinking. These new approaches allow a tolerance of ambiguity and for the teacher to let go of previously held assumptions as they engage in learning new skills. Others may continue to learn to become more efficient in carrying out routines they already adopt and therefore perform well in stable environments (Schneider & Plasman, 2011).

If one considers a group of professional teachers (e.g. high school biology teachers) as a social community of practice (Lave & Wenger, 1991), situational and constructive learning is assumed to take them from the margin as newly qualified teachers into the core of the community. 'Berliner (1988, 1994) describes 5 levels of skill development: novice, advanced beginner, competent, proficient and expert' (Schneider & Plasman, 2011, p. 533)

Berliner (2001) assumes that it takes at least 5 years for a newly qualified teacher to achieve expertise, irrespective of how one defines this.

The term 'Continuous Professional Development' has become a 'container concept' and again there is an absence of a shared understanding of what professional development actually is. Of course there is at least one explicit meaning connected with this term, which is: 'teachers continue to develop in their job, continuously learning from theory and practice and as a result become more experienced and efficient. Professional learning is assumed to be a continuum, starting in initial teacher training and evolving throughout the rest of a teacher's professional career.

Science education literature provides a huge variety of models for continuous professional development (CPD) for teachers. Continuous Professional Development for LOtC educators cannot draw on such a long history of research. Therefore it is assumed that whatever can be learned from research on 'formal teacher's professional development' will more or less be relevant for LOtC educators.

Professional development for teachers:
The term professional development is frequently used, but in very different contexts, referring to different practices and often with different meanings.

Klechtermans (2004) defines professional development as a learning process, resulting from the meaningful interaction between the teacher and their professional context both in space and time. This interaction eventually leads to changes in teachers' professional practice as well as in their thinking about practice.

Gusky (2000) sees professional development as a systemic process that considers change over an extended period of time and takes into account all levels of the organisation – the individual, the school, the school board, the national educational ministry etc.

He argues that CPD:

- is a learning process
- implies interaction with the context
- and leads to individual and organisational development

CPD is a term to describe all the activities in which teachers engage during their careers and which are designed to enhance their work (Day and Sachs, 2004). The main goal for CPD is that teachers' and educators' professional learning supports changes in teaching practices that result in improved student learning. The relationship between teachers professional development (PD) and teacher effectiveness, however, is not straight forward. The concept of 'Continuous Professional Development' (CPD) has been heavily criticised in terms of its ability to change teachers' practice and improve student outcomes for many years (McNicholl, 2013). CPD tends to have a small impact on teachers' learning, consequentially having little influence on their actual behaviour and even less influence on students' learning (Hattie, 2008).

A body of research knowledge about what works in CPD is already available and establishing professional learning communities (PLC) amongst participants in training courses is one of the favoured research-based recommendations (Timperley et al., 2007).

What makes Continuous Professional Development (CPD) effective?

Considerable effort has been directed to understanding the act of teaching and associated student learning outcomes. However, in terms of system engineering there seems to be another 'black box' situated between particular professional learning opportunities for teachers and their impact on teaching practice.

Based on education research outcomes, Gusky (2000) argues that 'good PD' mirrors the socio-constructivist ideas and should therefore:

- be social
- be interactive
- be context related
- challenge participants to critically review their beliefs and ideas
- be relevant to participant agendas

Groundwater-Smith and Dadds (2004) recommend focusing on five of the most important factors in CPD effectiveness:

- on learning through inquiry
- on the power of the school culture to affect teacher development positively or negatively
- on how the kinds of CPD available to teachers indirectly represent the kinds of professionals that teachers are expected to be or become
- on the importance of acknowledging values
- on evidence based practice as CPD

Wade (1984–1985) recommend four types of approaches found to be most effective on teachers' knowledge and behaviour, one of which has not been mentioned before is the

- observation on actual classroom methods and classroom practice

What is already known to be effective is unfortunately not always what is practiced. It is quite clear that listening to inspiring speakers or attending a one off workshop will rarely change a teacher's practice sufficiently to impact on student learning. However, looking at the professional development programme of the Pedagogical College in Tirol (winter term 2013/14) which is officially in charge for teachers professional development in the region, shows that most frequent offers (n = 48) addressing STEM teachers covers 4 teaching units which are about 3 hours.

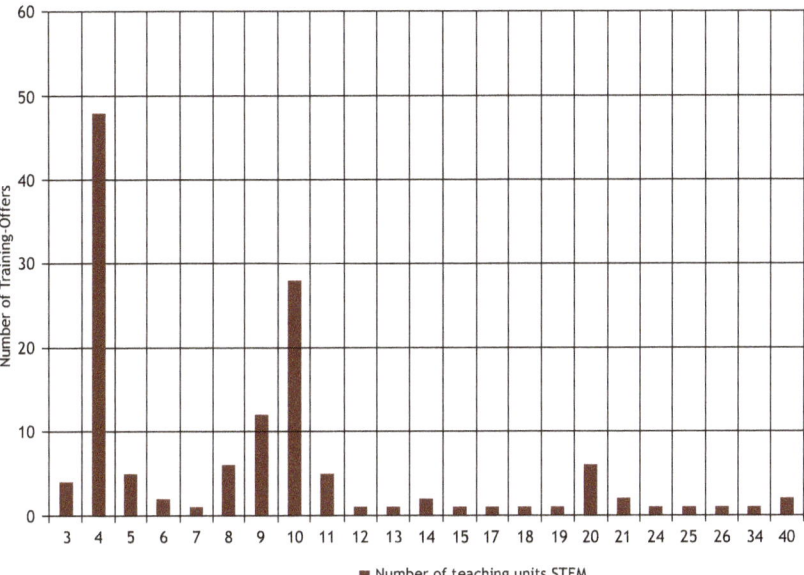

Figure 5: STEM related training offers at the Pedagogical College in Tirol most often (n = 48) covers 4 teaching units (3 h), followed by those lasting for 10 units (n = 28) which is about 7.5 h. The number of PD activities covering 11–20 units (up to 14 h) add up to a total of n = 19 offers, whereas those covering 21–40h add up to a total of n = 8.

However extended programs for teacher professional development are not necessarily more effective than short term offers. There is little evidence that either the 'non-structured approach' which treats teachers as self-regulated professionals who just need time and resources to construct their own learning, or the 'tightly structured approach', where external experts develop recipes for teaching, present prescribed practices with an underpinning rational and monitor their implementation, really work. For the latter there is evidence that these processes can be affective in changing teaching practice, however either this change has limited impact on students learning outcomes or the practice is not sustained once the 'expert' tutors withdraw from the process (Hattie, 2008; Timperley et al., 2007).

Timperley, Wilson, Barrar, and Fung published an extensive study in 2007, analysing 97 core studies and a couple of supplementary studies. They summarised seven themes about what works best in professional development:

1. *Extended time for opportunities to learn was necessary but not sufficient*
    - Learning opportunities typically occurred over an extended period of time and involved frequent contact with a provider

But extended opportunities also resulted in no or low impact on students. Limited time was adequate for relatively narrow curriculum goals.
- How time was used was more important than the exact nature of provision
   Funding for release time and the absence of such funding were both associated with the interventions in the core studies and with that low or no impact

2. *External expertise was typically necessary but not sufficient*
   Engagement of external expertise was a feature of nearly all the interventions in the core studies with funding frequently used for this purpose

   But interventions with low or no impact also involved external experts.

3. *Teachers engagement in learning at some point was more important than initial volunteering*
   Neither who initiated the professional learning opportunities nor whether it was voluntary or compulsory was associated with particular outcomes for students.

   What was more important was that the teachers engaged in the learning process at some point.

4. *Prevailing discourses challenged*
   Where prevailing discourses were problematic, they were typically based on assumptions that some groups of students could not learn as well as others and/or emphasised limited curriculum goals.

   The challenge to discourse typically involved iterative cycles of thinking about alternatives and becoming aware of learning gains as a result of changed teaching approaches

5. Opportunities to participate in a professional community of practice were more important than place
   Interventions in the core study were both school-based an external to the school

   Nearly all included participation in some kind of community of practice but such participation on its own was not associated with change

   Effective communities provide teachers with opportunities to process new understandings and challenge problematic beliefs, which focus on analysing the impact of teaching on student learning.

6. Consistency with wider trends in policy and research
   Approaches promoted typically were consistent with current research findings, recommendations of professional bodies (e.g. national subject association) and /or current policy

7. Active school leadership
   School-based interventions in the core studies had leaders who provide one or more of the following conditions

Actively organised a supportive environment to promote professional learning opportunities and the implementation of new practice in classrooms

Focused on developing a leaning culture within the school and were learners along with the teachers

Provided alternative visions and targets for students outcomes and monitored whether these were met

Created conditions for distributing leadership by developing the leadership of others. (ibid p. XXV)

Putting all 7 recommendations into practice was essential key aim of the INQUIRE training courses, as well as for the learning environment created in the INQUIRE consortium. This will be expanded on later.

Professional Learning Communities (PLC´s)

The notion of 'Situated Learning and Communities of Practice' have been addressed elsewhere already (s.p. 23).This learning principle is currently advocated in Professional Development research and communities established within the spirit of 'situated learning' are often referred to as Professional Learning Communities (PLC). PLCs have proven to be an alternative and successful way for the long-term professional development of teachers. They provide the space for learners to discuss and exchange knowledge as well as to make use of the social capital that individual members provide (Hofman & Dijkstra, 2010).

Hord (2009) defines the term PLC by explaining each individual concept as follows:

- *Professionals* are teachers/educators who feel responsible for developing classroom practice that supports effective student learning. Professionals are highly motivated and interested not only in their students but in their own learning.
- *Learning* is what professionals do to improve their knowledge and skills.
- *Community* is a group of individuals coming together to work on meaningful tasks and to share experiences, knowledge and skills.

Hord's (1997a) extensive literature review focused on school improvement efforts.

She summarized the professional learning community as having:

- supportive and shared leadership,
- shared values and vision,
- collective learning and application,

- shared personal practice, and
- supportive conditions – relationships and structures.

Bolam, McMahon, Stoll, Thomas, and Wallace (2005) reviewed the professional development literature published since 1990 and conducted a survey with 2,300 different schools (from nursery to secondary schools). The review and the survey confirmed the existence and importance of eight key characteristics shared by successful PLC.

Successful Professional Learning Communities share:

- Values and visions
- Collective responsibilities for student learning
- Reflective professional inquiry
- Collaboration focused on learning (the group as well as the individual)
- Professional learning
- Inclusive membership
- Mutual trust, respect, support and openness
- Networks and partnership

Authors point out that: 'the case study findings supported the conclusion that the more fully a PLC expressed the characteristics, the more they impacted positively on pupils' attendance, interest in learning and actual learning as well as on the individual and collective professional learning, practice and moral of teaching and support staff' (Bolam et al., p. iii).

Huffmann and Hipp's (2003) model of five dimensions for professional learning communities add into to the above list the perspective of 'Leadership', which includes external support provided by experts as well as shared authorities, tasks, duties and responsibilities amongst members. In addition, 'practical work' is shared which includes, for example, observing each other when putting knowledge and skills into practice.

The concept of the professional learning community was a central focus addressed in the OECD study 'Teaching Practices and Pedagogical Innovation TALIS 2008' (Vieluf et al., 2012). Hence central features of professional learning communities include 5 characteristics namely:

- co-operation among teachers (such as team teaching)
- holding a shared vision,
- having a clear focus on learning,
- practicing reflective inquiry and
- engaging in the de-privatisation of practice

Affirmative actions were taken by the INQUIRE management board to nurture the development of communities of learners, as groups of individuals or as a network of organisations. To value collaborative learning processes are a central theme in the INQUIRE project design.

Reflective Practice in Professional Development
Self-reflection and self-critique are characteristics any professional should exhibit. Because teaching requires teachers to change and adapt to new situations very quickly, they need to not only learn in practice but through practice. This means considering reflective practice as one of the major tools in increasing teaching proficiency. 'Reflective Practice' in education is a term that carries different meanings in particular contexts. For some, it means thinking about something, for other it is a well-defined and crafted practice or even a highly structured approach to develop a deeper understanding. For many student teachers it is considered an imposition that needs to be fulfilled to achieve course requirements.

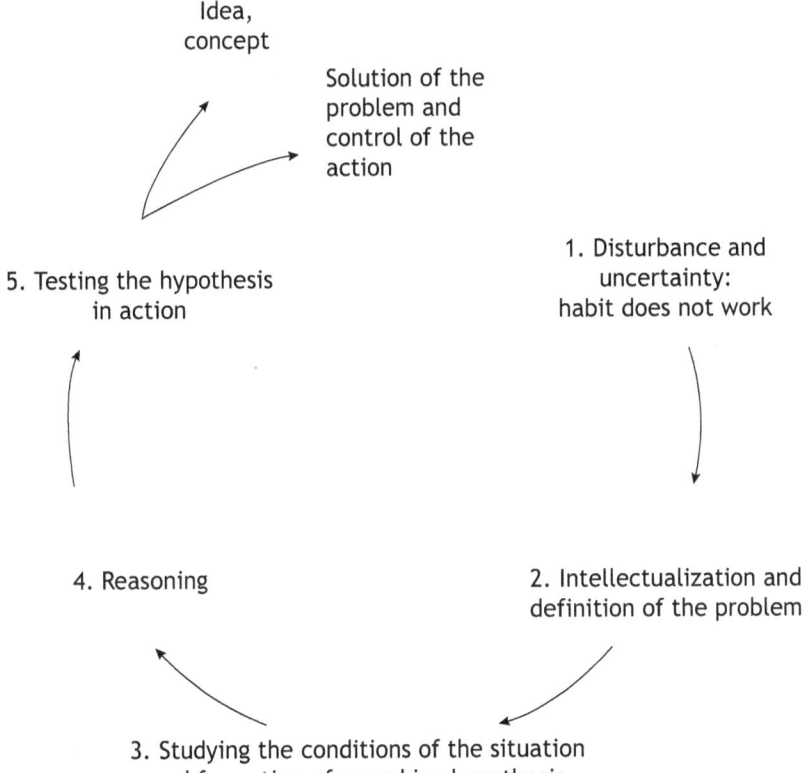

Figure 6: Dewey's model of reflective thought and action (Miettinen, 2000, p. 65).

In 1933 Dewey was already drawing the attention of teacher trainers to reflective thinking. He argued:

> 'Reflective thinking, in distinction from other operations to which we apply the name of thought, involves first a state of doubt/hesitation/perplexity/mental difficulty in which thinking originates.
> Secondly an act of searching/hunting/ inquiry to find material that will resolve the doubt, settle and dispose of the perplexity' (Dewey, 1993, p. 12)

According to Dewey a reflective thinking process is formed by five phases which need not necessarily occur in any particular order. The five phases are suggestions, problem, hypothesis, reasoning and testing (Loughran, 1996).

Based on Dewey notion of reflective action, Pollard and colleagues (2008, p. 14) provide seven key characteristics of reflective practice in the teaching context. These are:

1. *Reflective teaching implies an active concern with aims and consequences, as well as with means and technical efficiency.*
   Teaching practices are influenced by the wider society (education policy, parents beliefs, etc.). Hence reflective teachers should actively work on policy ideas – thus a critical attitude to policy ideas is important. A teacher is not an autonomous individual, which many teachers once thought to be and unfortunately occasionally still do. As soon as questions about education aims and social values are seriously raised a professional needs to take them into consideration and needs to develop those ideas further.
2. *Reflective teaching is applied in a cycle or spiral process, in which teachers monitor, evaluate, and revise their own practice continuously.*
   Teachers are principally expected to plan, take provisions and act. Reflective teachers monitor, observe and collect data of their own and their student's intentions as evidence to inform their own doing. This evidence needs to be critically analysed and evaluated and shared with others to finally inform further decisions. It is a continuous spiralling process towards higher-quality teaching.
3. *Reflective teaching requires competence in methods of evidence-based classroom enquiry, to support the progressive development of higher standards of teaching.*
   Methods applied are reviewing relevant existing research literature and gathering new evidence by e.g. collecting data, describing situations, processes, causes or effects. (e.g. objectively: what students actually do; or subjectively: individual perceptions). Applying analytical approaches such as interpreting data in the light of already existing research and other practitioners' knowledge and finally evaluating the scene by making judgements about the educational consequences.

4. *Reflective teaching requires attitudes of open-mindedness, responsibility and wholeheartedness.*
   All three attitudes are drawn from Dewey's 1938 notion of reflective action and are considered vital ingredients of the professional commitment that needs to be demonstrated by reflective teachers.
   - *Open-mindedness* is used as being willing to reflect and listen to more sides than one and to give attention to alternative possibilities. Thus own assumptions, prejudices and ideologies are challenged.
   - *Being responsible* means to taken moral, ethical and political issue into consideration to make professional and person judgement
   - To be *whole-hearted* asks teachers to be dedicated, single minded and enthusiastic
5. *Reflective teaching is based on teacher judgement, informed by evidence-based enquiry and insights from other research.*
   As far as teachers knowledge is solely based on individual experience and is simply believed to be valuable because it works in practical teaching there are little incentives to change even in the light of evidence supporting alternative ideas of practice. Educational research has the potential to complement, contextualise and enhance practical understanding. Thus reflective teaching is trying to merge the two knowledge areas of research based and practical based knowledge.
6. *Reflective teaching is enhanced through collaboration and dialogue with colleagues.*
   Engaging in reflective practice is most effectively done in association with colleagues because they provide the surrounding for collaborative or reflective discussions which are essential in all aspects of social learning
7. *Reflective teaching enables teachers to creatively mediate externally developed frameworks for teaching and learning.*
   Creative mediation involves the interpretation of external requirements in the light of a teachers understanding of a particular context and is often the source of essential forms of innovation for future development. (Regan & Dillon, 2013)

Reflective practice is advocated by many scholars in order to improve teacher development and is frequently recommended for teachers' professional development (Loughran, 2002).

The diversity of views on what reflective practice means how it should be done and documented and how the ability of students and teachers to become reflective practitioners can be improved, makes it difficult for both researchers and practitioners to agree on how pre- and in-service teacher programmes can support participants to develop a reflective attitude to their practice. A real and serious issue for professional development is the teacher's ability to capture, portray and share knowledge of practice in ways that are meaningful to others. Teachers engaging in reflective practice, or so called 'practitioner inquiry', however, collect evidence, which helps them share their experience and knowledge gained from practice with colleagues in a community of practice or professional learning community. Through reflective practice, professionals develop their understanding about the way they conduct their work and develop and refine their practice to become even more effective. The knowledge base generated is helping practitioners to better understand what they know and what they learn in practice and therefore supports the emancipation of practice by learning through practice (Loughran, 2002).

Loughran (2002) suggest that:

> 'effective reflective practice is drawn from the ability to frame and reframe the practice setting, to develop and respond to this framing through action so that the practitioner's wisdom-in action is enhanced and a particular outcome articulation of professional knowledge is encouraged.... It is through the development of knowledge and understanding of the practice setting and the ability to recognize and respond to such knowledge that the reflective practitioner becomes truly responsive to the needs, issues and concerns that are important in shaping practice' (p. 42).

External expertise

In science teaching, external expertise can come from various fields of expertise such as 'science', 'science education research', 'learning sciences', 'psychology', 'pedagogy' etc.

Shulman (1989a) argued that scientific knowledge is inseparable from pedagogical knowledge and so expertise in subject content knowledge is extremely important. Experts in a particular scientific field are therefore often highly appreciated if they are able to provide reliable, up to date science knowledge in an 'easy to understand' way.

In addition, pedagogical, PCK or practical expertise is equality important and experts in these fields helpful to give advice.

As Timperley, Wilson, Barrar, and Fung, (2007) have found, experts are not needed per se, but they can speed up the processes of learning in CPD. It is important who these experts are and how they are able to communicate the particular knowledge they are asked to bring into a community of learners.

Practitioners themselves most often value a practical approach to learning which provides them with opportunities to observe and test their knowledge as well as skills which are required for a particular CPD training. Although the strategies of collecting and adopting 'ready to go' teaching recipes hardly ever prove to be successful for implementation in every day classroom teaching, many teachers assume that the role of the expert is to provide these 'readymade' courses of action.

2.6 Design Based Research Informs Practice

> 'The ultimate purpose of science education research is the improvement of science teaching and learning throughout the world. (Abell & Lederman 2007, p. xiii)

Educational research, however, face the challenge as Abell and Lederman identified in their introduction to the 'Handbook of Research in Science Education' published in 2007:

> 'We must take care that the proximate causes of our research (e.g. achieving publications that count for tenure, writing conference papers so our universities will fund our travel, preparing new researchers getting grant dollars) do not derail us from achieving our ultimate purpose.' (Abell & Lederman, 2007, p. iii).

Whether and how research is still suitable for informing practice is a concern increasingly voiced by scholars in the field:

> 'I believe it would not be inaccurate to say that the most powerful forces to have shaped educational scholarship over the last century have tended to push the field in unfortunate directions – away from close interaction with policy and practice towards excessive quantification and scientism.' (Condliffe Lagemann, 2001, p. 1)

Splitter and Seidl (2011) argue that:

> 'The generation of knowledge by academics often entails the neutralization of practical urgencies – such as the ability to identify problems for the sole pleasure of resolving them and not because they are posed by the necessities of life'. (p. 106)

Referring to the work of the French sociologist Pierre Bourdieu, Splitter and Seidl assume that:

> 'Social practice performed by individual actors is influenced not only by the actors *'individual disposition'* (such as origin, education and identity) but also by supra-individual *'objective structures'* (such as socially defined interests, beliefs assumptions and resources). Objective

structures are not uniform but vary between different social spheres.' (p. 103)

Thus research and praxis are different social spheres, which exhibit different structures associated with different types of knowledge. Actors belonging to one or the other carry out their activities while facing different structural possibilities and constraints, such as being guided by different domain specific interests, beliefs and assumptions and are limited or supported by particular sets of resources. Particular conditions of one or the other field lead to a specific way of observing the world and even the language used. Splitter and Seidl (2011) cite Bourdieu to visualise a phenomenon which was frequently mentioned in this part of my work already and is most typical for science education research as it is not understood by practitioners:

> 'Instead of grasping and mobilizing the meaning of a word that is immediately compatible with the situation, we [scientists] mobilize and examine all the possible meanings of that word, outside of any reference to the situation [...] The scholastic view is a very peculiar point of view on the social world, on language, on any possible object of thought. (p. 105)

Science education research is often occupied by the monological paradigm of finding the universal laws or structure underpinning a phenomenon. It is predominately seeking to produce the single most coherent model of e.g. 'inquiry based science education', or 'communities of practice' and put significant efforts into examining possible meanings of terms such as 'scientific literacy' or 'pedagogical content knowledge'. By doing this, research runs the risk of overlooking the fact that knowledge is never independent of the social, historical and cultural context that gives it meaning.

An obvious theme, running through all topics addressed in the theoretical framework is the discrepancy between the researcher's perception of a concept and how this one is constantly misunderstood and modified when it is used and put into practice.

Cultural psychology design based research

> 'Design-based research is premised on the notion that we can learn important things about the nature and conditions of learning by attempting to engineer and sustain educational innovation in everyday settings. Complex educational interventions can be used to surface phenomena of interest for systematic study to better promote specific educational outcomes'. (Bell, 2004, p. 243)

'Cultural psychology design based research' recognizes the influence of the social context in which a particular work takes place. It has the potential to contribute to our understanding of learning in complex settings. In this regard, designing and developing an intervention is an explicitly theory driven activity. Theory is carefully studied and this knowledge is used to design, plan and implement a learning environment which has the potential to fulfil desired effects.

> [. . .] design based research seeks to understand the nature of the introduced changes and their consequences from the perspectives of the participant and often provides them with a voice and a source of influence on the shaping changes to their setting.' (Bell, 2004, p. 249)

Emphasis can be put on the localised nature of practices and norms of social groups investigated as they actually occur in their specific settings. It allows getting insights about the nature of organisations and suggests improvement for their educational enterprise. It helps to learn more about whether or not the design of the learning environment was appropriate for participating groups that are assumed to already have developed cultural practices before the invention begins (ibid, 2004).

Design based research is applied in this work in particular to understand more about whether a collaborative, expansive learning environment (applied design) has the potential to support partners professional development and to find out how an imposed theoretical view such as 'implementing inquiry based science education on a large scale in Europe' (Roccard, 2007) is interpreted by botanic gardens and natural history museums. Primacy is given to the interpretation of partner's activities to find out how the concept of IBST was actually understood in different venues while taking institutional norms associated with each setting into consideration

Through a retrospective analysis it is possible to map:

> '[. . .] the embodiment of particular conjectures through their design reification and to then design research studies to specifically tests the predictions that result. Such predictions pertain to both outcomes expected from the intervention and ways in which designed scaffolds are expected to function. The need to link outcomes to these expected functions across research iterations is the source of power from this analytic approach' (Sandoval & Bell, 2004, p. 200).

3. Part B – Putting Theory into Practice

Cultural psychology design based research (Bell, 2004) is applied to learn more about how international educational reform based projects need to be structured and implemented in order to become successful in implementing change in educational practice, at schools, as well as at Learning Outside the Classroom institutions.

As learning occurs most naturally and meaningfully when embedded in a sociocultural, activity related context, I will explain the INQUIRE project idea, design and framework and how collaborative knowledge creation processes have been supported among a group of Botanic Gardens, Natural History Museums and Science Education research institutions participating in the international EU 7th framework Science and Society project - INQUIRE: Inquiry based teacher training for a sustainable future (2010–2013).

The activity theory and the expansive learning model is applied to explore the collaborative knowledge creation process of one activity system, the Spanish INQUIRE partner, in detail. By analysing knowledge artefacts (e.g. understanding IBSE) and objects (e.g. lesson plans, training course design etc.) I try to learn more about how collaborative knowledge creation occurs and can be supported. In addition I will look at whether and how this new knowledge contributes to the transformation of practices in respect to a partner's socio-cultural context. According to Yrjö Engeström's theory, I value both the improvement on the scale of what is currently assumed to be good practice in IBSE teaching as well as the horizontal movement in terms of exchanging and hybridising different cultural contexts, concepts and attitudes; I also try to understand the totality of their work and practices.

How to cite this book chapter:
Kapelari, S. 2015. Putting Theory into Practice. In: Kapelari, S *Garden Learning: A Study on European Botanic Gardens' Collaborative Learning Processes*, Pp. 101–155. London: Ubiquity Press. DOI: http://dx.doi.org/10.5334/bas.c. License: CC-BY 4.0.

I conclude that the European commission's 7th Framework Program designers were wise to focus on 'Inquiry Based Science Education'. Not because some researchers claim IBSE is the most successful approach, but because it is still such a vague concept that requires teachers, educators, teacher trainers, researchers, curriculum planners and policy makers to 'move across boundaries'(Engeström & Sannino, 2010), and to find information and tools wherever they happen to be available.

Thus IBSE has a great potential to trigger 'expansive learning' processes amongst stakeholders all over Europe. However, experience has shown that some EU programmes, as well as project designers and evaluators, are too preoccupied with what they value as success. The focus is put on a monological stance or on measurable facts, such as timely delivery of reports and deliverables, progress towards the objectives of the project, whether and how project beneficiaries proceed in producing high numbers of educational materials published on websites or high numbers of contacts established with stakeholders. All this is independent of the quality of these contacts.

As a result of number crunching, we are left with little understanding of how educational practises change in relation to IBSE reform interventions at the organisational level or in schools and LOtC organisations. We know very little about what knowledge turns into organisational memory and whether it is implemented sustainably in future practice.

3.1 The INQUIRE Project

'Improving science education was and is an issue in educational policy in many European countries and worldwide for a couple of years already. High quality science teaching applied by those engaging in science education, formal and informal settings alike, is essential for effective student learning' (Osborne & Dillon, 2008).

The project 'INQURE: Inquiry based teacher training for a sustainable future' (EU Nr. 266616) was one of several initiatives funded by the European 7th Framework programme (2007–2013) Science and Society. I was the applicant and the coordinator of this three year project, running between 2010–2013, and which joined 17 partners from 11 European countries and had an allocated budget of 2,3 Million €.

INQUIRE was the follow up to the Project, PLASCIGARDENS- Plant Science Gardens: Plant Science Education for Primary Schools in European Botanic Gardens (SAS6-CT-2005-20577) which was mainly dedicated to developing an 'inquiry based, multilingual, multicultural plant science education tool about plant diversity' (www.planscafe.net).

I coordinated this project from 2005 to 2007 and ran it together with partners from Bulgaria, Italy and the UK. All three of these partners joined me again in the INQUIRE project. The first project already put an emphasis on developing teacher training offers at botanic gardens for promoting collaboration between botanic gardens and their local teachers and schools.

3.1.1 The INQUIRE Idea

Project abstract (Project Proposal handed in At the European Commission Research Directorate in 2010):
The science education community agrees that pedagogical practices based on IBSE methods are more effective. But the reality on the ground is different. For various reasons, this type of teaching is not practiced in most European classrooms. INQUIRE counteract this by developing and offering a one-year practically based IBSE teacher training course that will reach out to hundreds of teachers, and in turn thousands of children, in 11 European countries. The course is run through 14 Botanic Gardens and Natural History Museums - some of Europe's most inspirational cultural and learning institutions. These places act as catalysts, training and supporting teachers and educators to develop their proficiency in IBSE and become reflective practitioners. Most of the partner institutions have experience in delivering IBSE. The training locations, the practical nature of the course, the support offered and the subject content encourages teachers and educators to enrol in INQUIRE courses and try out IBSE in their everyday teaching. Biodiversity loss and climate change are the major global issues of the 21st century and many teachers are looking for innovative ways to tackle these subjects. INQUIRE training supports teachers to do just that and introduce them to institutions where children can carry out 'real' investigations and see science in action. INQUIRE training courses are promoted through national systems that support professional development for teachers as well as informal education training networks. The website encourages the uptake of IBSE. It promotes dialogue between partners and teachers, showcase best practice published on other EU websites and highlight the results of practitioner research in IBSE (Kapelari et al., 2010).

3.1.2 The INQUIRE Framework

Educational reforms efforts around the world are seeking to provide opportunities for pre and in service teachers to enhance their professional knowledge, skills and attitudes (s.p. 99ff) to develop new and more effective instructional practices. However many institutions that provide opportunities for teachers and students to learn about science outside the classroom often do not engage in bigger educational reform efforts (Phillips et al., 2007) and in service training programs for LOtC educators are rare. The INQUIRE project therefore asked Botanic Gardens and Natural History Museums to engage in designing and implementing inquiry based training offers for teachers and

LOtC educators and thus contribute to improving science education in their country.

Traditional professional teacher development schemes have come under criticism for their inability to promote teacher learning in ways that impact on outcomes for the diversity of students in the classrooms (Timperley et al., 2007). Criticism is directed to in-service training that follows approaches based on an external view of what knowledge and skills teacher need to be equipped with - a separation from the teacher's daily work or a setting that focuses on an individualistic development practices. These settings do not take into account what we already know about how adults and teachers learn (s.p. 106ff). Taking this into consideration, the INQUIRE approach to professional learning and development relies on collaborative knowledge creation processes to support consortium partners as well as their course participants in developing an understanding of IBSE that is fruitful in their particular socio cultural setting. The INQUIRE learning environment is based on Engeströms 'Expansive Learning Theory '(s.p. 34ff) thus expanding Vygotsky's constructivist approach of 'socio-cultural learning' (p. 31) and Lave and Wenger's ideas of 'situated learning in communities of practice' (p. 23ff) and assumes that a collaborative knowledge creation approach to learning has a great potential to support individual as well as organisational development.

3.1.3 The INQUIRE Network

As mentioned earlier, the Rocard Report (2007) suggests that 'Teachers are key players in the renewal of science education. Among others, being part of a network allows them to improve the quality of their teaching and supports their motivation' (p. 14). The use of network structures is becoming popular, in business and education alike, not only as a source of knowledge and to improve the effectiveness of organisations but as a source of innovation and transformation. Learning in collaborative networks is a special mode of knowledge production and values knowledge that is embedded in social structures within and between individuals and organisations. The INQUIRE network therefore is recognised as a collaborative network which is characterised by connecting all 4 levels of action.

- Level 1: the individual science teacher acting in the classroom / the individual science educator facilitating learning outside the classroom
- Level 2: the group of science teachers or science educators working in a particular school or in the education department in particular LOtC organisation
- Level 3: the collective of educational organisations (schools and LOtC organisations) actively engaged in science education in a particular country
- Level 4: the collective of formal education providers and LOtC organisations acting on an international level (Level 4).

A horizontal movement of information between organisations, as well as a vertical movement between all four levels of action, is accomplished by individuals acting on all 4 of these levels simultaneously – as botanic garden educators responsible for running school programs, as INQUIRE training course designers, as course teacher and as representative of their particular institution in the INQUIRE consortium. Knowledge created by teachers and educators participating in INQUIRE training courses is introduced through monitoring tools that the course trainers apply to evaluate their course and through assignments participants have to hand in to fulfil course requirements. Thus knowledge transfer and learning is not considered to be a one way road but interplay between these levels. It is assumed that it leads to the formation of new levels of learning located in the partnership. Van Aalst (2003) argues that, in terms of its efficiency, the quality of the network structure is important. As a consequence the INQUIRE project planning and the follow up implementation exhibit the following thoughts:

- Producers (Botanic Gardens, Natural History Museums offering training courses) and customers (schools, teachers, other LOtC organisations interested in running INQUIRE courses etc.) were linked via a national advisory board which consisted of teachers, members of the national school system, LOtC organisations etc. This was established to increase the degree of partner's integration on the national level.
- Links between partners in the consortium were assumed to be interactive and all partners expected gains from being involved in this network.
- The network enjoyed a degree of self-management which included different leaders for different aspects (visible in the INQUIRE management board)
- The INQUIRE consortium partners shared the common purpose of developing a deeper understanding of IBSE in a school - botanic garden learning environment and establishing teacher training courses which reflect this understanding and their organisational development (object).
- A sense of belonging, cohesion and reinforcement of values was created and maintained throughout the project via a sequence of meetings which were perfectly organised by the Management Board and the local host partner.
- Networks often come and go. The INQUIRE project came to an end after three years, however partners prepared the ground for new networks in a variety of partner combinations and with additional LOtC organisations.

3.1.4 The INQUIRE Design

The INQUIRE project design aspired to create a collaborative expansive learning environment (Engeström, 2001) that put the following characteristics into practice:

Circles of learning actions....

INQUIRE efforts are founded upon the idea that humans of any age learn more effectively through 'personal inquiry experience with others' than through didactic teaching and telling. Multiple expansive learning cycles (s. p. 35) were integrated into the INQUIRE project design from the start in order to develop a new and specific understanding of inquiry based science teaching at botanic gardens. The project management never advanced a monological view of the 'one and only best practice model of inquiry based science teaching' but repeatedly asked consortium partners to question their understanding of inquiry based science teaching, to develop lesson plans and model new solutions, examine them in practice and reflect on them not only in their own organisational context but to consolidate their understanding in dialogue with other consortium partners (s. p. 113).

Practitioner's inquiry is increasingly advocated as a self-reflection tool that can promote the development of teachers and researchers alike (Taber, 2007; Reid & Dillon, 2004) and this approach was applied to scaffold reflection throughout the process.

Partners present their findings in 'Portfolios of Evidence' which were introduced as a tool to

- promote reflective practice
- shared knowledge and experience with colleagues
- to encourage cooperation
- offer a bottom-up voluntary process that is owned by the partner and was not used for evaluation purposes
- support partners by enabling conditions (Klenowski, 2002,)

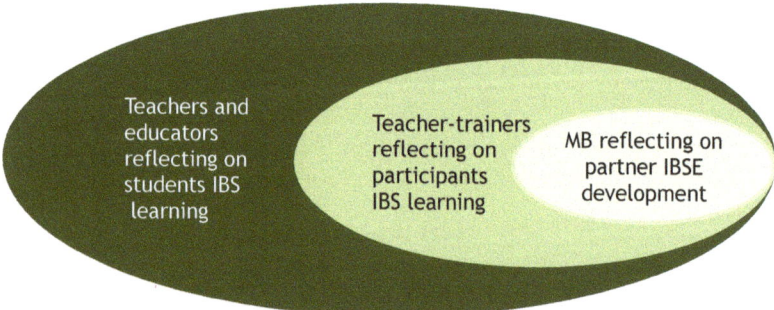

Figure 7: Reflection took place on 3 levels: course participants, botanic gardens and the Management Board were engaged in reflective practice.

Teachers and educators participating in the INQUIRE training courses were asked to investigate their own teaching and learning and hand in assignments that illustrate their learning process. Partner institutions did the same. The consortium as a whole applied a range of 16 different evaluation tools to monitor their practice (Regan & Dillon, 2013).

To value this process, a pilot and a second INQUIRE teacher training course was planned and implemented to provide the opportunity for partners to adapt their training course design in the light of experience, reflection and feedback from network partners and to see whether their new understanding proves successful. Partners were asked to hand in portfolios of evidence after each training course was finished. Portfolios of evidence were applied

> '[. . .] to consider the complex multifaceted nature of teaching by providing the opportunity to reflect critically on their practice, to engage in professional dialogue with colleagues and to collaborate and develop understanding and ideas on teaching and learning (Klenowski, 2002, pp. 24–25).

. . . informed design based research

> 'The design researcher proceeds through a series of highly aligned cycles of design, data gathering and analysis, using each implementation as an opportunity to inform and reformulate subsequent design principles. Through a parallel and retrospective process of reflection upon the design itself, the study of its implementation, its critical features and its formative outcomes, the researcher builds on the initial hypotheses and design principles. This reflective process occurs in real time and when done well it allows the researcher to provide fundamental understanding and to build a more coherent and robust theory based in actual practice' (Kelly & Sloane, 2003, p. 32)

Portfolios of evidence and other artefacts and objects (e.g. Lesson plans) handed in by partners after the first and after the second course were analysed. Interviews with partners were conducted in the middle as well as at the end of the project (s.p. 172). An 'Interims Evaluation Report' as well as a 'Final External Evaluation Report' Allun Morgan (2013) was commissioned to collect additional data and provide an external perspective on the work done in course of the project. All interims findings were used to adapt and improve the project design while the project was in progress.

Value multifaceted knowledge

The INQUIRE network design was chosen to value the innovative potential of a heterogeneous group. Multifaceted knowledge, experience and creativity was contributed through scientists, education researchers, botanic garden educators, teachers, horticulturalist and others who joined in and constituted this multicultural group. Building on the 'Model of Knowledge Creation' (Nonaka & Takeuchi, 1995), INQUIRE explicitly valued both stages of knowledge which are the 'tacit' and the 'explicit'. Explicit knowledge is easy to articulate and to express formally in clear terms whereas tacit knowledge is embedded in individual experience, involves personal beliefs, perspectives and values. The basic source of information in the INQUIRE model is tacit knowledge, which needs to be explicated in order to be transformed into knowledge that is useful at the level of the group and the whole project. A creative knowledge development processes is an ascending process of learning from the individual level to the group and organizational level and finally between organizations. The INQUIRE project management team aimed to activate all four levels of knowledge development.

The dynamics in INQUIRE can be explained by an interaction between tacit and explicit knowledge about IBSE available in the consortium and research and practice base literature made accessible by consortium partners. The consortium started by sharing tacit knowledge about IBSE by presenting IBSE activities during consortium meetings as well as articulating each individual's understanding of IBSE at that moment in time . Nonaka and Takeuchi (1995) termed this first phase *socialization* (planned and took place in project Work Package (WP1). It is followed by the second phase called *externalization* in which INQUIRE partners conceptualized tacit knowledge by means of presenting activities and developing a deliverable presenting a concept of IBSE in INQUIRE (planned and took place in project WP 2).

Explicit knowledge about IBSE was continuously discussed in a series of consortium meetings, where partners presented lesson plans and activities and questioned each other's teaching and learning approaches. This third phase is called the *combination* phase and asked partners to share explicit knowledge (planned and took place in project WP 2-4). INQUIRE finally reached the fourth and final phase which is called *internalization* (planned and took place in project WP5) which asked INQUIRE partners to absorb explicit knowledge gained in the project so that it becomes tacit again and is sustainably implemented through the partner's philosophy of IBSE teaching and learning. This organisational knowledge becomes visible in the final training course design and lesson plans which partners published on the INQUIRE website.

Collaborative learning in a community

The knowledge community that it was hoped would emerge in the INQUIRE consortium was an 'Advance Community of Practice', because it values expansive learning processes and not the system defined by Lave and Wenger's early understanding of situated learning which was seen as a predominantly vertical movement from the stage of incompetence to competence. The major goal in INQUIRE was to nurture the development of an international collaborative network described as a 'Community of Inquiry'.

The 14 Botanic Garden partners (see list of partners on p. 161) were selected because these Gardens feature an educational department with at least one employee. Consortium participants were expected to have a common interest in improving science education programmes (object) and in collaborating over an extended period of time to share ideas, find solutions and build innovation. Consortium meetings as well as an online platform provided the space for collaborative action.

Shulman and Shulman (2004) noted that an ongoing interaction between an individual professional and the community leads to a shared knowledge of the team/organisation which finally offers members the opportunity to confirm, interconnect and develop their professional knowledge. Thus the project management was responsible for setting tasks and timelines to nurture this ongoing reflection and knowledge sharing processes.

Provide additional source of information

VanDriel (2011) and Van Aalst (2003) highlight the importance of including experts in the field when it comes to maintaining networks/communities of learners because these people help the group to speed up their learning process. Experts were therefore asked to inform the INQUIRE community in two areas of knowledge development:

- Scientific background knowledge about 'biodiversity loss and climate change'.
- Science Education Research based knowledge about IBSE, Reflective Practice, Teachers Professional Development and Assessment.

The discourse and the different views of practitioners and researchers served to enhance the process of reflection and to expand the horizon, understanding and capabilities of both agents.

Appreciating science education research knowledge

Timperley, Wilson, Barrar, and Fung (2007) published a list of characteristic professional development activities which should be included in any professional development offer so that it becomes more successful in supporting teacher development (s.p. 106ff). The original INQUIRE teacher and educator training course design asked partner institutions to integrate these characteristics. However, as the expansive learning process took place in many different countries, these characteristics were discussed and trialled, with the result that on some occasions the final courses design turned out to be slighted different.

3.1.5 IBST in INQUIRE

The shared understanding of IBST in INQUIRE is valued as an expansive learning process and based on knowledge provided by science education research as well as on practice based knowledge provided by partners and other IBSE related educational project. The focus is put on student learning outcomes, not on a particular model of IBST. It is based on the notion that natural science is not all about following fixed and unalterable operating plans, which have to be completed one predefined step after another. It's actually a creative, but still understandable and reproducible, process of gaining information. The main principle of IBST in INQUIRE is to promote a model of the learner as autonomous and independently thinking - someone capable of dealing successfully with many aspects of science. Therefore, learners should be provided with free space for organising their learning processes individually. They also need to be taught some science content by teachers - they cannot simply invent scientific knowledge without any basic level of scientific knowledge. INQUIRE aims to support teachers and botanic educators and, in the long run, help pupils to understand the various and creative scientific approaches which represent the foundation of scientific learning, by enabling them to experience these approaches first-hand. Using IBSE approaches, teachers, botanic garden educators and their participating students should develop the ability to critically examine what they are told by people or read in on-line publications, newspapers or even in education research journals. They should also be able to examine their own ideas critically and ensure that, as much as possible, they are evidence-based (Kapelari et al., 2011). Thus INQURE aims to enable practitioners to adapt the abstract 'circle of inquiry based teaching' (see p. 58ff) innovatively, flexibly and competently to their own and to the needs of their students. Practitioners at all levels should be enabled to question their approaches self-reflexively, as well as to analyse the efficiency of their teaching approach while focusing on students learning outcomes.

3.1.5 The INQUIRE Proposal

I was primarily responsible for the development production of the INQUIRE project proposal. This was the 'road map' that the project consortium followed throughout the whole duration of the project without any major adaptation. The proposal was handed in to the EU in January 2010 and was positively evaluated by two external evaluators.

I was primarily responsible for negotiating the Grant Agreement with representatives of the European Commission between June and September 2010. The writing process, as well as the negotiation process, was supported by Julia Willison and Gail Bromley, for the most part in terms of fruitful discussion and editing of the English script .

The following INQUIRE partners were asked to contribute to the proposal by providing written sections appropriate to their expertise and therefore hold authorship of particular paragraphs.

Julia Willison: 'Supporting education for a sustainable Europe' (Proposal, p. 101)

Prof. Doris Elster: 'Assessing INQUIRE course development' (Proposal, p. 19–20)

In the end, the theoretical background provided by Prof. Doris Elster did not fully match my understanding of good practice in professional development, which has been described in great detail in this work already. The Framework for evaluating teachers professional development suggested by Prof. Elster did not meet the approval of the INQUIRE Management Board, so the evaluation strategy was changed and is described in detail in 'The Quality Management Report' (Regan & Dillon, 2013), which mirrors my understanding of collaborative knowledge creation in the light of activity theory. Nonetheless, at that stage of the proposal development I was grateful for these contributions.

Prof. Justin Dillon: 'Stimulating and motivating science learning from an earliest stage' (Proposal, p. 15–16)

The following pages have been taken from the proposal to give an insight how the basic principle of the INQUIRE Framework was put into practice.

[. . . .]

B.1. Concept and objectives, quality and effectiveness of the support mechanisms and associated work plan

B.1.1. Concept and objectives

> 'We cannot solve our problems with the same thinking we used when we created them.'
>
> *Albert Einstroom*

The overall objective of the INQUIRE project is the widespread uptake of inquiry-based teaching and learning in science education across Europe. With this in mind, the overwhelming goals of the INQUIRE project are the following:

The Goal
INQUIRE aims to reinvigorate inquiry-based science education (IBSE) in the Formal and the Learning Outside the Classroom (LOtC) educational systems throughout Europe. INQUIRE envisages to promote the professional development of teachers by implementing effective teacher training interventions using the expertise in inquiry-based learning and teaching of a consortium of 17 partners in 11 countries.

The consortium will develop and is planning to implement a rolling one-year training course for practitioners in inquiry-based learning methods, research methodology and assessment techniques. Through training, ongoing mentor-

Summary Table	Work packages addressing this issue
INQUIRE will link informal and formal education systems as well as the science education research community through assembling an interdisciplinary project team	WP2 Levelling
INQUIRE will develop a shared understanding of inquiry based learning in formal and informal educational institutions on a European scale	WP2 Levelling
INQUIRE will develop a rolling one-year training course for practitioners in inquiry-based learning (INQUIRE course manual) Addressing pupils age 9–14 years	WP3 INQUIRE course development
INQUIRE will promote already existing best practise models (PLASCIGARDEN, SINUS Transfer, POLLEN, S-TEAM, FIBONACCI) throughout the project in both the formal and informal education system	WP3 INQUIRE course development WP6 Dissemination
INQUIRE will develop a course whose subject content will highlight the major global issues of the 21st Century: biodiversity loss and climate change	WP3 INQUIRE course development
INQUIRE will promote learning in and outside the classroom	WP3 INQUIRE course development
INQUIRE will promote its course through the various national systems that support continual professional development for teachers	WP4 Implementation
INQUIRE envisages to implement pilot courses at a local level throughout 11 European countries	WP4 Implementation
INQUIRE will ensure that formative assessment encourages the course design to be adapted to the needs of individual countries	WP7 Quality Management
INQUIRE will create an interactive website and regularly published electronic newsletters to support a practitioners network	WP6 Dissemination
INQUIRE will train teachers and informal educators to carry out their own practitioners research	WP4 Implementation
INQUIRE will encourage teachers and educators to participate in website activities through establishing a teacher recognition scheme	WP3 INQUIRE course development
INQUIRE will run a final Conference to disseminate the project outcomes on a European wide scale	WP6 Dissemination
INQUIRE will support other informal learning institutions seeking to gain experience in the area of inquiry based science education techniques and run the INQUIRE Train the Trainer Course.	WP4 Implementation
INQUIRE outcomes will be promoted through a range of networks including the EU central information provider for dissemination of best practice	WP6 Dissemination

Table 3: Summary table of project objectives.

ing and promotion of best practice, INQUIRE will try to firmly embed this pedagogy within the educational systems of 11 European countries.

The subject content of the course will focus on the major global issues of the 21st Century: biodiversity loss and climate change and will build on already published teaching resources (PLASCIGARDEN, POLLEN, SINUS Transfer, S-Team, Biology in Context, etc.) as well as on newly created resources.

Plants are the basis for all life on earth and it is critical for a sustainable future that students and teachers understand the fundamental importance of plants to our lives. IBSE allows learners to critically explore inter-connections between subjects, which is an important tool in the development of fully informed citizens that play an active role in democracy.

Botanic gardens and science education researchers, with their practical as well as theoretical expert knowledge in this field, will mainly facilitate the course development and implementation.

LOtC institutions are known to increase learners' motivation to continue with their studies about science. Research into LOtC demonstrates clearly that learners develop their knowledge and skills in ways that add value to their everyday experience in the classroom. Research also shows that some experiences have a particularly positive impact on long-term memory. Out-of-class learning reinforces the link between the affective and cognitive domains and this provides a bridge to higher order learning.

The road to success
LOtC institutions are attractive learning sites for children and adults alike. Engaging LOtC institutions in offering teacher training courses in IBSE techniques will be an effective way to motivate teachers to implement IBSE in their classrooms. In addition LOtC institutions house experts working in scientific fields that can offer specialised knowledge to teachers - helping them to increase their effectiveness in IBSE. Seventeen partners are involved in this project. They will organise advisory groups in 11 European countries, comprising teachers, teacher trainers, botanic garden educators, representatives of regional or national school boards and science education researchers (optional). All LOtC learning sites are well equipped and experienced in the practical side of developing and conducting IBSE teaching programmes.

All partners will feed into the development of the INQUIRE teacher training course. The education researchers will ensure the theoretical underpinning of the course while other partners will add their expertise and perspectives. In addition the quality and effectiveness of the support mechanism will rely on researchers excellence to support partners and participating teachers in reflecting on their own doing as well as provide formative assessment while work is in progress. The aim is to develop a training course that is inspiring, meets practitioners as well as school authorities needs and is theory and evidence based. Through collaboration with stakeholders at local levels (Advisory Groups), cultural differences and needs can be incorporated and fed into the overall design of the course which will be finalised at IBSE Expert Consortium level. LOtC institutions will deliver the pilot course in their countries and use their various networks to invite teachers and educators from other LOtC institutions (Natural History Museums, Science Centres, Zoos and other Botanic Gardens) to participate in these courses. The goal is to help these institutions to develop their knowledge and skills in this area in order to deliver INQUIRE courses themselves and snowball IBSE expertise in formal and non-formal learning environments throughout Europe.

Teachers will be incentivised to participate in the INQUIRE courses through a range of benefits – these will include:

- free professional development
- joining a pan-European network of teachers with an opportunity to communicate with teachers in other European countries
- an opportunity to develop good contact with a prestigious LOtC site.
- an opportunity to showcase good teaching practice and influence practice in their own country and abroad
- an opportunity to participate in the final conference
- free entrance to LOtC sites
- free passes for their classes to visit LOtC sites

B.1.2. Quality and effectiveness of the support mechanisms and associated work plan

The first year of the project will involve developing the pilot course, a teaching manual and an interactive website. Discussions will be held about teaching methodologies, course structure and promotion and how this course can be

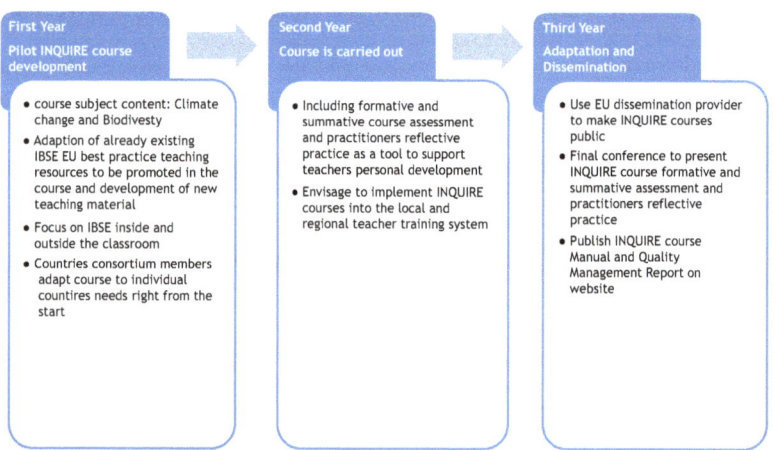

Figure 8: Project progress.

adapted to different country conditions, taking into consideration cultural differences in educational systems and working practices (WP1 Levelling). The course will be promoted through the various national systems that support continual professional development for teachers. One of the main objectives of the course is also to link informal and non-formal education systems through encouraging educators working in a range of LOtC institutions to participate in the project. The draft course manual will be adapted to the needs of different European countries as well as to the needs of various formal and LOC institutions (WP2). The interactive website (WP6) will encourage dialogue between partners and teachers and showcase best practice methods published on other EU websites, eg. POLLEN, SINUS Transfer, FIBONACCI and S-TEAM. INQUIRE will promote these practices throughout the project in both the formal and LOtC education system in 11 countries. A training workshop will be held for all partners to develop a shared understanding of inquiry-based learning and how it can be used effectively to teach environmental education and sustainable development.

The second year of the project will see the launch of the pilot INQUIRE course in 11 European countries. The course, run by the project partners, will consist of three two-day modules - one run in each teaching term (autumn, spring and summer) for teachers and LOtC educators from other institutions. The first workshop will focus on training in inquiry-based learning and methods, the second workshop will concentrate on reflective practice methodology and the third workshop will be dedicated to teachers' developments and reflective practice outcomes. During the workshops, the teaching manual will be discussed and refined and formative evaluation will be used to sharpen the course content. In between workshops, teachers will be encouraged to bring their students to visit the LOtC site and experience IBSE. Educators from other LOtC sites who have attended the INQUIRE course will be encouraged to develop their own network of teachers, teacher trainers and educational researchers to deliver INQUIRE courses the following year. These sites will be responsible for all costs associated with developing their own networks and running INQUIRE courses.

Following the second Module, participating teachers will be encouraged to engage in reflective practice to look on their own process of change and gather data how IBSE works in their classroom. INQUIRE will support teachers through the website and publish regular electronic newsletters. The challenge of encouraging teachers to participate in the website will be addressed by establishing a teacher recognition scheme to participate in the final European conference. During the year, botanic gardens will also provide an open informal space for teachers to meet and discuss their experiences gained through the project. They will be invited to post new methods and ideas on the website to share with their colleagues involved in the project. INQUIRE will facilitate this sharing through translations.

The third year of the project will see partners run the course again to consolidate and embed it within the botanic gardens and education systems. At this stage other LOtC institutions are invited to run courses. LOtC institutions are invited to participate in free "Train the Trainer courses" run by partner LOtCs to obtain an insight into the INQUIRE course design. If they are interested in running courses on their own costs themselves, partner organisations will support them by for example, providing already prepared teaching resources. They will not provide funding. The INQUIRE course manual will be finalised, edited and published on-line. It will also be promoted throughout the 11 regional networks. Increasing numbers of teachers are invited to bring their students to visit LOtC sites and experience IBSE. Partners will support practitioners' reflective practice through continuing to provide a forum for teachers to meet and discuss practice and INQUIRE will continue to publish regular e-newsletters and encourage shared dialogue through the website. Towards the end of the project a European practitioners' (teachers, science educators, researchers) conference will be held to showcase inquiry-based learning in Europe. Through the teacher recognition scheme 14 teachers will be invited to attend the conference.

Quality counts
Formative evaluation focusing on the process of the course development will be carried out during the project life cycle. Additionally an **external evaluator** will carry out a summative as well as formative evaluation on the meta-level to assess the outcomes of the project. He will not carry our research himself but will rely on data provided by project partners.

The external evaluator is brought in at the start of the project and will participate in two consortium meetings (one in the first year and one in the second year). During the third year he will attend the final conference and will hand in two external reports one in month 24 and one by the end of the project (month 36).
[...]
B.1.2.12.2. Timing of work packages and their components
The central goal of the project is to develop an INQUIRE course design, addressing primary and secondary school teacher's needs, that is flexible enough to work in different European education systems. Pilot INQUIRE course will run in each of the 11 participating countries. While one course will run in most of the participating countries two will run in Portugal, Spain and Germany (all in all 14 Pilot Courses) in the second project year. Alongside the pilot course a formative and summative evaluation is conducted and supported by partners KCL and UniHB which will help to improve the course design while work is in progress. The third year will see running the Final INQUIRE course in 11 participating countries (all in all 14 Final Courses) It is planned to develop this final course version into a standard available course offered by participating botanic gardens in cooperation with their local teacher training institutions within times to come. The project is structured within nine work

Work package (WP)	WP- Number	WP-Leader	Duration
Set up Project	WP 1	BGCI	Month 1–4
Levelling	WP 2	LFU	Month 2–5
INQUIRE course development	WP 3	UniHB	Month 4–12
Implementation	WP 4	MTSN	Month 10–36
Sum up	WP 5	KEW	Month 32–36
Dissemination	WP 6	BGCI	Month 1–36
Quality Management	WP 7	KCL	Month 1–36
Project Management	WP 8	LFU	Month 1–36
Ethical Issues	WP 9	UniHB	Month 1–36

Table 4: Work package summary.

packages with four in consecutive phases. Each phase is characterized by one work package. Four work packages span the whole project duration. An external evaluation is planned.

The project structure is kept as simple as possible. A number of partners will be allocated the same workload to make supervising and monitoring the project progress accomplishable. This will also make it easier for the Management Board to identify delays in the sense that partners will operate more or less independently and so delays will be limited to a particular partner.

The inaugural meeting (month 2) and the first Consortium Meeting will be crucial to establishing detailed timescales and management structures. In the inaugural meeting participants will agree on a detailed project schedule, deadlines for submitting work, discuss draft versions of "Project Planning, Dissemination Plan, and the Quality Management Plan" Partners will discuss and agree on the procedures that need to be taken should a partner not meet the required standards and deadlines. The modalities of money transfer will be discussed and agreed upon, keeping various risks in mind. Each partner will provide a Letters of Intent from a regional Teacher Training Institutions demonstrating their commitment to support the implementation of the INQUIRE teacher training course in their country. (See work package description).

Consortium Meetings: Consortium Meetings will enable work to be supervised and deadlines checked regularly. In total there will be 5 Consortium Meetings in three Years (a 6th is optional) and each meeting will last 2 days (2 nights including arrival and departure). Partners will be invited to host one of the 5 meetings. Two people will represent LFU and BGCI while all other partners will be represented by one person. In case partners send more than one person to meetings they will explain why.

The partner responsible for **Quality Management** will support the project at the Consortium level. This partner will ensure the smooth progression of the project and support partners to achieve high quality standards agreed upon.

Management Board Meetings will generally be held one day before Consortiums Meetings except the first one which is held in month 1 to prepare the Inaugural Meeting. This meeting will be held between partners BGCI, KCL, LFU and UniHB. It is planned as a video conference and the External Evaluator might be invited. Therefore Work package Leaders will not attend this meeting. All other Management Board Meetings will include all management board members. The Management Board will be dedicated to preparing Consortium Meetings and to support Botanic Gardens achieving the INQUIRE objectives. A final meeting at the end of the project is optional.

[...]

Work package 1 (WP1): Project Set Up   *Month 1–4*

Work package 1 will be initiated with a Management Board meeting that will prepare for the Inaugural Meeting (Kick off Meeting) in Brussels. This will be attended by at a minimum of 5 people (LFU, BGCI, KCL, UniHB and the External Evaluator) and is planned to be organized as a video conference. This Management Board will prepare detailed timescales and management structures to facilitate the progress of the project. "Project Planning", "Dissemination Plan", "Quality Management Manual" will be drafted and sent to partners before the inaugural meeting.

The Inaugural Meeting will gather the whole consortium for the first time. This will involve 19 people – 2 people each from LFU and BGCI and 1 person from each of the other partners. In case partners send more than one person they will explain why.

The consortium will work and agree on a detailed project schedule guided by the Management Board and agree deadlines and quality standards for handing in work carried out during the project.

A list of criteria for selecting existing IBSE teaching material to be used in the pilot INQUIRE course will be discussed, agreed on and finalized by the end of month 4.

Consortium members will discuss the draft of the "Dissemination Plan" and will add local and international activities run on their behalf. Project Management Board will finalize this work by the end of month 4.

The Quality Management team will discuss ideas with the consortium partners relating to the Quality Management Plan (see WP 7). Participants' ideas and individual, local and regional circumstances will be considered and a final version of the Quality Management Plan will be added to the Consortium Agreement.

Each Partner will identify and invite relevant members to participate in their Advisory Group. Each partner will document their members for inclusion on

the INQUIRE website. A document detailing their Advisory Group constitutions will be produced,
[...]

Work package 2 (WP2): Levelling Month 2–5

Partners will constitute and manage their Advisory Groups (AG). Each partner will decide whether they reimburse travelling costs for their members of the AG.

The installation of **Advisory Groups** supporting INQUIRE activities voluntarily has proven to be successful in the PLASCIGARDEN project already and will be documented in 11 EU-partner countries. Via experts knowledge gathered in group discussions partner institutions will plan for opportunities to localize official training activities to the national curriculum as well as legal and structural conditions in each participating country. Partners will collect information, e.g. curriculum requirements, criteria and requirements for INQUIRE course implementation and discuss these with their AG´s. AG´s will decide which existing teaching resources (PLANTSCAFE; SINUS TRANSFER; POLLEN; S-TEAM; FIBONACCI, BGCI, local material etc) are relevant and will fit within the INQUIRE training programme based on the criteria identified in WP1.

Partners will call on their 'national knowledge' to discuss national needs for developing the pilot INQUIRE course. National differences will be discussed and strategies developed to meet the needs of each country when it comes to offering the courses via the local teacher training systems.

The First Consortium Meeting in month 5 will focus mainly on developing a shared understanding of inquiry based science education for developing the pilot INQUIRE course (PIC), including teaching techniques and methods. The discussions will be underpinned by a theoretical basis.

Action minutes of the first consortium meeting will summarize the shared understanding established (Document summarising how IBSE is defined in INQUIRE course).

In addition a "Strategy Plan" will be formulated for implementing the course within each local teacher training system and will be sent to the Management Board by each participating partner. The Management Board will examine each strategy plan and will produce a final INQUIRE Course Implementation Plan (CIP) that takes into account national differences by the end of month 5. The **INQUIRE Course Implementation Plan** will summarize potential links to school curricula and national requirements across 11 countries and will be published
[...]

Work package 3 (WP3): INQUIRE Course Development Month 4–12

By participating in the Advisory Group (AG) all stakeholders (formal and informal educators, teachers, school authorities, etc) are invited to bring their knowledge and skills when it comes to developing the 'pilot INQUIRE course' (PIC) at a regional level. They will work on a voluntary basis and will meet twice a year. In between they will be informed about project progress via the INQUIRE newsletter.

The INQUIRE teacher training course will bring together teachers from the school sector (formal education) with educators form site-based education centres (informal education). Teachers participating in the courses should develop an understanding of how to facilitate inquiry based science education in their classrooms as well as outside at botanic gardens and natural history museums. These experiences are envisaged to deepen and enrich children's understanding of science.

Participation in the INQUIRE teacher training course is envisaged to support teachers to make the most of using IBSE materials with their students. IBSE often requires technical resources and living organisms. Teachers will be encouraged to use their school gardens as well as site based education centres that usually offer far more in terms of natural resources as well as specialist equipment. By bringing the formal and informal sectors together, teachers are envisaged to benefit from the amazing resources that site-based education centres have to offer. Pupils will also have the opportunity to see real conservation in action and this will facilitate their understanding of the need to address biodiversity conservation and climate change. INQUIRE envisages that a visit to a botanic garden or natural history museum will no longer be just a nice day out but an integrated part of pupils and teachers science curriculum in 11 European countries.

Because inquire based teaching methods often require a considerable amount of technical resources and living organisms we hope that teachers learn to use LOtC learning environments to enrich their pupils science learning environment by integrating LOtC attractions and expert knowledge to go for Inquiry based learning. The main goals the INQUIRE course will aim for are:

- to support teacher with scientific knowledge to teach biodiversity and climate change in IBSE classes as well as at LOtC learning site
- to encourage teachers to develop a proficiency in facilitating IBSE learning (how to work with experiments, facilitate group discussions, support students to develop higher order thinking skills)
- to support students and teachers to understand basic concepts of selected climate change and biodiversity issues
- to encourage teachers own development while reflecting on their own teaching and evaluating ISBE learning outcomes

Informal educators will provide profound background knowledge as well as methodological experience when it comes to structure and scaffold IBSE learning process in class as well as at LOtC institutions. Learning in a formal as well as an informal learning environment will support not only pupils but also teachers to give IBSE a go. These LOtC learning sites provide a unique setting and learning resources that a formal school environment simply cannot provide. Teachers will be introduced to teaching concepts that rely on the school as well as on the informal learning environment and will learn to extract the best from both.

Ideas and materials will be gathered at the national level and partners will document and bring them to the consortium meetings (month 5 and 10). The aim is to ensure that cultural differences and needs can be incorporated within the overall course design or can be met through individual adaptations right from the beginning.

The first year of the project will involve developing the pilot INQUIRE course modules and publish a draft **Pilot INQUIRE Course (PIC) Manual.**

Discussions will be held about teaching methodologies, course structure and promotion and how this course can be adapted to different country conditions taking into consideration cultural differences in educational systems and working practices. A **Strategy Plan for PIC Promotion** in each country and on an international level will be discussed and agreed upon.

Relevant existing teaching material will be identified according to the criteria published in Month 4 and adapted where necessary to the subject content (climate change and biodiversity) and translated into INQUIRE project languages.

The PIC manual will be adapted to various needs in various European countries and for various formal and LOtC institutions. The goal is to finally develop an overall European INQUIRE course design that is flexible enough to work in different European education systems.

During the second consortium meeting partners (month 10) partners will learn how they can contribute to the formative and summative assessment carried out alongside PIC implementation (facilitated by Uni Bremen), how reflective practice can be carried out by PIC participants (facilitated by KCL) and how LOtC institutions can support PIC participants development.

The Management Board will present the draft selection criteria for the teacher recognition scheme and the consortium members will discuss and finalise the criteria.

A 'Train the Trainer' Course (TTC) manual will be developed to support partner organisations preparing to run the PIC in their institutions.

TTC´s will be held in each partner institution to ensure high quality standards when it comes to facilitating the pilot INQUIRE course.

[...]

Work package 4 (WP4): Implementation *Month 10–36*

The PIC will be carried out by each participating LOtC in every participating country from Month 10 – Month 24. In total 14 courses (one course in most of the partner countries, two in Spain, Germany and Portugal) are envisaged to be carried out. This one year training course will oversee a manageable work load that could be easily integrated within a full time teaching schedule. The course will be held during holidays/ over weekends/or during working hours depending on participating countries customs. It is structured in three modules (each 2-3 days =20h; 60h for the whole course). In between these modules teachers will be encouraged to work in class and try out what they have learned during course modules.

It is envisaged that at least 15 primary and low secondary teachers (all in all approximately 210 primary and lower secondary teachers) and at least 5 informal educators (all in all ca 70 informal educators) will participate in each course.

Formative and summative assessment, focussing on professional development of participating teachers will be carried out for selected courses (at least 11 courses in 11 different countries). Outcomes that lead to changes will be incorporated into the course design.

The final INQUIRE Course (IC) design will be established based on formative assessment results.

From month 24 – month 36 educators from other botanic gardens, natural history museums or science centres will be invited by LOtCs to participate in the free TTC´s to develop their own knowledge and skills to run future INQUIRE courses at their own institutions (open 'Train the Trainer' courses). These sites will be responsible for all costs associated with running INQUIRE courses. The third consortium meeting will be held in month 15.

The final version will be offered to teachers as INQUIRE course in year three

From Month 24 – Month 36 indicatively 14 INQUIRE courses (IC) will be organised again.

It is envisaged that at about 15 primary/secondary teachers (all in all approximately 210 teachers) and about 5 informal educators (all in all ca 70 informal educators) will participate in each course.

It is envisaged that the INQUIRE course will develop into a standard available course offered by participating botanic gardens in cooperation with their local teacher training institutions within times to come.

[...]

Work package 5 (WP5): Sum up   *Month 32–36*

The final outcomes of the project are summarised. Teachers will get support in preparing posters for the Final Conference. The Quality Management report will be completed. All project outcomes are summarised and material will be collected for final project reports.

The INQUIRE course manual will be revised and will be published on the website in 10 European languages

An optional final consortium meeting is planned to the close of the project and will provide opportunities to discuss and plan further cooperation's between partners.
[...]

Work package 6 (WP6) Dissemination　　　　　　　　　　*Month 1–36*

The INQUIRE course will be promoted through the various national systems that support continual professional development for teachers. One of the main objectives of the course is to link informal and non formal education systems, by encouraging educators working in LOtC institutions to participate in the project. INQUIRE will focus attention on supporting IBSE in 11 European countries, bridging the gap between researcher, practitioners and key decision makers as well as setting up a European wide network of IBSE practitioners to support and encourage each other to put adequate teaching and learning techniques into practice.

Successful dissemination of the outcomes is of particular importance. A Dissemination Officer working at BGCI will be dedicated to fulfilling these requirements. A dissemination strategy will be prepared by the end of month 4 including all potential opportunities for disseminating INQUIRE ideas and findings.

The INQUIRE website will be set up during the course of the project and will be translated into 10 European languages. It will be updated on a regular basis and enable practitioners to interact with each other and to exchange knowledge and experiences gained while participating in the INQUIRE pilot courses. The Dissemination Officer will maintain the English area of the website and partners will update their own language areas in collaboration with the Dissemination Officer. The website will contain a range of materials including downloadable resources, links to relevant websites, training videos, images and news items. The final course manual will also be uploaded onto the website in month 36.

E-newsletters will also be sent out regularly to inform subscribers (botanic garden educators, teachers and school authorities) about new developments happening in the project and announce any materials that may be of relevance. E-newsletters will be written by the Dissemination Officer with input from partners, then be translated by partners and distributed throughout the 11 countries.

Information leaflets promoting the INQUIRE pilot courses will be prepared and translated and sent out by the end of month 10 to recruit teachers onto the courses. Scientific papers, abstracts, posters and oral presentations will be submitted at national and international meetings and conferences. Both the scientific community and the public media will be kept informed on a regular basis about developments with the INQUIRE project via press releases.

The Final Conference: We envisage that the target audiences for the final conference will be teachers, informal educators and members of the science education research community. It is indicative that INQUIRE teachers and informal educators will present their reflective practice data collected during the pilot INQUIRE courses and their knowledge gained through the formative and summative evaluation of the course. In addition teachers, informal science educators and researchers working in other EU IBSE projects will be invited to share preliminary and final results. All in all 100–150 delegates are expected to participate.

Community building on the international level will be supported through presenting papers and posters at international conferences throughout the whole project duration such as BGCI's International Congress on Education in Botanic Gardens (Mexico 2012), American Public Gardens Association Annual Conference (Philadelphia, 2011), ECSITE conference Warsaw, Poland May 2011, European Association of Zoos and Acquaria (Innsbruck, 2011), European Science Education Research Association (ESERA, Lyon, France, 2011), etc. The INQUIRE website will also be promoted to networks of LoTC institutions worldwide (eg. botanic gardens (BGCI, BGEN), zoos (WAZA, EAZA), wetland centres (WLI), Field Study Centres (FSC), RSPB sites, natural history museums, science centres (ECSITE), environmental education networks (eg. Australian Association of Environmental Education (AAEE), Environmental Education Association of Southern Africa (EEASA).

Project partners will make their training sessions available to potential associate partners (or 'friends of INQUIRE') who may send a representative (at their own cost) to training sessions (open and free Train the Trainer courses). This will support LOtC community building on a national and international basis.

Support project management when it comes to prepare deliverables and documents for publication
[...]

Work package 7 (WP7) Quality Management   Month 1–36

This work package is dedicated to creating a supportive structure for practitioners' development. The Quality Management Team (KCL and UniHB) = QMT will work in tandem with all partners to ensure that every team will produce high quality outputs with respect to running and evaluating pilot course progression.

UNI Bremen is responsible for supervising summative and formative assessment of Pilot INQUIRE participant's professional development (month 10–24). KCL will oversee reflective practice done by participating teachers and educators. LOtC Partners inform teachers and educators about how work is shared between these two partner institutions.

Participating teachers are supported to reflect on their own classroom teaching and learning and all activities developed and used are supposed to meet the defined and agreed standards. For teachers reflective practice, INQUIRE will draw on research in investigative science, argumentation, attitudes to science, interest and motivation, use of external partners and facilities (e.g. botanic gardens, science centres).

For summative and formative course evaluation, INQUIRE will draw on research in teacher collaboration, pedagogical content knowledge, teacher beliefs about science, teacher beliefs about integration of out-of-school facilities, video-based reflection on classroom practice.

The QMT, after discussing and designing the **Quality Management Plan** within the first four months, will be responsible for overseeing the INQUIRE course activities carried out in all 11 participating countries. The QMT will support practitioners to analyse, summarize and present outcomes. Outcomes will be evaluated to meet the expected high standards. The Quality Management Plan will be adapted to emerging needs in month 18. Best practice models, recommendations and ideas will be included in a detailed Quality Management Report by the end of month 36. The report will be uploaded to the INQUIRE web site in month 36. The QMT will develop a draft document that will be discussed during the Inaugural Meeting.

[...]

Work package 8 (WP8) Project Management   *Month 1–36*

INQUIRE´s Management Board is responsible for ensuring smooth project progress. It will support the project at the consortium level. A meeting schedule will be set up and updated according to participants' needs. A management handbook (website domain to share documents, minutes, agreements etc) will be installed 5 Management board meetings will be held to plan and prepare consortium meetings. It is planned to hold the first meeting as video conference. Project periodical reports will be prepared in months18 and 36.

[...]

Work package 9: Ethical issues   *Month 1–36*

Based on the EU recommendations addressed in the Ethical Review Report (date 16.09.2010) the INQUIRE consortium will establish an additionally work package "Ethical Issues" including two dimensions:

1. Ethical issues in relation to plants
2. Ethical issues regarding children protection, safety and data protection

[...]

3.1.6 INQUIRE Outcomes

The following INQUIRE 'Publishable Report' (Kapelari et al., 2013) gives a short overview about what the project has finally achieved.

Summary

The EU FP7 INQUIRE Project was developed and implemented to support science literacy in Europe through teacher training courses, focussing on the integration of Inquiry Based Science Education (IBSE) into informal and formal education programmes. Courses were developed and offered in 14 sites across 11 European countries with a cohort of over 570 participants that included both teachers in the formal education system and also education officers in informal education sites (Botanic Gardens, Natural History Museums etc).

Botanic gardens and similar LOtC sites are inspirational sites that can provide training for teachers and educators on critical issues such as conservation of our natural resources, sustainability and threats to our future, such as climate change. Integrating these themes into activities using IBSE pedagogy provides an exciting and stimulating programme which encourages teachers and informal educators to develop their proficiency in IBSE and to become reflective practitioners as well as raising awareness of these issues.

Introduction

Current science education reform initiatives require fundamental changes in how science is taught and in how teachers are supported to engage in alternative ways of science teaching. One current approach is the incorporation of inquiry based science education (IBSE) into the everyday school science curriculum. To help make this change happen, teachers need opportunities to participate in a variety of professional development experiences that foster an understanding of science and inquiry based science teaching. Research has also shown that learning that includes activities based outside the classroom is highly motivating, not only for children but also for teachers. The UK Government's education manifesto 'Learning outside the Classroom' was launched to emphasis this key issue and Europe has already recognized the potential of Learning Outside the Classroom (LOtC) venues to support the implementation of IBSE methods on a large scale. With more people living in cities, botanic gardens, which provide excellent opportunities for education in major cities worldwide, offer some of the only outdoor learning sites for children to gain first-hand experiences of IBSE.

The INQUIRE project and its objectives and achievements

The Inquire project was set up to foster the development and implementation of IBSE in both formal and informal education systems by developing, testing and implementing IBSE training courses in 11 European countries. One of the key aspects of this project was the provision of a 'long-term' training course (60 hours +) over a prolonged period and a course where there was a real emphasis on reflective practice being developed by both course participants and Consortium Partners. This is a change from short, sharp training sessions that often are the objectives of projects and which, although they may result in high numbers of participants, unfortunately do not actually effect real behavioural and attitudinal change in those participating. Inquire course participants and partners were a smaller cohort but were offered a more intense and in depth training and were encouraged to develop an action research approach, which has been evidenced in both the Quality Management Report and the external evaluation. There has also been a good community of practice developed. All of these outcomes are likely to result in real sustainability of the project aims and objectives going forward and for long-term and profitable collaborative work in the future across the range of participating EU organisations.

The content of the INQUIRE training courses focused on various aspects of biodiversity loss and climate change, drawing on the expertise and inspirational settings for the courses in Botanic Gardens and natural history centres across Europe. The courses were piloted by partners early on in the project and post evaluation of the pilot course, a second course was run. The project partners used reflective practice and evaluation processes to analyse good practice, effectiveness and impact of the courses both with their course participants, through the consortium partnership meetings and through support sessions provided by the Quality Management team and Management Board. The courses were refined and improved through this process, resulting in enhanced courses with more polished delivery and good impact. Throughout the Inquire training courses, teachers and botanic garden educators had also been encouraged to learn with, and from, each other and to develop a shared understanding of how IBSE can be facilitated in class and in botanic gardens and natural history museums. Sustainability was key to the project and this was attained through the community of practice and through the running of 'Train the Trainer' courses to cascade knowledge and experiences gained through the project to other LOtC institutions. There was also excellent dissemination of outcomes and practices through a range of media and at conferences, workshops, seminars and promotional events both nationally and internationally.

INQUIRE courses developed and implemented in 11 EU countries

Two sets of Inquire courses were run over the project period. The pilot courses ran between September 2011 and July 2012 and the second set, building on the initial course content and processes, ran between the autumn of 2012 and the summer of 2013. Using the reflective practice developed throughout the project and supported by partnership interaction and exchange of best practice, partners were able to refine and enhance their courses for the second period. Overall the courses reached a total of 576 participants; 250 in the pilot courses and 326 in the second set of courses. Course participants included educators in LOtC sites, primary, secondary and student teachers, education authority officers and other staff from LOtC sites. The outcomes and impacts from these courses were explored in the Final Quality Management Plan and the Final External Evaluation Report which draw on the 'Portfolios of Evidence' (PofE) and case studies submitted by partners following the two sets of courses. These partner PofE, in turn, draw on the findings and reflections from participants on individual courses as well as partner course tutor's/ organiser's reflective practice. A sea change in both practice and attitude can be seen in these findings.

A Quality Management Plan has been implemented and supported

The Quality Management Plan was developed and agreed in the initial period of the project. The plan outlined how evidence for project outcomes would be collected through surveys, on-line questionnaires, case studies submitted by partners during partner meetings, interviews, observation and Portfolios of Evidence. This plan was implemented and augmented as necessary over the project period. Regular support was provided throughout the project period by both the QM team and the full Management Board including provision of partner visits, support telephone calls, on-line via Glasscubes and through the Inquire website and regular newsletters. The Final QM Report, published in month 36 (Deliverable D7.2) provides an analysis of participants and Partner feedback. This was very positive and was further demonstrated by the innovative and stimulating workshops and presentations from partner and course participants at the final INQUIRE conference, held at Kew Gardens, London UK on July 9th and 10th 2013 and attended by 124 participants from 13 countries. The Final External Evaluation report, submitted in the final month 36 (November 2013) additionally demonstrated very positive outcomes for the project.

Development of a Community of Practice between Partners

The Consortium Partners quickly developed and maintained an excellent Community of Practice during the three years of the project. The success of this was in part due to the very good support from the QM team and full Management Board. Communication was a strong focus for the project team and was very well managed by BGCI. This was built on regularly through the 5 partner meetings, Train the Trainers course and final conference held during the project period. Many good friendships were established and the opportunities to share best practice face to face, discuss common problems and successes was valued very highly by all partners. Partners are still communicating regularly post project and are actively seeking new inter-European joint project / programme collaborations for the future.

Impact through establishment of National Advisory Groups (NAG)

The National Advisory Groups (NAG) were established in the early project months and continued to meet and support partners within their countries throughout the project period. Most partners had 2 meetings per year; a few had just one often due to availability of the AG members. Advice included how to integrate the courses into the national teacher training mechanisms, how best to promote courses, on the structure and content of courses and where to find appropriate resources and other support. The NAGs were established with experts in the field of formal and informal science education and were influential in encouraging regional take up and curriculum input through their contact as well as effective at adding value to the partner course delivery and evaluation by sharing their broad expertise with partners.

Snowballing the INQUIRE idea: Train the Trainers and Dissemination

Besides the partner Train the Trainers course run in Obergurgl, where 57 educators were trained in IBSE delivery and processes, the 15 Train the Trainers courses delivered through the project engaged over 285 participants, snowballing the project aims and objectives further. Participants were from a range of professional backgrounds and included not only educators from botanic gardens, science centres, natural history museums, zoos and environmental NGO's but also secondary teachers, primary school teachers, teacher trainers and representatives of Educational authorities.

The dissemination of the Inquire aims and objectives was managed through a variety of media across the project period. Besides the many and varied written texts, either published in printed format or on-line, partners attended and offered dissemination activities at 56 International conferences / events and 135 national conferences /events. The Inquire co-ordinator participated in several other IBSE linked EU project meetings and events as well as joining ProConet and was therefore able to ensure cross project dissemination. The conference, organised by BGCI and KEW and held at Kew on 9–10th July 2013 also attracted 124 delegates from 13 countries disseminating best practice and project outcomes more widely. Four other EU funded projects (PATHWAY, Natural Europe, GreeNET and S-TEAM.) were also represented at the conference- broadening the experience of all project partners and opening up new avenues for collaboration in the future. The published Train the Trainers and Inquire course manuals and activity booklet will additionally support this process.

The following Partners worked on the INQUIRE project:

Figure 9: Project countries.

- University of Innsbruck, Austria (co-ordinator)
- Botanic Gardens Conservation International, UK
- King's College London University, UK
- Museo Tridentino di Science Naturali, Trento, Italy
- Royal Botanic Gardens, Kew, UK
- University of Bremen, Germany
- University of Sofia, Bulgaria
- Schulbiologisches Zentrum Hannover, Germany
- Jardin Botanique de la Ville de Bordeaux, France
- Moscow State University Botanical Garden, Russia
- University of Lisbon, Portugal
- National Botanic Garden of Belgium
- Coimbra Botanic Garden, Portugal
- Botanischer Garten, Rhododendron-Park, botanika Bremen, Germany
- Agencia Estatal Consejo Superior de Investigaciones Cientificas, Spain
- Universidad de Alcala, Spain
- Natural History Museum Botanical Garden, Norway

Inquire courses

Aim: Help reinvigorate IBSE in the formal and the Learning Outside the Classroom (LOtC) educational systems throughout Europe through teacher training courses.

Activities: Run by botanic gardens and Natural History Museums in 11 countries, INQUIRE training courses demonstrate to teachers and educators how IBSE can inspire students in science and engage them with issues of biodiversity and climate change. Courses comprise minimum 60 hours of training with a combination of full day sessions and self study. They promote the integration of learning in and outside of the school classroom.

Achieved: 28 Pilot and final INQUIRE courses run in the period 2011–2013. The courses took place in 11 countries across Europe engaging in total: 576 teachers, educators and other professionals and reaching more than 16,000 students who experience IBSE in their school and in LOtC. The INQUIRE course manual has been published in 10 languages.

Quality Management

Aim: Ensure implementation of high quality INQUIRE courses by establishing evaluation processes.

Activities: Determine and conduct summative and formative evaluation, train Partners to use evaluation tools, support visits to Partners, encourage reflective practice, collect Portfolios of evidence and improve quality of courses.

Achieved: Pre- and Post- course questionnaires designed for summative evaluation of courses, used by all Partners. Partners trained to use formative evaluation methods- interviews, concept maps, reflective journals, observations and compiled portfolios of evidence. Quality Management Plan developed. KCL conducted support visits to 14 Partners. The Quality Management team and the Management Board supported Partners through personal contacts, on –line communications via Glasscubes and through workshops during the 4th Partner meeting in Lisbon, October 2012. The Final Quality Management Report (Deliverable D7.2) provides an analysis of participants and Partners feedback which was very positive.

Consortium meetings

Aim: Bring Partners together to ensure work is delivered on time and to high standards and develop a Community of practice amongst the consortium.

Activities: Discuss deliverables, discuss INQUIRE course structure and evaluation, provide training on evaluation, reflect on running the courses, exchange good practice on IBSE, peer review lesson plans and modules, discuss communication in the project, training on evaluation and website, prepare for INQUIRE conference.

Achieved: An Inaugural meeting, five Consortium meetings and a Train the trainers meeting held. Between 30 and 40 people attended each meeting which resulted in preparing the deliverables on time, developing, running and improving the Pilot and Final INQUIRE courses, establishing project evaluation methods, developing Partners' reflective practice and creating a collaborative atmosphere within consortium. 12 Management Board meetings held to plan and prepare Consortium meetings.

Advisory groups

Aim: Support running and promotion of INQUIRE courses.

Activities: advise on development and delivery of INQUIRE courses, recommend resources, advise on dissemination of project and course participants' recruitment, comment on implementation and effectiveness of project outcomes, advise on accreditation of the course.

Achieved: A National Advisory group has been established in each country. 122 members in total (Education authorities representatives, teacher trainers, science education researchers, teachers, educators, head teachers, representatives of other LOtC institutions and networks). 49 meetings held in total by the 11 Advisory groups. The meetings were organized to support major developments i.e. establishing, revising and running the INQUIRE course, preparing for the INQUIRE conference and ensuring the courses sustainability.

Dissemination

Aim: Achieve public awareness about project goals.

Activities: develop and run INQUIRE website, distribute newsletters, present work of the INQUIRE project in conferences, produce dissemination resources, distribute press releases, organise INQUIRE conference.

Achieved: INQUIRE website www.inquirebotany.org live since September 2011 in 10 languages. Monthly e-newsletters have been sent to 1000 subscribers. Partners have presented INQUIRE project in 56 International and 135 National conferences and events. The INQUIRE conference was held at Kew, London on 9–10th July 2013 and attracted 124 delegates from 13 countries, stimulating discussion and reflections on IBSE. An INQUIRE leaflet has been produced in 10 languages and an INQUIRE film subtitled in 10 languages.

Snowballing

Aim: Encourage further implementation of IBSE in 11 European countries of the project.

Activities: meetings and training seminars for LOtC staff and teacher trainers to inspire them to run INQUIRE courses. Advisory groups promote IBSE through networks.

Achieved: The Partner Advisory groups included 16 representatives of education authorities, 8 teacher trainers, and 16 staff from LOtC institutions. All promoted IBSE through their positions. In order to encourage further implementation of IBSE, Partners have been running Train the Trainers courses. Some of these were day seminars while others were run in a similar structure to the INQUIRE course. 15 Train the Trainers courses have been run by 15 Partners. These were attended by 289 participants mainly educators from botanic gardens, science centres, and other LOtC sites.

3.2 The INQUIRE Case Study

The following chapter is an extensively elaborated version of the chapter "Collaborative Pedagogical Content Knowledge Creation in Heterogeneous Learning Communities"(p. 127–145), published by Kapelari (2015).

3.2.1 Rational

'Learning outside the classroom is about raising achievement through an organised, powerful approach to learning in which direct experience is of prime importance. This is not only about **what** we learn but importantly **how** and **where** we learn'. (LOTCM, 2007)

Becoming and remaining a place that offers high quality learning experiences outside the classroom requires professional educators and educational program designers to continuously improve their knowledge, skills and attitudes (s.p. 99ff) toward teaching and learning in their particular context. However, if learning is valued as a situated process in a social context, the individual learner cannot be the only centre of attention. In the INQUIRE context the educational department, and even the whole Botanic Garden in which this learning takes place, has to be recognised as an entity for learning if changes in practice are expected to be implemented sustainably. It is assumed that if the members of a particular educational department develop their understanding of IBSE collaboratively over time, collective understanding and experience evolves and becomes organisational knowledge. Declarative knowledge and procedural knowledge such as skills and routines are then shared in the particular community and become organisational memory.

In addition, one has to recognise that no organisation is an autonomous island floating in an infinite space. All educational institutions - schools, LOtC sites, universities etc. are building blocks embedded in a socio-cultural setting that enables or inhibits development that governs actions, divides labour and creates the community in which action and learning takes place (s.p. 31ff). Thus educational reform efforts, such as those supported by the EU 7th Framework Science and Society can never be assessed as a simple input - output system. Sustainable change is the result of sophisticated information processing taking place in a complex network of social interactions.

Focusing on individual teacher or educator learning as the only unit of analysis may fail to recognise the socio-cultural setting in which these individuals act. It ignores the fact that:

'most organisations[schools and botanic gardens included] have shared assumptions that protect the status quo, preclude people from challenging others, troublesome or difficult qualities and characteristics, and provide silent assent to those attributions; hence, very little learning is possible' (Kim, 2004, p. 35).

As a logical consequence, the unit of analysis in the following case study is the activity system named the 'Spanish partner' (s.p. 29ff).

Activity theory and expansive learning (s.p. 31ff) is applied as a framework to interpret the significant steps of transformation that occurred during the three year project duration. Traditionally, we would expect that learning is manifested as change in the subject, in the behaviour and cognition of the learner. In this respect, this case study challenges the traditional view of learning as an isolated activity in which an individual acquires knowledge from a de-contextualized body of knowledge (s.p. 17ff).

Expansive learning is manifested primarily as changes in the object of the activity system (Engeström, 2001, Paavola et al., 2004). The objects in this case are IBSE lesson plans and the design of the teacher training course. Object artefacts, such as portfolios, as well as knowledge artefacts, such as partner interviews, are at the centre of attention when interpreting organisational sense making and societal transformations. As such, this more pluralistic and multi-levelled interactional approach offers conceptual tools to achieve a more nuanced picture of the significance of IBSE use in botanic gardens educational practises. In exploring the potential role of 'expansive learning' as a framework for extending botanic gardens perception and knowledge of IBST and reflective practice, the purpose of this case study was to address the following questions:

- How does the expansive learning environment contribute to partners understanding of Inquiry Based Science Teaching?
- Do partner organisations feel competent to implement this pedagogy into their educational programmes?
- Do partners develop an awareness of the role reflective practice and assessment plays in good science teaching?

3.2.2 Methodology

Case Study

I chose to conduct this case study because a vivid and full description of a single case is most valuable at this stage of my understanding of Botanic Garden learning and in order that I could understand organisational development from a partner's point of view. Gerring (2004) suggests that a case study is an in depth study of a single unit where the scholar's aim is to elucidate features of a larger class of similar phenomena. Thus it is a particular way of defining cases, not a way of analysing cases or modelling causal relations. The term 'case study' might be used in various ways. However, in the context of my work, I define my case study accordingly as 'an intensive study of a single unit for the purpose of understanding a larger class of similar units' (Gerring, 2004, p. 342). and I went for his? Type I occupation which is defined as 'case studies [that] examine variation in a single unit over time, thus preserving the primary unit of analysis' (Gerring, 2004, p. 343).

This case study is dedicated to the process of the development of two Spanish Botanic Gardens who decided to work as a single activity system called 'Spanish Partner". However, in the INQUIRE consortium case study, outcomes cannot be interpreted as being detached from findings reported by the External Evaluator Dr. Alun Morgan, Exeter University UK (External Evaluation Report) and the Quality Management Team - Dr. Elaine Regan and Prof. Justin Dillon, Kings College London, London, UK (Quality Management Report). Both reports can be downloaded from the website: www.inquiryebotany.com/resources. These reports illustrate project outcomes at the whole consortium level and thus inform this particular research case study about the context in which it is situated.

Framework for Analysis

Wertsch (1991, p. 3) cites Dewey, who assumed that the discipline would not be able to deal with the many phenomena it sought to examine if it continued to focus exclusively on the individual organism. Psychology would have to come to term with how individuals are culturally, historically and institutionally situated before it could understand many aspects of mental functioning. Cultural Historical Activity Theory and expansive learning (s.p. 31ff) is applied as a framework to interpret the significant steps of transformation occurring during the three year project duration. Engeströms (2001) dynamic model of an activity system is used to explain the interactions between a subject (and groups of subjects), object, mediating artefacts, rule, communities, and division of labour. In this study, the primary focus is on the top triangle of the activity system (s.p. 31ff). The research methods of artefact analysis and interviews are applied.

> 'Artifacts become data through the questions posed about them and the meanings assigned to them by the researcher. There is no one right way to analyse artefacts. A wide range of disciplines informs the analysis of artifacts, including anthropology, archaeology, art history, history, human geography, ethnography, and sociology. In the process of analysis, we are asking the data to tell us something. An artifact has a story to tell about the person who made it, how it was used, who used it, and the beliefs and values associated with it'. (Norum, 2008, p. 1)

The production process in any activity system involves a subject, an object/various objects and mediating tools (artefacts) that are used in

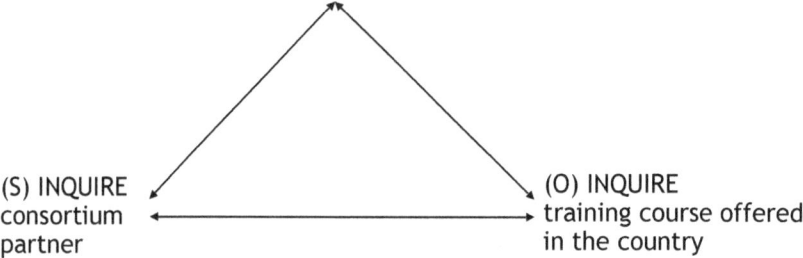

Figure 10: Mediating activity in INQUIRE.

the activity. These may be concrete ones such as written lesson plans or operations mediated via talks and conversation captured via interviews. INQUIRE consortium partner activities were oriented to the object; the implementation of an inquiry based teacher and botanic garden educator training course. The science content addressed in these courses was related to biodiversity and climate change and enabled learners to experience an inquiry based science learning environment created in the class as well as at the botanic garden.

The process of creating the object was facilitated via an expansive learning process (s.p. 35ff). It is assumed that with the production of the course, the consortium partner develops new knowledge about the activity (developing an inquiry based course design, its components (e.g. IBSE activities), its assumptions (= good teaching practice) and contradictions (= student learning outcomes). Partners are expected to consciously understand the characteristic of their knowledge gaining process because their own learning cannot be separated from the activity.

The INQUIRE consortium

Any consortium partner is a member of at least two community systems – their particular Botanic Garden institution and the INQUIRE consortium. Both communities are influential not only to the object but the subjects own development.

As a consortium partner, the Spanish partner, as with other partners, had to follow rules set up in the grant agreement or which were developed during the project, such as how and when to fulfil tasks. The division of labour was defined

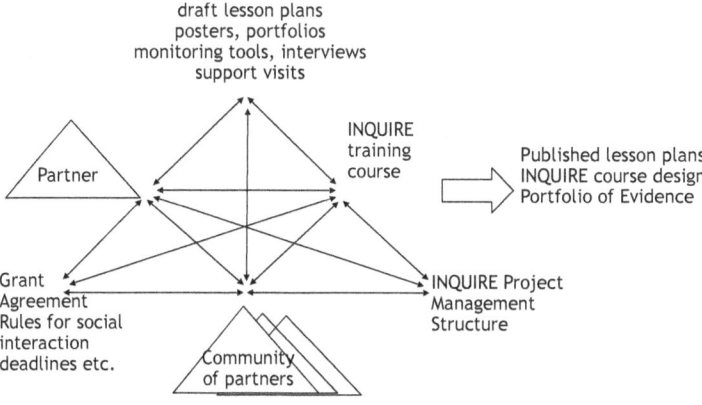

Figure 11: The INQUIRE project activity system.

according to roles various partner play e.g. as botanic garden partner, science education research institution, project management or project coordinator. Partners took over different roles simultaneously e.g. course designer, critical friend, host etc. For example, the Spanish group was responsible for hosting one consortium meeting in March 2012.

The community of partners plays an important role in choosing tasks which lead to meditating artefacts, giving feedback and are therefore most influential in enabling and preventing learning processes. The INQUIRE management board was responsible for designing and cultivating a collaborative expansive learning environment for consortium partners. As collaborative knowledge creation processes are dynamic, much effort was put in cultivating a space for people to connect, to communicate in a given context, to share information, stories or personal experience and knowledge in ways that built on understanding and insight. Scaffolded social interaction was applied to enable dialogue, capture and diffuse existing knowledge, introduce collaborative processes, generate new knowledge and help people organize around purposeful actions that deliver tangible results (Cambridge et al., 2005). The INQUIRE project lasted for three years. Five consortium meetings, a train the trainer course and a final conference were organised to provide space for face to face contact among consortium members. Consortium meetings lasted for at least two full days. In between these face to face contact periods, partners were asked to produce object artefacts to share their knowledge and experience in poster presentations, lesson plan discussion or workshops for the following meeting. An online platform, Glasscubes (http://www.glasscubes.com/), was introduced to organize collaboration and enhance communication among partners in between direct contact sessions.

Rational for choosing the 'Spanish Partner'

The basic notion guiding this study is the view that individual persons who have feelings, values, needs, and purposes for acting are members of social groups and organisations, which directly or indirectly set the general condition for day to day learning processes (s.p. 31ff). Even if a single member of a social unit has the potential to fulfil an extraordinary development in this unique INQUIRE setting, this will remain a single facet of an organisational learning process and may or may not result in changing existing practices.

Thus the focus of my study is on the organisational level, the INQUIRE partner as a social unit, which will act as the sum of its components (s.p. 31ff).

The Spanish Partner was chosen for this in-depth study for three reasons:

- these two Spanish organisations decided to establish one activity system at the national level.
- This activity system merges a Botanic Garden with a very long history of c.260 years (which is representative for one set of partner institutions in the INQUIRE project) and another institution with a relative short history of about 12 years (which is typical of some other INQUIRE partners).
- The history of both educational departments is closely linked and these institutions have already shared a very close partnership for many years, which was maintained during and post the INQUIRE project. This close relationship was the reason why two Spanish gardens were invited to join the INQUIRE consortium; most other countries participating in the project had only one Garden invited.

Data Collection

Data collection was distributed over a period of three years (2011–2013). A multifaceted approach was used to gather different types of artefacts, which were then used to describe different perspectives or for cross checks. Individual data sources have particular strengths and weaknesses. For example, interviews provide subtle and personal feelings but statements may consciously or unconsciously be tailored to the interviewers' expectations. Artefacts give insight into what people put into practice, but may miss information about the reason for doing it in a particular way. To balance detachment and involvement and to inhibit tendencies to over identify with particular interpretations, I considered other colleagues work which focused on evaluating the consortium as a whole from an 'External Evaluators' and the Quality Management Team's' perspective.

In reference to Cultural Historical Activity Theory (s.p. 31ff) and principles of knowledge creation approaches to learning, I considered the following combination of data relevant to understanding the dynamics present in the INQUIRE setting. In this respect interviews are considered knowledge artefacts while posters or lesson plans etc. are considered to be object artefacts/outcomes.

Data Source	Data unit	Description	Purpose
Semi structure Interviews	Interviews 1 (I1/2011)	Interview: exploring reflective practice, evaluation and progress with Pilot Inquire course implementation Conducted by E. Regan	Semi structured interview after pilot INQUIRE course as a formative discussion about feedback and evaluation
	Interview 2(I2/2013)	Interview: exploring reflective practice, evaluation, issues with final course implementation personal gains Conducted by E. Regan	Semi-structured interview after the final INQUIRE course as a discussion of the course evaluation and outcomes from project
	Interview 3 (I3/2013)	Individuals/staff educational background, history of education department Conducted by S. Kapelari	Exploring division of labour, rules and community within the activity system
Mediated Artefacts produced by partners (Botanic Gardens)	Lesson Plans (LPy1/1,2) (LPy2/1) (LPy3/1–5)	Lesson plans were developed by partners on a regular basis to share the current understanding of 'good IBS teaching' Year 1: 2 lesson plans Year 2: 1 lesson plan Year 3: 5 lesson plans published on the INQUIRE website	Lesson Plans provide insight into how partners put their understanding of IBST into practice
	Posters (P)	Posters were presented at partner meetings to share partner understanding of a good INQUIRE course design, course evaluation and how these was developed (4 Posters)	Provide insight into the socio-cultural context in which the INQUIRE course was implemented as well as into partners understanding of useful assessment and evaluation strategies
	Presentation at INQUIRE Conference (PIC)	Posters and/or Papers presented at the Final INQIURE conference July 2013 1 workshop	Show what partners consider important for presentation to a wider public

(*Continued*)

Data Source	Data unit	Description	Purpose
	Portfolio of Evidence (P 1/2)	Evidences are collections of artefacts partners consider give insight into their learning. A written commentary explains why these artefacts were chosen. Portfolio 1 was handed in after the INQUIRE pilot course Portfolio 2 was handed in after the Second INQUIRE course A detailed Case Study was part of the P2	Provide insight into partner ability to carry out critical reflection; their professional learning and experience gained in practice.
	Reports and Deliverables (R/D)	Partners contribute to the final Project report via handing reports on -Progress towards the Project objectives - Working with their national Advisory Board -Plans for Implementing the INQUIRE training course in the future	Provide insight into partners learning progress, competence development and future perspective
Consortium based findings produced by others	Final External Evaluation Report	Author: Dr. Alun Morgan, Exeter University UK www.inquirebotany.org	Provide the opportunity to reflect on outcomes in the context of the whole consortium
	Quality Management Report	Authors: Dr. Elaine Regan and Prof. Justin Dillon, Kings College London, London, UK www.inquirebotany.org	Provide the opportunity to reflect on outcomes in the context of the whole consortium

Table 5: Data source.

Data analysis

The analytic tools used were selected so as not to create additional work for the INQUIRE Partner organizations; however they served as a reference for participating partners on the project outcomes as they developed their processes during the project

Interview transcripts
The interview protocols and the overarching framework for the Quality Management Plan was discussed and agreed within the management board in advance of starting the project proper. Due to my role as the project coordinator it was important not to conduct interviews myself. However partners were informed about the fact that all members of the INQUIRE Management Board would have access to data collected. The first semi-structured group interview was done by Dr. Elaine Regan during the implementation stage of the pilot courses to explore reflective practice and evaluation strategies (Interview 1). This short interview (approx. 40 minutes) was conducted during the 3rd Partner Meeting in Spain, February/March 2012. For the Spanish partner 2 people participated in the interview.

Post the second INQUIRE course, a second semi-structured group interview (Interview 2) explored similar themes as well as exploring the influence of participation in the INQUIRE project on partners and their institutions. These final longer interviews (approx. 60 minutes) took place at the final Partner Meeting in Trento, Italy October 2013. All four members of the Spanish group participated. The interview was conducted by Dr. Elaine Regan. In addition, I held a semi-structured interview (Interview 3) with the Spanish partner to explore additional themes such as the cultural-historical background, the division of work and particular rules applicable for the Spanish partner. Interview 3 took place at the Partner Meeting in Trento, Italy October 2013and was transcribed by myself. Interviews 1 and 2 were transcribed by a third person. I finally analysed all three transcripts myself. Quotes from these interviews are not attributed to any individual but to the partner group. Interview transcribes were analysed following the content analysis approach suggested by Mayring (2008).

Posters, reports and deliverables, conference contributions
Whenever applicable, the same coding scheme used for analysing interview transcripts was applied to text based artefacts. Partners completed various project tasks and produced many artefacts during the INQUIRE project in preparation for the partner meetings (2011–2013), the conference (2013) and the train the trainer course in Obergurgl (2011). Examples include posters outlining the intended structure of their INQUIRE course (Poster 1: Course Design) and their anticipated strategies for evaluation (Poster 2: Evaluation), lesson plans (Lesson Plans: 1,2, . . .), course plans for review by the consortium members (Lesson Plan Review: 1,2, . . .) and the Conference workshop (CW1)

Lesson plans:
A rubric for analyzing lesson plan development was developed based on the BSCS (Biology Science Curriculum Study) 5E Instructional Model. This model was chosen as a reference for analyzing expansive knowledge creation because

it provides more flexibility in valuing hybridizations of exiting knowledge and relies on a foundation of contemporary research on student learning, particularly in science (Bybee et al., 2006).

Portfolio of Evidence
Partners were asked to select material they considered appropriate for providing evidence of the effectiveness of their INQUIRE course, as well as artefacts that they considered important to their own work. In addition, they needed to highlight evidence that course participants handed in. All partners were asked to write a one page review on why and how they selected these particular items and why they considered them representative for their organizational development. Portfolios were accomplished following the completion of the Pilot INQUIRE Course (Portfolio 1, 2012) and the Second INQUIRE course (Portfolio 2, 2013). While the first one was compulsory the latter was optional. Portfolios have been uploaded on the project website to share with consortium partners as well as with the MB.The Spanish partner handed in two portfolios. For analysing the portfolios I went for a holistic approach, focusing on the overall quality of the work with attention to how the individual piece of work contributes to the whole. It was more important for me to see what partners did, rather than comparing entries with prior expectation that may not necessarily align with partner performance. Whenever applicable the same coding schemes as for analysing interview transcripts or lesson plans were used.

3.2.3 Case Study Findings

Question: Do you think this type of activity helps to improve your learning?

'*Si, porque vivimos una experiencia propria*' = Yes, because we live our own experience
A teacher's response (Case study, p22).

Who are the subjects of learning, how are they defined and located?
The 'Spanish Partner' is a group of people employed at two different Botanic Gardens but forming a discrete activity system in the INQUIRE consortium

Real Jardín Botánico Juan Carlos I, Alcala

The Garden: Real Jardín Botánico Juan Carlos I belongs to the University of Alcalá, in Alcalá de Henares, Madrid. The garden was founded in 1991 and the education department was established in 1995. The Garden covers about 26 Hectares and is located in the campus area of the University. Plant conservation and education are considered to be the main priorities. Apart from hosting the biggest collection of cacti in Spain, other living plant collections such as

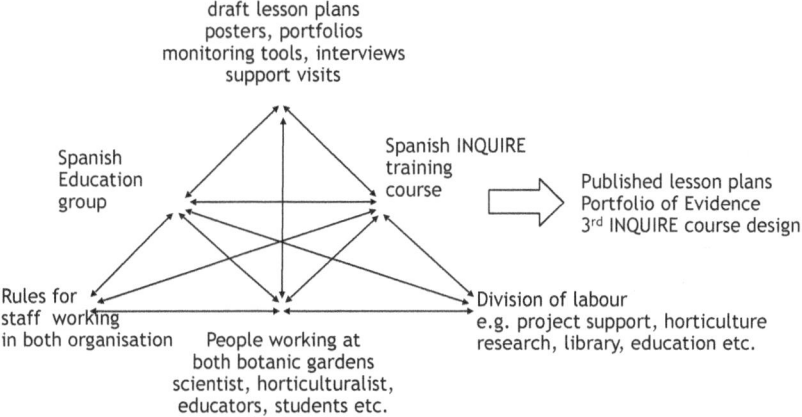

Figure 12: The Spanish partner activity system.

the collection of roses, tropical plants, conifers, Spanish trees, regional flora, *Cycadales* and garden plants add to about the c.8000 taxa which contribute to the plant conservation strategy the garden applies. A 'seed bank' (about 10.000 accessions) and related research and horticultural practices have been developed in the garden over the last couple of years.

Education department: The educational department includes has two full time positions. The 'INQUIRE representative (IRA), Alcala is head of the 'Educational Program in the Real Jardín Botánico Juan Carlos I' and has been responsible for designing and developing the Educational Program since 1995. She holds a degree in botany and did additional training to become a secondary school teacher; she spent 2 years teaching secondary and high school students (16–18 years). IRA worked as a Teacher of 'Botany for Horticulturalists', a course at Madrid Botanic Gardens, for about 5 years before she and a group of colleagues were asked to establish the new garden in Alcala. Another biologist, a specialist in geology, holds the position of 'Coordinator of the Educators'. He has been working in the program since 1999 but has no pedagogical background. The 'group of educators' includes about 4–10 students from Alcala University; all of them are studying biology or environmental sciences and they work as 'freelance' contracts. The University employs them and they currently stay for 3–4 months, although in former times they stayed for about 1–3 years. As soon as they have finished their studies they now have to leave. One person was exclusively employed via INQUIRE funding to support IRA in fulfilling project related tasks.

Educational Program: Running for more than 15 years, the educational program is one of the oldest and most developed ones offered by botanical gardens in Spain. It provides a huge number of activities (more than 60) involving local and regional participants. The educational program is supported by the University of Alcalá. Educational staff members also participate in national and international outreach activities such as offering courses, contributing to congresses, publishing in journals, etc. The team has contributed to the creation of the new botanical gardens in Malabo (Equatorial Guinea) and at the University of León (Nicaragua).

Alcala botanic garden offers educational activities to different target groups, of all age groups, in a formal as well as an informal setting (eg. kindergarden -, primary – secondary and high school classes, students with special needs, the elderly, groups of adults with special interests in a particular subject and the general public). Most of these activities are designed and carried out by the garden staff themselves, but some are developed and conducted in collaboration with other institutions or groups of interest. The educational program has been linked to the formal school system since its inception and an official convention with the local school authority (Regional Training and Innovation Centre for Teachers) has existed since 1998. The garden engages with local schools in international projects such as the "Key to Nature" project and in local and regional activities like "The Week of Science", "Science Fair", "Plant Fair", etc. Aside from this, the educational department maintains a close collaboration with the educational department of the Spanish botanical garden society.

Real Jardin Botanico de Madrid

The Garden: The Garden, founded in 1755, belongs to the National Research Council (Consejo Superior de Investigaciones Científicas), the largest research institution in Spain. It is declared a 'Major Scientific Facility' due to its important historical collections (herbaria, library and archives). Within this mission, the Garden focuses on scientific research in plants and fungi, exhibition and conservation of the living plants collections, conservation of historical and scientific collections (e.g. herbarium, library and archives) and the development of plant-based educational programmes.

In 1755, Fernando I ordered the building of the Royal Botanical Garden of Madrid, which was first settled in the outskirts of the city, close to the Manzanares River. In 1774, Carlos III decided to move the Garden to its current location at the Paseo del Prado, where it was opened in 1781. Sabatini (Architect to the King) and Juan de Villanueva (architect who designed the Prado Museum and the Astronomical observatory) were in charge of this project. At that time, the garden was designed as three terraces and the plants were ordered according to Linnaean system of plants for the first time. The iron fence, several greenhouses and the vine arbors were also built at that time and still exist today.

From the very first days, teaching of botany took place in the garden, expeditions were supported, large collections of drawings were ordered and the herbaria began to grow.

Since 1939, the garden has been under the ownership of the Spanish National Research Council (CSIC) and in 1942 it was declared an 'Artistic Garden'. In 1974, after decades of hardship and neglect, the garden was closed to the public for restoration work and it reopened in 1981. The Garden holds a huge Library (32,000 books, 2,075 periodicals, 27,000 brochures or off-prints, 3,000 titles on microfiche, 2600 maps and 60 CD-ROMs). Its collections contain historical materials of incalculable value from the 17th and 18th century as well as electronic resources and online databases, with access to the most recent publications in botany and horticulture.

The *Historical Archive* contains the textual and graphical documents produced by the institution between the 18th century and the present day. It also keeps the botany-related documents produced by Spanish scientific expeditions in the 18th and 19th centuries. It comprises approximately 20,000 documents and over 10,000 botanical drawings.

The Herbarium is the largest in Spain and one of the most representative ones in Europe. It houses over a million specimens organized accordingly to standardized classification systems. The herbarium's collections are still growing thanks to the research work of the RJB's scientists, as well as donations, acquisitions and exchanges of specimens with other herbaria.

The Living Plants collection comprises 5.500 species which are exhibited on the three main terraces:

- *Terraza de los Cuadros* – collections of ornamental plants, medicinal, aromatic, endemics and orchard specimens gathered around a small fountain. All are planted in box-edged plots.
- *Terraza de las Escuelas Botánicas* – a taxonomic collection of plants, ordered phylogenetically and set within plots in and around 12 small fountains.
- *Terraza del Plano de la Flor* – a diverse collection of trees and shrubs, in the romantic English style as designed in the mid-nineteenth century. It contains the Villanueva Pavilion, built in 1781 as a greenhouse, and a pond with a bust of Carl Linnaeus.

Research focuses on the diversity of plants and fungi at the species level, how this diversity has come about, and how it can be conserved, as well as on biodiversity at the ecosystem level, particularly in the case of aquatic ecosystems in the Mediterranean region and the tropics.

Educational department

The education team was established in 2002 and nowadays belongs to the Scientific Culture Department of the Garden along with media,(including on-line materials and social networks) and external relationship sections. In total, the department employs 5 people and some external collaborators.

The INQUIRE representative, Madrid (IRM) holds a degree in Botany and did a one year training course in education to become a teacher. She has been responsible for the educational department at Madrid Botanic Garden since the beginning and is Head of Education now.

15–20 educators are hired on a day to day basis to deliver educational activities, some of whom have been working with the garden for many years. The garden offers in-house training for these educators once or twice a year with attendance on a voluntary basis.

Educators usually hold a degree in, or are still studying, biology or similar sciences and have either training or previous experience in education or dealing with groups. One person was exclusively employed via INQUIRE funding to support IRA in fulfilling project related tasks.

Educational Program: During the week the main target groups addressed via educational activities are school classes. Workshops and visits for the general public and families are carried out on weekends. The Garden also participates in several regional, national or international events such as Science Week, Science Fair and Fascination of Plants Day. The department additionally is involved in several national and European projects, such as INQUIRE (7th Frame Program).

Division of work

In the course of the INQUIRE project the Spanish Partner employed one person at each of the two botanic gardens. Both employees have a science, not an educational, background and they were mainly responsible for developing the lesson plans and producing all required artefacts which have been produced during the INQUIRE project. According to their statements, the four members of this partner group felt responsible for the content and quality of each single artefact that was handed in. Thus their work is the product of a joint venture and cannot be assigned to any individual in particular. According to them, they spent much time discussing and reflecting on their work and running the training courses jointly. These 4 members met on a regular basis and divided the work amongst themselves, according to each person's particular strengths. IRA and IRM see themselves as being responsible for the final quality checks of all the project work conducted.

These four members of the Spanish team attended the INQUIRE meetings as well the 'Train the Trainer Course' in Obergurgl and the Final Conference at Kew Gardens apart from the INQUIRE employee (Madrid),who went on maternity leave in December 2012 (end of 2nd Year) and was replaced by another employee who attended the Final Conference at Kew Gardens. No other members of the educational departments from either garden attended an INQUIRE meeting. According to IRA and IRM, these other staff have been informed about progress, lessons learned and outcomes on a regular basis.

Project administrative issues have been discussed with support staff at Alcala and Madrid University. Due to economic reasons, both INQUIRE employees left their respective organizations after the money ran out at the end of the project.

Why do they learn? Why do they make the effort?

According to Lave and Wenger (1991), the motivation to learn emerges from participating in a community that values collaborative practices and aims to improve these practices in order to produce something useful. These two Spanish Gardens were selected for participating in the INQUIRE consortium because both of them have an educational department with more than one person employed. One Spanish Garden was additionally partner in two unsuccessful attempts to get a proposal accepted by a funding agency and has repeatedly shown commitment to join the collaborative INQUIRE group. They initiated the invitation for the other Spanish garden to join the project. This same Spanish partner repeatedly showed their interest in improving science education programs (object) and in collaborating with the other garden over an extended period of time. The gardens shared ideas, found solutions and built innovation. However due to the economic crisis, the Spanish activity system faces a funding crisis and the raising of funds for education activities is now of extreme urgency. IBSE has been a good 'buzz word' when it comes to raising money for educational reform activities. In addition participating in an international Botanic Garden education project was highly valued in the organisation.

> 'I think they [botanic garden as a whole] value a lot to participate in an European project of this framework, it's a great point for the garden, but also for the whole institution (I272013p19)

What do they learn? How do they learn? What are the outcomes of learning?

The inquire model of professional development asks participants at either level, the national INQUIRE course or the international INQUIRE consortium, to experience at first-hand what will be later applied. While planning, designing and trialling their INQUIRE courses, partners engaged in their own inquiry and learned to assess and reflect on their own, as well as their course participants' learning outcomes.

> '... it is just that with the second course we make not only more activities but activities we have done were more reflective. I mean we could explain better the steps in inquiry based learning education and we make it different [...] from other methodologies, so this kind of reflection, while we are making activities, were an improvement from the first course' (Int2, p. 2).

148 Garden Learning

Partners understanding of IBSE:

> '... at the beginning, I didn't know anything about IBSE, I'd just seen a few activities in our botanic garden, they were very practical, but not exactly IBSE, so for me, it was a new topic, so I've developed a whole knowledge, not whole knowledge but from zero to more advanced' (Int2, p. 31).

Reflective cycles applied to developing IBST 'Lesson Plans' supported the Spanish team to change their understanding of the role of the educator as being the person 'in charge of the knowledge' and responsible for *'explaining the contributions of biodiversity to human beings and to the environment'* (LP1a,2011) or *'explaining what real scientists do at seed banks'*(LP1a; 2011).

In 2011, LP1a was presented at the Train the Trainers Meeting in Obergurgl. The team was paired with another consortium partner to discuss strengths and weaknesses of their lesson outline. In 2013 the revised lesson plan (LP3a) was published.

The initial lesson plan suggested that teachers perform two experiments to show students that CO_2 is a heavy gas and that plants take up CO_2 and produce oxygen.

The final lesson plan asks students to think about how they can use the first experiment to *'design another experiment that proves plants absorb CO2'*.

Both lesson plans are strong for engaging students, asking them to access prior knowledge and to expose their prior perceptions. Both provide students with opportunities to actively explore scientific concepts. The revised lesson plan is obviously stronger in helping students to use prior knowledge to generate new ideas and provides opportunities to demonstrate conceptual understanding and process skills (*Explanation*) as well as asking them to apply their understanding of concepts by conducting additional activities (*Elaboration*).

Feedback given to an assignment that a teacher handed in during the course was put into the partner portfolio of evidence that was handed in after the Pilot INQUIRE course (PE1). It gives a good insight into what the team considered best IBSE practice in Spain in 2012:

> 'We had the idea that your lesson plan was good but now that I've read it carefully it seems just excellent. It brings together many of the most important aspects of inquiry based learning for example it is entirely focused on student, the teacher has the role of being a facilitator which promotes a high degree of student involvement to unleash their creativity and confidence in their approach. It promotes the active pursuit of information from different source and media it places great emphasis on communications skills of students, the feedback between them is an important part of the activity I also find very good the final evaluation report: how you selected the criteria to evaluate each aspect of the activity and how you have developed a method to quantify with tables that offer.

Anyway in my opinion is a great example of good activity IBSE, congratulations'. (PE1, p. 5)

Spanish partners were given a similar opportunity to share lesson plans and get feedback from other partners 3 times in the course of the project duration. Lesson plan analysis shows that the Spanish group developed their understanding of good IBSE teaching in terms of 'Instructions- Scaffolding', 'Quality of Questions', 'Number of alternative approaches to solve a problem' and 'Emphasising a systematic scientific approach'.

Early lesson plans (LP1's, LP2) frequently used directives such as '*Look at the map and think*' or '*Experiment: Place the covered jar with the plant inside under the lamp . . .*'.

Closed questions such as '*In your opinion which of the following species should not exist?*' or '*How many energy sources do you know*' were asked more frequently.

While activities did identify skills and asked learners to use prior knowledge they rarely offered alternative ways of doing a task.

> '*Divide the class into groups of 4 students. Deliver them the material. Each group should cut the pieces of the puzzle and the foam. Students should stick the pieces of the puzzle and the foam. Try to solve the puzzle*' (LP1c)

Early lessons plans did not expect students to formulate a hypothesis, design experiments or assess their understanding. However teachers were motivated to assess students learning via observation of and oral communication with students.

All 5 LP3s (LP3a-e) handed in at the end of the project demonstrate obvious clear change in the role the students are expected to play in the knowledge gaining process. Students are required to become more responsible for their own learning and frequently design their own experiments to prove their hypothesis:

> 'How could you prove it? Encourage them to use the material you provide in order to design their own scenario and check how water acts on different types of soil' (LP3d).

Learners are asked to explain their knowledge right from the start and formulate hypotheses. For example, LP3b, asks students to explain 'How do plants move?' and to come up with various explanations (hypotheses).

While offering more freedom for students to shape their own learning processes all LP3s put more emphasis on the systematic scientific approach which is commonly used in IBST, e.g. LP3c starts with a *brainstorming/question-Phase*, followed by formulating *hypothesis*, conducting *experiments* and finally *communicating* and *discussing results*.

The training course includes an activity which asks participants to discussion advantages and disadvantages of IBSE when implemented in class and at the botanic gardens.

According to the worksheet responses, partners considered that the advantages of IBSE were:

> '... that it works on previous experiences, is motivating, asks for active participation of the student, includes both trial and error, promotes creativity and cooperation, is in contact with reality. Learning is meaningful and very visual'.

Disadvantages included: preparation time is needed, allies are needed, it is more difficult to control, teacher training is necessary, (teaching) materials necessary and it is difficult for us as teachers because we did not experience inquiry-based learning ourselves' (PE2).

In course of the INQURE project the Spanish team became aware that IBST needs to find a balance between an open/unstructured and a closed/very structured approach and mentioned teachers recognising this in course of the training programme.

> 'The beliefs of the teachers have changed a lot from the beginning of the course. For example, the most significant discovery was that most of them thought that IBSE was chaotic and disorganized at the beginning, but their answers completely changed when they were asked the same question at the end of the course' (PE2Case Studyp10)

Appreciating reflective practice:

From artefact analysis, we can see that the Spanish team describe, in their portfolio of evidence, outcomes that emerge spontaneously from reflective practice.

> 'The impressions of the Spanish team are that trough gaining experience in organizing the courses, in the last course we have felt much more confident and prepared than in the first one. Attending the Inquire meetings and getting feedback from other partners was also crucial to increasing the "Inquire skills" (PE2p4).

Gaining experience and reflecting on outcomes led the Spanish team to put more emphasis on particular learning phases.

> 'The balance between theory and practical activities was basically maintained, but in the second and third course the practical activities had much more space for teacher's comments and were continually compared to the IBSE learning cycle so that every step of the activities would fit on it (PE2p3)

Finding a balance between structure and freedom in IBST is necessary to support certain groups of students in specific learning environments to achieve particular learning goals. This requires practitioners to constantly observe and evaluate what happens in the classroom or outside in the botanic garden. This is tedious task however and may not be appreciated by all practitioners alike.

The team used the nickname '*pieces of evil*' when referring to the portfolios of evidence materials they had to collect over the course of the project. Nevertheless, although only one portfolio was compulsory, they handed in a very detailed second one following the second course and valued this exercise as helpful to their own learning.

> 'Just I said before that although the portfolio and the case study was a bit tricky but it´s good method or it made us reflect on our practice and even the interview because it is not the same writing about it and explaining to someone else about your and it makes us think also as a group' (Int2p32)

Their course assessment included a written case study/portfolio, which had to be handed in at the end of the course and the team noted that there was a reluctance amongst their INQUIRE course participants to evaluate their teaching efficiency.

> 'It is interesting to remark that, although they could only get a certificate trough delivering the assignment, most of them didn't (they were extremely busy, in the final exams period); they argued they had taken the course for the learning itself rather than the certification. This was pretty encouraging for us' (PE2p8).

The Spanish team, however, values their reflective practice and sees sharing their findings with the learning community as important for their own benefit.

> 'Moreover, we took into account the suggestions and ideas from the National and Regional Education Authorities, the Advisory Group and other INQUIRE Partners. These improvements consisted on improved lesson plans and conferences given by experts and invited teachers' (PE2CaseStudyp10).

Partners appreciated new ideas introduced not only by consortium partners or advisory group members but by teachers. This knowledge was valued and as soon it was shared at meetings and via lesson plan publications became INQUIRE consortium knowledge.

> 'I remember that during the final discussion, this was a big issue - the evaluation methods- and they [teachers] even suggest new methods and

they were helping each other with very quick methods and they were very inspiring, for us too' (Int2p12).

After three years, the Spanish partner feels confident and competent about running IBST teacher training courses successfully.

'Throughout the whole reflection, we are positive we can conclude that there has been a clear improvement in the practice of the courses from the first one' (PE2p11).

The INQUIRE Community of Inquiry

INQUIRE consortium meetings were important for partners and an assumption was that being able to interact face to face with other partners will be sorely missed now the project is finished. Some ideas and approaches shared by partners during these contact sessions were ignored; however, several were copied or adapted for partners' own purposes. The idea of investigating different types of honey, which was finally published as the Spanish lesson plan: 'Do we know what we eat?', was presented by another partner during an earlier stage of the project and was adopted by the Spanish team as a starting point for developing their own approach to plant diversity. In contrast, an experiment introduced by the Spanish group to visualise CO_2 gas qualities was used in IBSE activities developed by others.

The Spanish team valued the opportunity to visit each other institutions and observe others doing their work.

'Ideas, not only about the inquiry based learning but visiting each other in our gardens and institutions gives us the opportunity to see how [...] said before, how other people work in a botanic garden, maybe they have very different ways to do things but still we have always something to learn.' (I2/2013p30)

They take advantage from participating in the INQUIRE learning community.

'The INQUIRE courses have definitely been very positive for both institutions as they have helped to grow the teaching role of Botanic Gardens. They also served as a link to connect formal and non-formal education. In addition, we have learnt a lot from our collaboration between both Botanic Gardens and between other INQUIRE Partners' (PE2CaseStudyp12).

Organisational learning has taken place, was recognise by partners as such and mentioned explicitly

'The staffs of the Botanic Gardens have gained a lot of experience and we will try to continue running these courses in the future because we have raised and improved our contact and understanding with teachers. It has been also positive not only to the education team but to the rest of the staff who have been involved in the development of the courses, meetings, dissemination plan, conferences, etc.' (PE2Case Study p12).

Knowledge is now embedded in educational programmes/ lesson plans and routines and attests to partner's growth.

> 'because [writing lesson plans] it's hard work, I mean, we have lesson plans for everything we make, so we have [over talking] I mean, it's something we have to do from now on (Int2p28).

This knowledge enables partners to use these resources accordingly as well as to improve their education programmes in the future. Nevertheless partners realize that there is still room for improvement. Learning and sharing knowledge needs to continue in the future.

> 'yeah, for me as well. I think like we've spent three years learning, learning, learning and practising a bit and we will need at least another three years, put in practice a lot, a lot, a lot and then getting back to, so [I don't feel to be already] an expert [in IBST] really' (Int2p31).

Partners and their socio-cultural context

Implementing an inquiry based science teaching approach sustainably within a well-established botanic garden education department cannot only be met by training individual educators to adopt new skills and knowledge. This is particularly true if these staff are solely employed on a limited contract funded by the EU or other sponsor. It cannot be ignored that Spain has been, and still is, facing a severe economic recession since 2010 (the year the INUQIRE project started). Budget cuts of 20% led to an increase of working hours for teachers for the same payment. In primary schools, the number of students per class increased from 25 to 30, and in secondary education from 30 to 36. For 'non-obligatory' secondary education for students aged 16–18, classrooms where filled with up to 46 students. Teachers and Tutors went on major strikes in May 2012 as well as in October 2013 in response to these cuts.

For Spanish teachers it became more and more difficult to engage in any educational reform.

> 'Likewise, they [teachers] think that the scarce time and the large number of students is a difficulty. On the other hand, they believe that this methodology is very positive because it helps the students to understand the content of Science and it is more engaging'. (PE2Case Study p. 10)

The funding crisis was ably demonstrated by the issues around recruitment for the second Spanish INQUIRE course.

> '... so the general feeling of the teachers would be something that, you know, stopped them to go, cause some of them tell us that, we didn't feel like in the mood of going to a course, it's like saying no to the government, you know' (Int2p9).

In addition local and regional authorities were having problems. Consequently these had an impact on partners work.

> 'We realised that being enthusiastic and able to express the objectives of the project was crucial to the "Ministry of Education" to include the course in their programme. In fact, they were enthusiastic too. So they offered us to include our pilot course in their summer programme, so our second target was achieved too, which was getting promotion of the course by a national teacher training institution [EVIDENCE 3]. These meetings took place in the Ministry of Education's facilities and in both BGs. As it was a national course, teachers came from all over Spain so the Ministry of Education provided them with accommodation and meals. This fact was appreciated by the teachers ending with a list of more than 100 [EVIDENCE 4]. The conditions they asked for were not very demanding and adapted well to our course.... In order to do the second INQUIRE course, we have contacted/plan to contact them but the main problem is that they have removed all the summer teacher training courses. This is mostly caused by the economic cuts that the Ministry of Education is experiencing by the Government. Likewise, this institution has been replaced by the "*Centro Nacional de Innovación e Investigación Educativa*", "Ministry of Education, Culture and Sports" and some employees have changed. In summary, future collaborations with this institution are uncertain'(P1, p. 4–5).

So it became more difficult to recruit teachers for the second INQUIRE course in 2013.

> We launched [the call for teachers] twice for the course for primary and twice for secondary level but, unfortunately, we did not have the same success in recruiting teachers as during the IFIE's course since at the end of the call we did not have enough teachers so we could not run the course [EVIDENCE 10, 11, 12 and 13]. This was due to some social and political facts.

Nevertheless, the Spanish team eventually managed to run three courses and argue:

'We also found that delivering the courses independently form the Ministry of Education has given us more freedom in order to design the structure, number of speakers and so on; in the first course we were more tided up' (PE2p3).

All the courses proved very successful in the end and the Spanish team provided good evidence for sustainable organisational development. The economic situation however is unfortunately accountable for the Spanish INQUIRE employees having to leave the organisation when the project finished at the end of November 2013.

4. Discussion and Conclusion

4.1 Discussion

'Teaching isn't an exact science. Uncertainty is in its nature. This uncertainty calls for wise, well-founded judgment. Uncertainty is the parent of professionalism and the enemy of standardization. It is what makes teaching interesting, variable, and challenging—a job that's different every day'. (Hargreaves & Fullan, 2012 cited in Campell, 2013, p. 181)

Triggering the process of knowledge creation through collaborative learning

In 2007, the Rocard Report: 'Science Education now, a renewed pedagogy for the future of Europe' was published to support science education reform and forge a new direction by asking science and mathematics teachers, teacher trainers, Learning Outside the Classroom (LOTC) institutions and formal educational systems across Europe to implement Inquiry Based Science Education (IBSE) on a large scale. However, Inquiry Based Science Teaching (IBST) and learning is not necessarily a new, innovative approach and a remedy for all problems (see.p. 58ff). In my opinion, emphasising IBSE as 'a renewed pedagogy for the future of Europe' was a brilliant strategy because IBSE is a theoretical concept (s. p. 58ff). Therefore all those putting it into practice are required to grapple with it and construct a practical approach that covers theoretical features as well as a fit with their individual knowledge and skills and their particular socio-cultural context. Traditional models of learning often deal with tasks in which the content to be learned is well known ahead of time by those who design, manage and implement programs

---

How to cite this book chapter:
Kapelari, S. 2015. Discussion and Conclusion. In: Kapelari, S *Garden Learning: A Study on European Botanic Gardens' Collaborative Learning Processes*, Pp. 157–168. London: Ubiquity Press. DOI: http://dx.doi.org/10.5334/bas.d. License: CC-BY 4.0.

of learning. However this is not the case when implementing IBST. As a consequence, the Rocard Report (2007) asked stakeholders across Europe to engage in social learning processes while constructing and implementing a new, wider and more complex understanding of good science teaching in their individual country. The study presented here, provides evidence that collaborative, social learning processes have the potential to trigger organisational learning which finally leads to both organisational changes across the range of botanic gardens as well to the behaviour of teachers and educators.

Experience has shown that, in IBST, the collective activity systems, namely European project consortia, national educational systems, teacher training institutions, learning outside the classroom sites, science teachers etc., need to redefine themselves and their traditional models of teaching and learning science. It is not enough to simply agree on adopting IBST because as a theoretical concept it is an abstraction summarising multiple approaches to practical science teaching. Therefore, although IBSE has a long history, Capps and Crawford (2013) recently concluded that;

> 'today there is still no consensus as to what it [IBSE] actually is and what it looks like in the classroom` (p. 525)

A questionnaire applied at the beginning of the INQUIRE project revealed that many partners held a simple and experiential learning based understanding of IBST. Doing hands on activities was named as the main characteristic (Kapelari at al. 2011). Capps and Crawford's (2013) study showed that teachers in the United States, a country in which 'inquiry has been a buzz word in science education for many years' (p. 523), hold many misconceptions and myths about inquiry and equate it with questioning, student centred teaching approaches, and hands on teaching.

> 'It was particularly troubling that many teachers in this study believed they were teaching science as inquiry even when they did not (ibid, p. 522).

Capps and Crawford therefore call for the establishment of a 'unified concept of inquiry based teaching', rigorous assessment and professional development that supports teachers in learning about this particular 'unified concept of inquiry' and the nature of science (ibid).

This monological model assumes that science education is a closed system that follows a given set of rules, so that it is possible to discover direct relationships between inputs and outputs. Finding the perfect model of IBST is thought to be the key to designing successful interventions. This approach does not only ignore the fact that practitioners and students are individuals, deeply rooted in their socio-cultural context, but also that there is no such a thing as 'the one and only scientific inquiry approach'.

Science philosophers do not provide a unified concept of 'inquiry' in science research and there is no single concept of the nature of science that is fully accepted by all scientific disciplines. The nature of science is a matter of discussion (Harré, 1985, Bechtel, 1988). Agreement across all parties may never be reached and Bechtel (1988), in fact, argues that 'scientists are encouraged to engage with the issues themselves and to reach their own conclusion' (p. xii). As a result there are many variations of inquiry and any science education researcher or research group interested in analysing 'inquiry approaches' need to be aware of this.

For example Capps and Crawford (2013 p. 500) assume that 'doing inquiry' is characterised by being involved in science oriented problems, designing an investigation, prioritising evidence in respect to a problem (observe, describe, record), using evidence to develop an explanation, connecting explanations to scientific knowledge, communicating and justifying, using tools and techniques to gather, analyse and interpret data, as well as using mathematics in all aspects of inquiry. Minner, Levy, and century (2010) provide a more or less similar list of characteristics based on the NRC 2000 publication (s.p. 60ff). However neither do they focus on mathematics in all aspects of inquiry nor do they put emphasis on initial questions instead of problems. For these authors, it is 'precisely the lack of a shared understanding of the defining features of various instructional approaches that has hindered the research community making significant advancement in determining the effects of distinct pedagogical practices (Minner et al., 2010, p. 476). Capps and Crawford (2013) finally ask the question: 'If the academic community has not reached a consensus, how can we expect teachers to understand what inquiry is and how to teach science this way?' (p. 523).

After a long history of science education reform in the United States, aimed at implementing inquiry based learning, teachers and researchers still do not know what kind of knowledge, skills and attitudes are needed to design IBSE learning environments and which of those are most successful in supporting student learning (Minner et al., 2010; Capps & Crawford, 2013). Even more of a problem, the often favoured IBSE learning approach mentioned by the authors above covers neither the various approaches science takes to generate knowledge nor does it guarantee good science teaching (Dillon, 2012). Minner, Levy, and Century (2010) suggest that further work should be done to determine how practices such as 'active thinking', 'decision making' or 'drawing conclusions from data', applied outside the investigative context, contribute to student learning as compared to those taking place within the investigation context. In some instances, these have been significant predictors of increased student understanding of the science content.

Thus this raises the question of whether academics should continue to focus on 'reaching a consensus on the nature of inquiry teaching, taking care and precision in communicating what inquiry is to members of the education community, and developing viable and usable assessments of inquiry and NOS' (ibid, p. 524) or not. This may solve the problem of the comparability of research studies which apply an experimental design but will it support practitioners to improve their practice?

We may need to reconsider whether finding the best practice model for an investigative cycle, open or structured, is really a matter of urgency and an answer to practitioner uncertainty. Models are just that- they cannot be a one size fits all answer – they always need to be adapted to the particular user's context.

Practitioners will therefore always adapt any suggested model to their own experience, knowledge, attitudes and beliefs as well as to those of their students and organisational needs and perceptions (Drake & Sherin, 2006). A study done by Miller-Day, Pettigrew, Hecht, Shin, Graham, and Krieger, J. (2013) on how a 'drug prevention curriculum' was taught` in rural schools in the US, showed that 97% of the lessons observed were adapted in some way. Reasons for adaptation included responding to time, institutional, personal, and technical constraints, as well as responding to student needs. The latter included responding to their students' ability to process the curriculum content or in order to enhance student engagement with the teaching material. Drake and Sherin (2006) reported on teacher use of a reformed mathematic curriculum and found that it showed distinctive patterns of adaptations which were related to the teacher's own experience of mathematics learning. As mentioned already, Capps and Crawford (2013) showed that teachers believed that they were teaching science as 'inquiry' even though they were not.

Even if we agree that there are different ways of doing science inquiry, this does not mean that 'anything goes' – that IBST approaches can be user-defined or that anything published under the name of 'inquiry based science teaching resources' is successful per se. Although the activities may vary, IBST is assumed to follow a 'genuine process' for gaining scientific knowledge and most of all improve student science learning outcomes. Using readymade ISBT teaching material is particularly challenging for teachers who do not have a well-grounded PSCK background (s.p. 101ff). Whenever these teachers or educators engage in adapting IBS- teaching material to their personal, student or socio-cultural needs, there is a risk that their teaching may not be as efficient as expected;

> 'Not everything in a lesson can be planned in advance. By definition, if students existing ideas are taken into account, some decisions will depend on what these ideas are. Some Ideas can be anticipated from teachers' experience and from research findings built into curriculum material, but not all. What the teacher needs is not prescribed lesson content but a set of strategies to deploy according to what is found to be appropriate on particular occasions' (Harlen, 2013).

Therefore it is inevitable that teachers and educators will need to gather evidence whether or not their science lessons are still effective. As reflective practitioners they need to formatively and summative assess whether their students will still achieve the desired learning outcomes (Harlen, 2013).

Taking this into consideration, it might be wise to come to terms with the current more or less 'precise' definition of IBST and to devote oneself to learn more about how to scaffold collaborative learning environments that engage numerous organisations and individuals in expansive knowledge creation processes as a means to increase professionalism and improve day to day science teaching inside and outside the classroom.

Scaffolding collaborative learning has the potential to improve science education

According to Lave and Wenger (1991), the motivation to learn emerges from participating in a community that values collaborative practices and aims to improve these practices to produce something useful. In the case of putting inquiry based science education into practice, contradictory views advanced by practitioners and researchers alike, as well as a very non-specific use of the term in various contexts, actually challenged the idea that a well-defined stage of proficiency and a gradual acquisition of mastery can be reached by mere participation in the community.

The INQUIRE project management team avoided putting too much effort into reaching a consensus on 'the best practice model for what IBST should look like in Botanic Gardens' and instead went for a learning outcome oriented approach (s. p. 132). Partners were expected to become aware that whenever it comes to inquiry based science teaching it is important not 'that' but 'how' one asks a question, why a particular phenomenon, an experiment or a particular hands on activity is chosen and how this is embedded in a particular learning context, how and when aspects of the nature of science are made explicit, how and whether additional information is provided, and how learners are guided through the process of active knowledge construction and transformation (s.p. 58ff). It was assumed that moving on from abstract IBS instruction to concrete practice can only be achieved through specific epistemic or expansive learning actions (Engeström, 2001). 'In expansive learning, learners learn something that is not yet there. In other words, the learners construct a new object and concept for their collective activity, and implement this new object and conception in practice' (Engeström & Sannino, 2010, p 2). In our project, botanic gardens were expected to expand their understanding of IBSE and become self-confident in running Inquiry Based Science Teacher Training Courses on site.

With two courses run and an overall project duration of 3 years, the time span might still be too short to guarantee significant organisation development (Timperley et al., 2007). It is assumed that social communities need time to establish; not only teachers but teacher trainers and training organisations, formal and LOtC sites alike, need to engage in multiple social learning processes to develop the knowledge and skills needed to objectivise and evaluate IBSE related offers. A sustainable change in science education practices will only be achieved if enough time and space for the collaborative learning of teachers, educators and educational organisations is provided. All those involved need to adopt a critical reflective approach to teaching science and as a consequence they need to construct and develop a deep understanding of the science content as well as appropriate pedagogical knowledge in order to scaffold and assess inquiry based learning both inside and outside the classroom.

This case study, as well as outcomes published in the INQUIRE Quality Management report (Regan & Dillon, 2013) and the External Evaluation Report (Morgan, 2013), show that the INQUIRE expansive learning framework was successful in mediating the process of developing a better organisational understanding of how to apply IBSE in botanic gardens. The management board initiated their research by questioning partner understanding of inquiry and inquiry based learning, as well as the approach of traditional botanic garden teaching. By dedicating sufficient time to modelling new solutions as well as presenting and discussing practical approaches during consortium meetings, more and more partners were united in the process and 'a collaborative analysis and modelling of the zone of proximal development' (Engeström & Sannino, 2010) was initiated and carried out.

The INQUIRE grant agreement explicitly emphasised the examination and testing of new models of INQUIRE course design. Initially running a pilot INQUIRE course (PIC), reflecting on what required improvement and finally running a second INQUIRE course (IC) to establish whether the course is more successful were fundamental aspects of the INQUIRE framework and put value on Engeström's (2007) phases 4., 5.,and 6 in an expansive learning environment (see p. 35).

Traditionally, we expect learning to be manifested as change in the 'subject' which means that change becomes obvious in the behaviour and cognition of the learner. Expansive learning is manifested primarily as changes in the 'object', the outcomes of the activity system (Engeström & Sannino 2010; s.p. 31ff). The organisational learning effort developed through the implementation of the INQUIRE teacher training courses became obvious in adaptations of the initial course design and in new models of IBST activities. These observations, partner portfolios and partner interviews helped us to find out whether collective sense making and societal transformations had taken place. By studying the development of various objects, we were able to study the learning that took place across the complex and rapidly changing INQUIRE consortium activity systems.

Artefacts produced and presented in five consortium meetings, the 'train the trainer' course and the final conference offered opportunities for knowledge exchange and feedback, as well as engagement in learning activities to develop proficiency in reflective practice. These face to face meetings set the framework for partners to engage in a sequence of questioning, criticising or rejecting IBSE practices and existing knowledge about IBSE, followed by analysis of the situation, modelling new or different perceptions of IBSE, examining a model, implementing a new version and reflecting and evaluating its success (Engeström, 2001). The Spanish team explicitly mentioned how important the consortium meetings were and how they would miss them after the project finished. For them, it was important to 'find a balance between structured and open approaches' and to overcome the common misconception that IBSE is all about 'doing hands on activities'.

The INQUIRE consortium was an organisational network which united partners with different socio-cultural and historical backgrounds. It was characterised by a horizontal movement of information between organisations as well as a vertical movement between different organisational levels (s. p. 126) such as those within the botanic garden itself, the teacher trainers and the teachers and educators participating in INQUIRE training courses. Knowledge transfer and learning was not considered to be one-way but interplay between these levels. It was expected to lead to the formation of a new level of learning located in the partnership. The Spanish portfolios of evidence and their lesson plans exhibit the clear attitudinal change that the organisation went through. Not only did the role of the student change in lesson plans from that of receiver to that of creator of knowledge. The same occurred with the teachers and educators participating in INQUIRE training courses. The Spanish team explicitly valued the contributions that teachers made to enhance their original course design and they changed certain activities accordingly. They explicitly mentioned how course participants helped them to develop their own understanding of IBSE. Course participant case study findings also informed the Spanish INQUIRE course design.

The Spanish team became increasingly aware that IBST is embedded in an investigative cycle. Later produced lesson plans predominantly emphasise IBSE investigative steps. However, none of the analysed artefacts provide insight as to the reason for that particular development. Whether this process was characterised by controversies and conflict (Engeström, 2001) or just happened as a process of mutual agreement is not evident. The Spanish team only mentioned that discussions took place and that the final version of a lesson plans is one that all members of the team finally agreed on. These later lesson plans therefore may not be interpreted as the product of individual learning and thinking. The collaborative nature of this knowledge creation process is characterised by the exchange of knowledge and shared decision making and thus it is assumed that organisational learning is reaching a deeper level.

'According to Stehr, objectification processes occur as social communication processes when knowledge is stored in a textual, language or graphic form, i.e. when it is represented symbolically. This is how society is supposed to succeed in establishing an enormous amount of objectified knowledge (...) that acts as a mediator between humans and nature' (Paetau, 2001, p. 3).

Mediating artefacts and objects produced during the INQUIRE project helped partners to advance their organisational knowledge in IBSE. The Spanish team explicitly valued this process and mentioned in an interview that developing written lesson plans has become an organisational strategy, which will continue even after the project has been finished. Written lesson plans provide insight into the knowledge base underpinning a particular botanic garden's education practice. Sharing those with other consortium members supported not only the Spanish team but all the consortium partners in improving their practice (Regan & Dillon 2013). In this way, the very subject of learning is transformed from belonging only to isolated individuals, teachers and educators, to the collective members in the organisation and to the INQUIRE partner network. Individual learning advances organisational learning and becomes embedded in an organisation's memory and structure (Kim, 2004). For the Spanish team, this knowledge creation process was increasingly intertwined with acquiring the skills required for putting good science teaching into practice; knowledge creation and practical skill development merged.

The INQUIRE framework asked partners to engage in inquiry to enhance their organisational development. While engaging in an 'inquiry based learning process' the Spanish team developed their INQUIRE course design and investigated whether their course participants achieved expected learning outcomes. Via this process, it was assumed that partners appreciate and value reflective practice embedded in a 'professional learning community' and understand how this can help them to improve their own skills and competences for running professional development courses at Botanic Gardens. After three years, the Spanish partner now feels confident and competent about running IBST teacher training courses successfully and argues that:

> 'Throughout the whole reflection, we are positive we can conclude that there has been a clear improvement in the practice of the courses from the first one' (PE2p11).

Critiques of expansive learning express concern about how the expansive learning cycle enables the learner to access knowledge that does not emerge directly out of practice. (Engeström & Sannino, 2010). However, the heterogeneity of the INQUIRE consortium, made up of a diverse group of competent practitioners, as well as science education researchers and scientists who were from different educational and socio-cultural backgrounds, was assumed to provide a solution to this problem. It was assumed that these personnel have the potential to provide a fruitful diversity of thought as well as access to the theoretical or research knowledge needed to expand learning (ibid). Artefact analysis provides evidence that the tension that emerged in the INQUIRE community of learners nurtured the discussion and enhanced development. Experts, practitioners, education researchers, scientists and advisory group members 'crossed boundaries' (Engeström, 2001) and gave feedback on the processes that individual organisations made to ensure that the INQUIRE courses met national needs. This heterogeneous group of experts and practitioners therefore provided the kind of 'quality assurance' needed to support partners in developing a better understanding of IBST. Evaluation reports (Regan & Dillon, 2013; Morgan, 2013), as well as this case study, reveal that many partners profited from participating in this collaborative learning environment.

The Spanish partners valued the opportunity to work not only with other botanic garden partners but with their advisory group and the academic partner, Kings College London. They explicitly mentioned the interviews conducted by Kings Colleges helped them to reflect on their work. However, artefacts from the project do not provide evidence as to whether or not the Spanish group personally examined research or theoretical literature provided by Kings College about IBSE or reflective practice or whether they just considered educational research findings as helpful or appropriate for their own practice.

Botanic Gardens and natural history museums are becoming professionals in the field of learning outside the classroom

Tran and King (2011) argue that, in terms of teaching science in a LOtC context, a distinct body of knowledge and pedagogical practice has been established amongst educators working in the field. A few of these educators are aware of the various strategies they use or their relative efficacy, however, this body of knowledge is usually neither recognized nor shared by educators working across various institutions and settings.

> 'Without a shared knowledge base underpinning practice it may be argued that the pedagogical support provided by educators in the LOtC setting is inherently compromised. Furthermore a lack of an explicitly articulated body of knowledge raises concerns as whether the field can become a profession and further develop its practice'. (Tran & King 2011, p. 282).

The purpose of the INQUIRE project was to provide a space for LOtC organisations to make this tacit knowledge explicit, to share their knowledge and to adopt a positive attitude towards reflective practice as a tool for improving educational practice. Not only the Spanish team, but all partners accepted the challenge of applying reflective practice approaches to improve their INQUIRE training course design. Many show evidence that they valued the opportunity of sharing their knowledge with others (Regan & Dillon, 2013). A distinct body of knowledge and pedagogical practices has therefore been established, recorded and made explicit. Partners became conscious of the various strategies they use to implement IBST and learned about their efficacy; they additionally started to articulate this body of knowledge though how sustainable this movement will be is not predictable. To date, the INQUIRE consortium has provided the space for consortium partners to share and reflect on their own experience and to engage in science education theory and practice. This turned out to be fruitful for the Spanish team and they have developed a feeling of competence about applying any inquiry based science teaching approaches in the future. The staff of the Botanic Garden gained experience in the field and will try to continue running INQUIRE teacher training courses in the future:

> 'we have raised and improved our contact and understanding with teachers. It has been also positive not only to the education team but to the rest of the staff who have been involved in the development of the courses, meetings, dissemination plan, conferences, etc' (PE2/2013).

Developmental learning processes like these are more or less evident in all partner data provided for analysis (Regan & Dillon 2013).

Given the history of collaboration, it is most likely that the two Spanish gardens will continue to work together, sharing knowledge and experiences in the future. However, the fact that both Spanish INQUIRE employees, as well as several other partner INQUIRE employees, had to leave their respective organisations after the project finished may cause problems for both institutions. Kim (2004) argues that organisational learning is dependent on individuals improving their mental models. Making these mental models explicit is crucial to developing new 'shared' mental models which allow organisational learning to be independent of any specific individual. Although the Spanish team, as have other partners, produced a serious of written lesson plans which show a well-developed understanding of IBSE, more knowledge and skills are required to implement these lesson plans efficiently and effectively. The essence of the delivery is embodied more in 'the people' than in 'the written outline'. Due to work commitments in the Spanish group, these two INQUIRE employees were assigned the responsibility of designing and conducting the IBSE activities. Although sharing of ideas, knowledge and experience took place between all the Spanish partner team, there is now a high risk that this loss of 50% of the people implementing the project objectives will lead to a great loss of organisational knowledge. Any knowledge that has not been written down or articulated orally will disappear. New staff recruits to the Spanish team will have their own mental models about IBSE, and these may have no connection to the organisational memory remaining. They will have to take time to 'learn the ropes' in their new roles and will no doubt take up a lot more time learning from those more experienced in this approach.

4.2 Conclusion

Expansive Learning Theory places the emphasis on communities as learners, on transformation and creation of culture, on horizontal movement and hybridisation and on the formation of theoretical concepts (Engeström & Sannino, 2010). This expansive cycle of learning (s.p. 35) proved to be a useful framework for structuring the learning processes in the INQUIRE network.

'There is a need for new approaches to learning, especially for understanding and supporting practices where people are creating or developing useful and reusable things in collaboration.'(Moen et al., 2012, p. ix). As knowledge and learning are highly complex concepts and are experienced in many different ways, thinking of knowledge as just being an individual constructive process is too simple and ignores knowledge that is embedded in social systems. Without challenging the traditional individualistically oriented conceptualisation of learning, one will not be able to value situated learning and knowledge creation taking place in groups, organisations and networks.

In our society, knowledge is growing exponentially and we face fundamental changes in how information is communicated and evaluated. The question is what potential this knowledge has and how it is being used in social systems such as organisations, communities, social networks and society as a whole. Vygotsky's socio-cultural theory of knowledge construction, Lave and Wenger's understanding of situated learning and Engeström's understanding of expansive learning informs the basic notion underlying the INQUIRE project path. Their understanding of how learning takes place, along with that of those that follow them, becomes visible in the basic principles informing the INQUIRE teacher training course design, the INQUIRE management structure and the decisions that were made in the course of the project implementation. The INQUIRE logic asks for a holistic approach in reviewing the process of learning on all levels - the individual, the organisation and the network as a system.

Outcomes show that the INQUIRE design was successful in supporting the Spanish botanic garden education team to develop a better understanding of inquiry based teaching as an approach :

> '. . . that it works on previous experiences, is motivating, asks for active participation of the student, includes both trial and error, promotes creativity and cooperation, is in contact with reality. Learning is meaningful and very visual' (PE2).

The organisation feels competent about implementing this pedagogy in their educational programs as well as running INQUIRE courses in the future. They became aware about how reflective practice and formative and summative assessment can help them to improve their educational work.

4.3 Future perspectives

The Botanic Garden perspective

It would be rash to assume that botanic gardens have established a professional, theory informed, attitude towards teaching and learning within just the three years of the INQUIRE project. However, if similar collaborative learning processes continue, it is likely that partners will become professionals in botanic garden education in the near future. The first attempts have now been made and we now need to proceed to the next step. Botanic gardens need to develop a better understanding of what the 'domain specific assets of botanic garden learning' actually are. They need to actively contribute to the development of a theory of botanic garden learning. Whenever they think about the content and the context in which botanic garden learning takes place, it is recommended that they value the heterogeneity of their educational audiences, their socio-cultural background and the knowledge and experiences visitors already bring to any constructivist or situated learning activity. In addition, botanic garden educators and educational programme designers need to be aware that their own cultural background, beliefs and attitudes, not just towards their participants, but also towards teaching and learning is very influential on the learning environment they create. Focusing on the accuracy of just the science content may not be enough for modern botanic garden teaching and learning. It could also be worse if educators fail to reflect on their own science learning history or experience and simply adopt teaching approaches similar to those practiced in schools. Learning in a botanic garden may run the risk of losing the very essence that makes it unique.

The Research Perspective

Design based research has provided evidence that the collaborative INQUIRE learning environment was fruitful in improving educational practice at botanic gardens. Future investigations will focus on operational aspects of the proposed framework by analysing the social interaction amongst organisations more thoroughly. Social network analysis (Borgatti, 2013) has already been tested as a tool for visualising interactions amongst teachers and educators participating in the Austrian INQUIRE courses (see conference Publications) and the preliminary results are promising. This could be a way of assessing developmental processes taking place during the life span of a collaborative network and thus offer opportunities to scaffold this process more effectively.

5. References

Abell, S. K., & Lederman, N.G. (2007). Preface. In: S. K. Abell & N. G. Lederman (Eds.). *Handbook of Research on Science Education* (pp. 9–13). Routledge Taylor & Francis Group, New York London.

Adams, J. D., Tran, L. U., Gupta, P. & Creedon-O'Hurley, H. (2008). Sociocultural frameworks of conceptual change: implications for teaching and learning in museums. *Cultural Studies of Science Education*, 2, 435–449.

Amin, A., & Roberts, J. (2006). Communities of Practice? Varieties of Situated Learning, paper prepared for: EU Network of Excellence, Dynamics of Institutions and Markets in Europe (DIME). http://www.dime-eu.org/files/active/0/Amin_Roberts.pdf. Accessed: August 2, 2013.

Anders, D., & Zhang, Z. (2003). Teacher Perceptions of Field-Trip Planning and Implementation. *Visitor Studies Today*, 4(3), 6–11.

Anderson, J. R., Reder, L. M., & Simon, H. A. (1996). Situated Learning and Education. *Educational Researcher*, 25(4), 5–11.

Anderson, D., Lucas, K. B., Ginns, I. S., & Dierking, L. D. (2000). Development of knowledge about electricity and magnetism during a visit to a science museum and related post-visit activities. *Science Education*, 84(4–5), 658–679.

Appleton, K. (2007). Elementary science teaching. In S. K. Abell & N. G. Lederman (Eds.), *The Handbook of Research on Science Education* (pp. 493–535). NJ: Lawrence Erlbaum.

Argote, L., & Miron-Spektor, E. (2011). Organizational Learning: From Experience to Knowledge. *Organization Science*, 22(5), 1123–1137.

Argote, L. (2013). *Organisational Learning: Creating. Retaining and Transferring Knowledge*. Springer Science and Business Media, New York.

Asay, L. D., & Orgill, M. K. (2009). Analysis of Essential Features of Inquiry Found in Articles Published in the Science Teacher, 1998–2007. *Journal of Science Teacher Education*, 21(1), 57–79.

Bailin, S., Case, R., Coombs, J. R., & Daniels, L. B. (2010). Common misconceptions of critical thinking. *Journal of curriculum Studies*, 31(3), 269–283.

Bamberger, Y., & Tal, T. (2008). An Experience for the Lifelong Journey: The Long-Term Effect of a Class Visit to a Science Center. *Visitor Studies*, 11(2), 198–212.

Barron, B., & Darling-Hammond, L. (2010). Prospects and challenges for Inquiry based approaches to learning. In The Nature of Learning: Using Research to Inspire Practice, OECD Centre for Educational Research and Innovation. http://www.oecd.org/edu/ceri/thenatureoflearningusingresearchtoinspirepractice.htm Accessed 2 August 2013.

Barron, B. J. S., Schwartz, D. L., Vye, N. J., Moore, A., Petrosino, A., Zech, L., Bransford, J. D., & The Cognition and Technology Group at Vanderbilt (1998). Doing with Understanding: lessons from Research and Problem- and Project-based learning, *Journal of the Learning Sciences*, 7(3–4), 3–11.

Barton, D. & Tusting, K. (2005). *Beyond Communities of Practice: Language power and social context*. Cambridge University Press, N.Y., USA.

Batatia, H., Hakkarainen, K., & Mørch, A. I. (2012). Tacit knowledge and trialogical learning: towards a conceptual framework for designing innovative tools. In A. Moen, A. I. Mørch & S. Paavola (Eds.). *Collaborative Knowledge Creation Practices, Tools, Concepts*. Technology Enhanced Learning Vol.7, 15–30. Sense Publishers, Rotterdam/Boston/ Taipei.

Bechtel, W. (1988). *The Philosophy of Science: An Overview for Cognitive Science*. Lawrence Erlbaum Associates, Inc. New Jersey, USA.

Bell, P. (2004). On the Theoretical Breadth of Design-Based Research in Education. *Educational Psychologist*, 39(4), 243–253.

Bell, P., Lewenstein, B., Shouse, A. W., & Feder, M. A. (Eds). (2009). *Learning Science in Informal Environments People, Places and Pursuits*. The national Academies Press, Washington, D.C.

Bentley, T. (1998). *Learning beyond the Classroom: Education for a changing world*. London: Routledge

Berliner, D. C. (2001). Learning about and learning from expert teachers. *Educational Researcher*, 35, 463–482.

Bereiter, C. (2002). Design research for sustained Innovation. *Cognitive Studies, Bulletin of the Japanese Cognitive Science Society*, 9(3), 321–327.

Bertsch, C., Unterbruner, U., & Kapelari, S. (2008). Forschend-begründendes Lernen im naturwissenschaftlichen Unterricht. Wege zu einer naturwissenschaftlichen Grundbildung am Übergang Primar/Sekundarstufe am Beispiel von Unterrichtsmaterialien zum Thema Fotosynthese. Dissertation an der Universität Innsbruck, Austria. https://www.imst.ac.at/imst-wiki/images/2/2b/Dissertation_ChristianBertsch.pdf Accessed 13. December 2013.

Bevan, B., with Dillon, J., Hein, G. E., Macdonald, M., Michalchik, V., Miller, D., Root, D., Rudder, L., Xanthoudaki, M., & Yoon, S. (2010). Making Science Matter: Collaborations Between Informal Science Education Organizations and Schools. A CAISE Inquiry Group Report. Washington, D.C.: Center for

Advancement of Informal Science Education (CAISE). http://www.amnh.org/learn-teach/evaluation-research-and-policy/policy/making-science-matter-collaborations-between-informal-science-education-organizations-and-schools Accessed: 6 December 2013.

BGCI, Botanic Gardens Conservation International (2002). *Global Strategy for Plant Conservation*. Richmond, Surrey: BGCI.

Bianchini, J. A., & Colburn, A. (2000). Teaching the nature of science through inquiry to prospective elementary teachers: a tale of two researchers. *Journal of Research in Science Teaching*, 37(2), 177–209

Bifie, (Eds.) (2011). 338 Kompetenzorientierter Unterricht in Theorie und Praxis. Graz:339 Leykam. https://www.bifie.at/system/files/dl/bist_vs_sek1_kompetenzorientierter_unterricht_2011-03-23.pdf Accessed: 18 April 2014.

Blum, N., Nazir, J., Breiting, S,. Chuan Goh, K., & Pedretti, E. (2013). Balance the tension and meeting the conceptual challenges of education for sustainable development and climate change. *Environmental Education Research*, 19(2), 206–217.

BMUKK (2000). Lehrplänen an Österreichs Schulen. http://www.bmukk.gv.at/schulen/unterricht/lp/index.xml Accessed 1 April 2014.

Bolam, R., McMahon, A., Stoll, L., Thomas, S., & Wallace, M. (2005). *Creating and Sustaining Effective Professional Learning Communities*. London: Department of Education and Skills.

Booth, W., Cuzyova, A., Key, P., Macauley, J., & Murison, S. (2004). Establishing a Community of Practice, A Resource Handbook, Draft for Discussion. Available online: http://webcache.googleusercontent.com/search?q=cache:GSd_TejycWAJ:europeandcis.undp.org/files/uploads/CoP/How%2520to%2520Establish%2520a%2520Community%2520of%2520Practice%252Draft%2520Final%2520230505.doc+&cd=6&hl=de&ct=clnk&gl=at Accessed 13 December 2013

Borgatti, S. P., Everett, M. G., & Johnson, J. C. (2013). *Analyzing Social Network*. SAGE Publications Ltd.

Bozin, A. M. (2008). Integrating Instructional Technologies in a Local Watershed Investigation With Urban Elementary Learners. *The Journal of Environmental Education*, 39(2), 47–58.

Bransford, J. D., Darling-Hammond, L., & LePage, P. (2005). Introduction. In L. Darling-Hammond & J. Bransford (Eds.) *Preparing Teachers for a Changing World*. Jossey-Bass, A Wiley Imprint, San Francisco, CA.

Bransford, J. D., Brown, A. L., & Cocking, R. R. (Eds.) (2000). *How People Learn: Brain, Mind, Experience and School*. Washington DC: National Academy Press.

Brown, F. S. (1996). *The Effect of an Inquiry-Oriented Environmental Science Course on Pre-service Elementary Teachers' Attitudes about Science*. Paper presented at the Annual Meeting of the National Association for Research in Science Teaching (69th, St. Louis, MO, April, 1996).

Bybee, R. W., Taylor, J. A., Gardener, A., VanScotter, P., Powell, J. C., Westbrook, A., & Landes, N. (2006). The BSCS 5E Instructional Model: Origins and Effectiveness. A report Prepared for the Office of Science Education National Institutes of Health. http://sharepoint.snoqualmie.k12.wa.us/mshs/ramseyerd/Science%20Inquiry%201%2020112012/What%20is%20Inquiry%20Sciecne%20(long%20version).pdf Accessed 1 April 2014.

Cambridge, D., Kaplan, S., & Suter, V. (2005) Community of Practice Design Guide. A Step-by-Step Guide for Designing & Cultivating Communities of Practice in Higher Education. http://net.educause.edu/ir/library/pdf/nli0531.pdf. Accessed 12 February 2013.

Campbell, E. (2013). Judgement in Teaching. *Curriculum Inquiry*, 43(2), 181–188.

Capps, D. K., & Crawford, B. A. (2013). Inquiry-based Instruction and Teaching About Nature of Science: Are They Happening? *Journal of Science Teacher Education*, 24(3), 497–526.

Carli, E. (2013). *A case study: "Can children interlink specific modules/activities with each other on the one hand and with the overall/ all-encompassing scientific question on the other hand?"*. Presented at the INQUIRE Conference, Raising Standards Through Inquiry, Royal Botanic Gardens, Kew, London, 9–10 July 2013.

Coates, S. A. (Ed.) (2011). Second Report of the Independent Review of Teachers´ Standards. www.education.gov.uk. Accessed 2 August 2013.

Cole, M. (1996). *Cultural psychology. A once and future discipline.* Harward: Harward University Press.

Condliffe Lagemann, E. (2001): *An Elusive Science: The Troubling History of Education Research.* University of Chicago Press, Chicago, USA.

Covitt, B. A., Gunckel, K. L., & Anderson, C. W. (2009). Students' developing understanding of water in environmental systems. *Journal of Environmental Education*, 40(3), 37–51.

Cox-Petersen, A. M., Marsh, D. D., Kisiel, J., & Melber, L. M. (2003). Investigation of guided school tours, student learning, and science reform recommendations at a museum of natural history. *Journal of Research in Science Teaching*, 40, 200–218.

Darling-Hammond, L., & Bransford, J. (Eds) (2005). *Preparing Teachers for a Changing World.* Jossey-Bass, A Wiley Imprint, San Francisco, CA.

Darling-Hammond, L., Wei, R. C., Andree, A., Richardson, N., & Orphanos, S. (2009). Professional Learning in the Learning profession. A Status Report on Teacher Development in the United States and Abroad. National Staff Development Council, NSDC. http://www.learningforward.org/docs/pdf/nsdcstudy2009.pdf Accessed: August 28, 2013.

Davidsson, A., & Jakobsson, A. (Eds.) (2012). *Understanding Interaction at Science Centers and Museums Approaching Sociocultural Perspectives.* Senes Publsihers, Rotterdam Boston Taipei.

Day, C., & Sachs, J. (2004). Professionalism, performativity and empowerment: Discourse in the politics, policies and purposes of continuing professional development. In: C. Day & J. Sachs (Eds.). *International handbook on the continuing professional development of teachers.* (pp. 3–10). Maidenhead, UK: Open University Press.

Davis, C. L., & Honan, E. (1998). Reflection on the Use of teams to support the Portfolio Process, In N. Lyons (Ed.). *With Portfolio in Hand: Validating the New teacher Professionalism* (pp. 90–102). New York: Teachers College Press.

Dewey, J. (1938). *Experience and Education.* New York: Collier Books, Macmillan.

DeWitt, J., & Storksdieck, M. (2008). A short Review of School Field Trips: key Findings from the Past and Implications for the Future. *Visitor Studies,* 11(2), 181–197.

Dillon, J., & Reid, A. (2004). Issues in case-study methodology in investigating environmental and sustainability issues in higher education: towards a problem-based approach? *Environmental Education Research,* 10(1), 23–37.

Dillon, J. (2007). Researching science learning outside the classroom, *Journal of the Korean Association for Research in Science Education,* 27(6), 519–528.

Dillon, J., & Osborne, J. (Eds.), (2007). Special Issue: Research on Learning Science in Informal Contexts. *International Journal of Science Education,* 29(12).

Dillon, J. (2009). On Scientific Literacy and Curriculum Reform. *International Journal of Environmental & Science Education,* 4(3), 201–213.

Dillon, J. (2012). Panacea or passing fad – good is IBSE? *Roots,* 9(2), 5–9.

Donovan, M. S., & Bransford, J. D.(Eds.) (2005). *Introduction. How Students Learn Science in the classroom.* Washington DC: The National Academies Press.

Drake, C., & Sherin, M. G. (2006). Practicing Change: Curriculum Adaptation and Teacher Narrative in the Context of Mathematics Education Reform. *Curriculum Inquiry,* 36(2), 153–187.

Duschl, R. A., & Grandy, R. E. (2008). *Teaching scientific inquiry: Recommendations for research and implementation.* Sense Publisher.

Dyck, B., Starke, F. A., Mischke, G., & Mauws, M. (2005). Learning to Build a car: an empirical investigation of organisational learning. *Journal of Management Studies,* 42(2), 387–416.

Eder, F. (2009). Folgerungen für Lehrerbildung und Schulentwicklung. In C. Schreiner & U. Schwantner (Eds.). *PISA 2006 Österreichischer Expertenbericht zum Naturwissenschaftsschwerpunkt.* Leykam, Graz, Austria.

Endreny, A. H. (2010). Urban 5th graders conceptions during a place-based inquiry unit on watershed. *Journal of Research in Science Teaching,* 47(5), 501–517.

Engeström, Y. (1987). *Learning by Expanding: an activity-theoretical approach to developmental research.* Helsinki, Orienta-Konsultit.

Engeström, Y. (2000). Can people learn to master their future. *The Journal of the Learning Sciences*, 9(4), 525–534.
Engeström, Y. (2001). Expansive Learning at Work: toward an activity theoretical reconceptualization. *Journal of Education and Work*, 14(1), 133–156.
Engeström, Y. (2007). Enriching the theory of expansive learning: Lessons from journey towards co-configuration. *Mind, Culture, and Activity*, 14(1–2), 23–39.
Engeström, Y., & Sannino, A. (2010). Studies of Expansive learning: foundation, findings and future challenges. *Educational Research Review*, 5(1), 1–24.
EU (2000). Lisbon European Council 23 and 24 March 2000 PRESIDENCY CONCLUSIONS. http://www.europarl.europa.eu/summits/lis1_en.htm. Accessed 30 December 2013
EU Commission (2004). Europe needs more scientists. Report by the High Level Group on Increasing Human Resources for Science and Technology in Europe. http://ec.europa.eu/research/conferences/2004/sciprof/pdf/final_en.pdf Accessed 30 December 2013
EU Expert Group (2013). Supporting teacher competences for better learning outcomes. http://ec.europa.eu/education/schooleducation/doc/teacher-comp_en.pdf Accessed 6 December 2013
Eylon, B. S. (2000). Designing powerful learning environments and practical theories: The knowledge integration environment. *International Journal of Science Education*, 22, 885–890.
Falk, J., & Dierking, L. (2000). *Learning from Museums: Visitor Experiences and the Making of Meaning*. Walnut Creek, CA: Alta Mira Press.
Falk, J. H., Moussouri, T., & Coulson, D. (1998). The effect of visitors' agendas on museum learning. *Curator*, 41, 107–120.
Falk, J. H., & Storksdieck, M. (2005). Using the Contextual Model of Learning to understand visitor learning from a science center exhibition. *Science Education*, 89, 744–778.
Fang, Z. (1996). A review of research on teacher beliefs and practices. *Educational Research*, 38, 47–65.
Fraser, B. J., Tobin, K., & McRobin, C. J. (Eds.) (2012). *Second International Handbook of Science Education 24*, Springer Science + Business Media B.V.
Gerring, J. (2004). What Is a Case Study and What Is It good for? *American Political Science Review*, 98(2), 341–354.
Grafendorfer, A., & Neureiter, H. (2009). Unterricht in Naturwissenschaften. In C. Schreiner & U. Schwantner (Eds.). *PISA 2006 Österreichischer Expertenbericht zum Naturwissenschaftsschwerpunkt*. Leykam, Graz, Austria.
Griffin, J., & Symington, D. (1997). Moving from task-oriented to learning-oriented strategies on school excursions to museums. *Science Education*, 81, 763–779.
Griffin, J. (2004). Research on Students and Museums: Looking More Closely at the Students in School Groups. *Science Education*, 88(1), 59–70.

Groundwater- Smith, S., & Dadds, M. (2004).Critical practitioner inquiry: towards responsible professional communities. In C. Day & J. Sachs (Eds.). *International Handbook on the continuing Professional Development of teachers*. Open University Press, Berkshire, UK.

Gusky, T. (2000). *Evaluating Professional Development*. Thousand Oaks, Corwin Press, CA.

Handley, K., Sturdy, A., Fincham, R., & Clark, T. (2006). Within and Beyond Communities of Practice: Making Sense of Learning Through Participation, Identity and Practice. *Journal of Management Studies*, 43(3), 641–653.

Harlen, W. (2013). Assessment & Inquiry-Based Science Education: Issues in Policy and Practice. The Global Network of Science Academies (IAP) Science Education Programme (SEP). www.interacademies.net/activities/projects/12250.aspx Accessed 1 April 2014

Harré, R. (1985). *The Philosophies of Science*. Oxford University Press.

Hattie, J. (2008). *Visible Learning: A Synthesis of Over 800 Meta-Analyses Relating to Achievement*. First Edition, Roudlege, Taylor & Francis Group, London and New York.

Heimlich, J. E., & Ardorin, N. M. (2008). Understanding behavior to understand behavior change: a literature review. *Environmental Education Research*, 14(3), 215–237.

Hein, G. E. (2012). *Progressive Museum Practice John Dewy and Democracy*. Left Coast Press, Walnut Creek, California, USA.

Herzog. W., & VonFelten, R. (2001). Erfahrung und Reflexion. Zur Professionalisierung der Praktikumsausbildung von Lehrerinnen und Lehrern. Beiträge zur Lehrerbildung. 19(1). http://www.bzl-online.ch17/ Accessed 14 July 2013

Hmelo-Silver, C., Duncan, R., & Chinn, C. (2007). Scaffolding and achievement in problem-based and inquiry learning: A response to Kirschner, Sweller, and Clark (2006). *Educational Psychologist*, 42(2), 99–107.

Hoekstra, B. (2000). Plant blindness: The ultimate challenge to botanists. *American Biology Teacher*, 62, 82–83.

Hodgkinson, G., & Sparrow, P. R. (2002). *The competent organization: A psychological analysis of the strategic management process*. Buckingham: Open University Press.

Hodson, D. (2007). *Towards scientific Literacy A teachers guide to the History, Philosophy and Sociology of Science*. Sense Publisher, Rotterdam/Taipei.

Hofman, R. H., & Dijkstra, B. J. (2010). Effective teacher professionalization in networks? *Teaching and Teacher Education*, 26(4), 1031–1040.

Hogan, K., & Berkowitz, A. R. (2000). Teachers as Inquiry Learner. *Journal of Science Teacher Education*, 11(1), 1–25.

Hohenstein, J., & Manning, A. (2010). Thinking about learning. In J. Osborne & J. Dillon (Eds.). *Good Practice in Science Teaching. What Research has to say*, Second Edition. Open University Press, UK.

Holstermann, N., & Bögeholz, S. (2007). Interesse von Jungen und Mädchen an naturwissenschaftlichen Themen am Ende der Sekundarstufe I. *Zeitschrift für Didaktik der Naturwissenschaften*, 13, 71–86.

Holzinger, F., & Reidl, S. (2012). *Humanressourcen Barometer. HR Monitoring in Wissenschaft und Technologie*. Johanneum Research Forschungsgesellschaft. BMVIT, Wien.

Hord, S. M. (2009). Professional Learning Communities. *Journal of Staff Development (JSD)*, 30(1), 40–43.

Hord, S. M. (1997a). *Professional learning communities: Communities of continuous inquiry and improvement*. Austin, TX: Southwest Educational Development Laboratory.

Huffman, J. B., & Hipp, K. K. (2003). *Reculturing schools as professional learning communities*. Lanham, MD: Scarecrow Education.

IUS (2013). Innovation Union Scoreboard. http://ec.europa.eu/enterprise/policies/innovation/files/ius-2013_en.pdf, Accessed 2 January 2013.

Jonassen, D. H. (2000). Revisting Activity Theory as a Framework for designing Student Centered Learning Environments. In D.H. Jonassen and S.M. Land (Eds.) (2000). *Theoretical Foundation of Learning Environments* (pp. 89–120). Lawrence Erlbaum Associates. Publisher, Mahwah, New Jersey, London.

Kapelari, S., Elster, D., & Dillon, J. (2011). *Deliverable N°: 2.2. Document summarising how IBSE is defined in the INQUIRE course*. EU Commission, research Directorate.

Kapelari, S., Bromley, G., & Vergou, A. (2013). INQUIRE Publishable Summary. www.inqirybotany.org, Accessed 30. January 2014.

Kapelari, S. (2015). Collaborative Pedagogical Content Knowledge Creation in Heterogenous Learning Communities. In M.Grangeat (Ed.) (2015). Understanding Science Teacher Professional Knowledge Growth. Sense Publisher, Rotterdam Boston Taipei (in print)

Kelly, A. E., & Sloane, F. C. (2003). Educational Research and the Problems of Practice. *Irish Educational Studies*, 22(1), 29–40.

Klechtermans, G. (2004). CPD for Professional Renewal: moving beyond knowledge for practice. In C. Day & J. Sachs (Eds.). *International Handbook on the Continuing Professional Development of Teachers*. Open University Press, Berkshire, UK.

Kim, D. H. (2004). The link between individual and organisational learning. In K. Starkey, S. Tempest & A. McKinley (Eds.), *How organisations learn. Managing the search for knowledge*. 2nd Edition. Thomson, UK.

Kirschner, P., Sweller, J., & Clark, R. (2006).Why minimal guidance during instruction does not work: An analysis of the failure of constructivist, discovery, problem-based, experiential, and inquiry-based teaching. *Educational Psychologist*, 41(2), 75–86.

Kisiel, J. (2005). Understanding Elementary Teacher Motivations. *Science Education*, 89, 936–955.

Klein, J. H., & Connell, N. A. D. (2008). Identification and Cultivation of Appropriate Communities of Practice. In C. Kimble, P. Hildreth & I. Bourdon (Eds.) (2008). *Communities of Practice Creating Learning Environments for educators Volume 1*. IAP –Information Age Publishing, Inc., USA.

Klenowski, V. (2002). *Developing Portfolios for learning and assessment. Processes and Principles*, Roudledge Falmer, London, UK.

Kneebone, S., & Willison, J. (2007). A global snapshot of botanic garden education provision. Paper presented at the 3rd Global Botanic Gardens Congress, BGCI, 15–20 April 2007, Wuhan, China.

Krüger, D., & Burmester, A. (2005). Wie Schüler Pflanzen ordnen. *Zeitschrift für Didaktik der Naturwissenschaften*, 11, 85–102.

Krüger, D. (2007). Die Conceptual Change Theorie. In D. Krüger & H. Voght (Eds.). *Theorien in der biologiedidaktischen Forschung*. Springer, Berlin Heidelberg New York.

Kubicek, J. (2005). Inquiry-based learning, the nature of science, and computer technology: New possibilities in science education. *Canadian Journal of Learning and Technology*, 31(1).

Kuhn, T. (1970). *The Structure of Scientific Revolutions*, Second Edition, Chicago: University of Chicago Press

Kyburz-Graber, R. (2013). Socio-Ecological Approaches to Environmental Education and Research. A Paradigmatic Response to Behavioral Change Orientations. In: *Handbook of Research on Environmental Education* (pp. 23–31). The AERA/Routledge Research Handbook Series.

Lakoff, G., & Johnson, M. (1980). *The metaphors we live by*. Chicago: The University of Chicago Press, USA.

Léna, P. (2009). Europe Rethinks Education. *Science*, Vol. 326, 501.

Lave, J., & Wenger, E. (1991). *Situated Learning. Legitimate Peripheral Participation*. Cambridge University Press, Edinburg, UK

Lederman, N. G. (2007). Nature of Science: Past, Present and Future. In S. A. Abell & N. G. Lederman (Eds.), *Handbook of Research on Science Education*, Lawrence Erlbaum Association, New Jersey, USA

Lederman, N. G., & Lederman J. S. (2012). Nature of scientific knowledge and scientific Inquiry. In B. J. Barry, K. G. Tobin & C. J. McRobbie (Eds). *Second international handbook of Science Education*, Volume 1, Springer Dordrecht Heidelberg London New York.

Link Perez, M. A., Dollo, V. H., Weber, K. M., & Schussler, E.E.(2010). What's in a Name: Differential labelling of plant and animal photographs in two nationally syndicated elementary science textbook series. *International Journal of Science Education*, 32(9), 1227–1242.

Loughran, J. (1996). *Developing Reflective Practice; Learning about teaching and learning through modelling*. The Falmer Press, London; UK.

Loughran, J. (2002). Effective Reflective Practice: In Search of Meaning in Learning about teaching. *Journal of Teacher Education*, 53(1), 33–43.

Loughran, J., Berry, A., & Mulhall, P. (2006). Understanding and developing science teachers' pedagogical content knowledge. Rotterdam, The Netherlands: Sense Publishers.

LOTCM (2007). Learning Outside the Classroom-Manifesto. http://webarchive.nationalarchives.gov.uk/20080305115859/teachernet.gov.uk/teachingandlearning/resourcematerials/outsideclassroom/. Accessed 1 April 2014.

Lunetta, V. N., Hofstein, A., & Clough M. (2007). Learning and teaching in the school science laboratory: an analysis of research, theory and practice. In N. Lederman & S. Able (Eds.) *Handbook of research on science education* (pp. 393–441) Mahwah, NJ: Lawrence Erlbaum.

Marbach-Ad, G. (2004). Expectations and difficulties of first year college students in biology. *Journal of College Science Teaching*, 33, 18–23.

Mayer, R. E. (2004). Should there be a Three-Strikes Rule Against Pure Discovery Learning? *American Psychologist*, The American Psychological Assoziation, USA, 59(1), 14–19.

Mayring, P. (2008). *Die Praxis der qualitativen Inhaltsanalyse* (2. Aufl.). Weinheim: Beltz.

McEneaney, E. H. (2003). The worldwide Cachet of Scientific Literacy. *Comparative Education Review*, 47(2), 217–237.

McKinsey and Company, (2007). How the world's best-performing schools come out on top. http://mckinseyonsociety.com/how-the-worlds-best-performing-schools-come-out-on-top/ Accessed 1 April 2014.

McNicholl, J. (2013). regional agency and teacher development: at CHAT analysis of a collaborative professional inquiry project with biology researchers. *European Journal of Teacher Education*, 36(2), 218–232.

Michie, M. (1998). Factors influencing secondary science teachers to organize and conduct field trips. *Australian Science Teacher Journal*, 44, 43–50.

Miettinen, R. (2000). The concept of experiential learning and John Dewcy's theory of reflective thought and action. *International Journal of Life Long Education*, 19(1), 54–72.

Miller-Day, M., Pettigrew, J., Hecht, M. L., Shin, Y. J.; Graham, J., & Krieger, J. (2013). How prevention curricula are taught under real-world conditions Types of and reasons for teacher curriculum adaptations. *Health Education*, 113(4), 324–344.

Minner, D. D., Levy, A. J., & Century, J. (2010). Inquiry-Based Science Instruction—What Is It and Does It Matter? Results from a Research Synthesis Years 1984 to 2002. *Journal of Research in Science Teaching*, 47(4), 474–496.

Moen, A., Mørch, A. I., & Paavola, S. (2012). Collaborative Knowledge Creation: Introduction. In A. Moen, A.I. Mørch & S. Paavola (Eds). *Collaborative Knowledge Creation*. Sense Publisher, Rotterdam, The Netherlands. ix–xv.

Morgan, A. (2013). Deliverable 8.2. INQUIRE, External Evaluation: Final Report. http://www.inquirebotany.org/en/resources/categories/inquire-project-reports-and-resources-33.html, Accessed 1 April 2014

Morris, J. A. (2013). Exploring Exemplary elementary Teachers' Conceptions and Implementation of Inquiry Science. *Journal of Science Teacher Education, 24*, 573–588.

National Research Council. (1996). *National Science Education Standards.* Washington, DC:

National Research Council. (2000). *Inquiry and the National Science Education Standards.* Washington, DC: The National Academies Press.

Nonaka, I., & Takeuchi, H. (1995), *The Knowledge-Creating Company*, Oxford University Press, New York, NY.

Norman, D. A. (1993). *Things that make us smart: defending human attributes in the age of the machine.* Reading: Addison-Wesley.

Norris, S. P. (1997). Intellectual independence of non-scientists and other content-transcendent goals of science Education. *Science Education*, 81, 239.

Norum, K. E. (2008). Artifact Analysis. The SAGE Encyclopaedia of Qualitative Research Methods. http://srmo.sagepub.com/view/sage-encyc-qualitative-research-methods/n14.xml Accessed 2 March 2014.

OECD (1999). Measuring Student Knowledge and Skills – A New Framework for Assessment, Organisation for Economic Co-Operation and Development. OECD. http://www.oecd.org/edu/school/programmeforinternationalstudentassessmentpisa/33693997.pdf Accessed 1 April 2014.

OECD (2007). PISA 2006 Science Competencies for Tomorrow's World, Volume 1. OECD. http://www.oecdilibrary.org/docserver/download/9807011e.pdf?expires=1396635932&id=id&accname=ocid56025002&checksum=07504ECA78CD8B26DA83EA2FD604A1C5 Accessed 1 April 2014

OECD (2010). The Nature of Learning: Using Research to Inspire Practice, OECD Centre for Educational Research and Innovation. http://www.oecd.org/edu/ceri/thenatureoflearningusingresearchtoinspirepractice.htm Accessed 2 August 2013.

OECD (2012). PISA in Focus 2012/04 How "green" are today's 15-years-olds? http://www.oecd.org/pisa/pisaproducts/pisainfocus/50150271.pdf Accessed 4 April 2014.

OECD (2013). PISA 2012 Assessment and Analytical Framework. http://www.oecd-ilibrary.org/docserver/download/9813011e.pdf?expires=1397861625&id=id&accname=ocid56025002&checksum=EBDD744E5998E9288ECC3F20D9EABBB0 Accessed 1 April 2014.

Osborne, J. & Dillon, J. (2008). Science Education in Europe: Critical Reflections. A Report to the Nuffield Foundation, Kings College London. http://www.nuffieldfoundation.org/sites/default/files/files/Sci_Ed_in_Europe_Report_Final(1).pdf Accessed 1 April 2014

Osborne, J. & Dillon, J. (ed) (2010). *Good Practice in Science Teaching.* Open University Press, McGraw-Hill Education, Berkshire, UK.

Österlind, K. (2005). Concept formation in environmental Education: 14 year olds' work on the intensified greenhouse effect and the depletion of the ozone layer. *International Journal of Science Education*, 27(8), 891–908.

Paavola, S., Lipponen, L., & Hakkarainen, K. (2004). Models of Innovative Knowledge Communities and three Metaphors of Learning. *Review of Educational Research*, 74(4), 557–576.

Paetau, M. (2001). Sustainability Networks and the Emergence of Knowledge. Paper presented at the third international conference on socio-cybernetics, Leon, Mexico, June 24 – July 1, 2001. www.unizar.es/sociocybernetics Accessed 6 August 2013.

Palmer, D. H. (2009). Student interest generated during an inquiry skills lesson. Journal of Research in Science Teaching, 46(2), 147–165.

Papert, S. (1993). *The children's machine: rethinking school in the age of the computer.* New York Basic books, USA.

Papousek, H., & Papousek, M. (2002). Intuitive Parenting. In M. H. Bronstein (Ed.). *Handbook of parenting* (pp. 183–206), Second Edition, Volume 2, biology and Ecology of Parenting. Lawrence Erlbaum Associates, Publisher. Mahwah, New Jersey, London.

Patterson, L., & Harbor, J. (2005). Using assessment to evaluate and improve inquiry-based geo-environmental science activities: Case study of a middle school watershed E. coli investigation. *Journal of Geoscience Education*, 53, 201–214.

Peacock, A., & Bowker, R. (2001). Thinking of Eden: Developing children's thinking about sustainability at the Eden Project. *Teaching Thinking*, 5, 22–24.

Peacock, A., & Pratt, N. (2011). How young people respond to learning spaces outside school: A sociocultural perspective. *Learning Environment Research*, 14, 11–24.

Petrosino, A. J. (1998). *The use of reflection and revision in hands-on experimental activities by at risk-children.* Unpublished doctoral dissertation. Vanderbilt University, Nashville, TN.

Pettigrew, A. (1990). Longitudinal Field Research on Change. Theory and Practice. *Organization Science*, 1(3), Special Issue: Longitudinal Field Research Methods for Studying Processes of Organisational Change, 267–292.

Phillips, M., Finkelstein, D., & Wever-Frerichs, S. (2007). School Site to Museum Floor: How informal science institutions work with schools. *International Journal of Science Education*, 29(12), 1489–1507.

Pollard, A., Anderson, J., Maddock, M., Swaffield, S., Warin, J., & Warwick, P. (2008). *Reflective Teaching evidence-informed professional practice.* Third Edition Continuum International Publishing Group, London, New York.

Pope, M. L., & Gilbert, J. K. (1983) Explanation and metaphor: some empirical questions in science education. *European Journal of Science Education*, 5, 249–261

Price, S., & Hein, G. E. (1991). More than a field trip: Science programmes for elementary school groups at museums. *International Journal of Science Education*, 13, 505–519.

Rebar, B. M. (2012). Teachers' sources of knowledge for field trip practices. *Learning Environments Research*, 15(1), 81–102.

Regan, E., & Dillon, J. (2013). Final Quality Management Report, Deliverable Nr.7.2. of the INQUIRE Project. Published on the project website: www.inquirebotany.com.

Reinhold, P. (1997). *Integrierte naturwissenschaftliche Grundbildung, Lehrerfallstudie zur Unterrichtspraxis.* IPN Leibnitz-Institut f. d. Pädagogik d. Naturwissenschaften an d. Universität Kiel, BRD.

Richards, J. H., & Lee, D. W. (2002). "To see . . . Heaven in a Wild flower". . . Teaching botany in the 21st century. *American Journal of Botany*, 89, 172–176.

Rickinson, M., Dillon, J., Teamey, K., Morris, M., Choi, M. Y., Sanders, D., & Benefield, P. (2004). *A review of research on outdoor learning.* Preston Montford, Shropshire: Field Studies Council.

Rocard, M. (2007). Science Education Now: A Renewed Pedagogy for the Future of Europe. http://www.eesc.europa.eu/resources/docs/rapportrocardfinal.pdf Accessed 6 April 2014.

Roehring, G. H., & Luft, J. A. (2004). Constraints experienced by beginning secondary science teachers in implementing scientific inquiry lessons. *International Journal of Science Education*, 26(1), 3–24.

Rost, J., Senkbeil, M., Walter, O., Carstensen, C. H., & Prenzel M. (2005). Naturwissenschaftliche Grundbildung im Ländervergleich. In: PISA-Konsortium Deutschland (Eds.) (2005). *PISA 2003, Der zweite Vergleich der Länder in Deutschland- Was wissen und können Jugendliche.* Waxman Verlag GmbH, Münster.

Sadler, D. T., Burgin, S., McKinney, L., & Ponjuan, L. (2010). Learning Science through Research Apprenticeships: A Critical Review of the Literature. *Journal of Research in Science Teaching*, 47(3), 235–256.

Sammons, P., Day, C., Kington, A., Gu, Q., Stobart, G., & Smees, R. (2007). Exploring variations in teachers' work, lives and their effects on pupils: Key findings and implications from a longitudinal mixed method study. *British Educational Research Journal*, 33(5), 681–701.

Sanders, D. L. (2007). Making Public the Private Life of Plants: The contribution of informal learning environments. *International Journal of Science Education*, 29(10), 1209–1228.

Sandoval, W. A., & Bell, P. (2004). Design-Based Research Methods for Studying Learning in Context: Introduction. *Educational Psychologist*, 39(4), 199–201.

Sawyer, R. K. (2006). Introduction. In R. K. Sawyer (Ed.). *The Cambridge Handbook of The Learning Sciences.* Cambridge University Press, New York. 1–18.

Sawyer, R. K. (2008). Optimising Learning Implications of Learning Science Research. In OECD: *Innovation to Learn, Learning to Innovate* (pp. 45–65). Center for Educational Research and Innovation.

Schmelzing, S., Wüsten, S., Sandmann, A., & Neuhaus, B. (2010). Fachdidaktisches Wissen und Reflektieren im Querschnitt der Biologielehrerbildung. *Zeitschrift für Didaktik der Naturwissenschaften*, 16, 189–207.

Schneider, R. M., & Plasman, K. (2011). Science Teacher Learning Progressions: A Review of Science teachers' pedagogical Content Knowledge development. *Review of Education Research*, 81(4), 530–565.

Schratz, M., & Westfall-Greiter, T. (2010). *Schulqualität sichern und weiterentwickeln*. Germany: Klett/Kallmeyer.

Schreiner, C., & Schwantner, U. (2009). *PISA 2006 Österreichischer Expertenbericht zum Naturwissenschaftsschwerpunkt*. Leykam, Graz, Austria.

Schwartz, D. L., & Martin, T. (2004). *Inventing to prepare for Future Learning: The hidden Efficiency of encouraging Original Student Production in Statistics Introduction, Cognition and Instruction*, 22(2), 129–184.

Sellemann, D., & Bogner, F. X. (2013). Climate change education: quantitatively assessing the impact of a botanical garden as an informal learning environment. *Environmental Education Research*, 19(4), 415–429.

Sfard, A. (1998). On Two Metaphors for Learning and the Dangers of Choosing Just One. *Educational Researcher*, 27(2), 4–13.

Shulman, L. S., (1987). Knowledge and Teaching, Foundations of the New Reform. *Harvard Educational Review*, 57(1), 1–21.

Shulman, L. S., (1998a). Theory, Practice and the Education of Professionals. *The Elementary School Journal*, 98(5), 511–526.

Shulman, L. (1998b). Teacher Portfolios: A Theoretical Activity, In N. Lyons (Ed.) *With Portfolio in Hand: Validating the New teacher Professionalism* (pp. 23–37), New York: Teachers College Press.

Shulman, L.S., & Shulman, J. H. (2004). How and what teachers learn: a shifting perspective. *Journal of Curriculum Studies,* 36(2), 257–271.

Simpson, M. G. (2006). *Plant Systematics*. Elsevier Academic Press Burlington, MA, USA.

Sjøberg, S., & Schreiner, C. (2010). The ROSE project: An overview and key findings. http://roseproject.no/network/countries/norway/eng/nor-Sjoberg-Schreiner-overview-2010.pdf Accessed 6 April 2014.

Slavin, R. (1991). Synthesis of Research on Co-operative Learning. *Educational Leadership*, 48(5), 71–82.

Splitter, V., & Seidl, D. (2011). Does Practice-Based Research on Strategy Lead to Practically Relevant Knowledge? Implications of a Bourdieusian Perspective. *The Journal of Applied Behavioral Science*, 47(1), 98–120.

Squires, G. (1999). *Teaching as a Professional Discipline*. Falmer Press, Taylor & Francis Group, London UK.

Standish, A. (2012). *The False Promise of Global Learning. Why Education Needs Boundaries*. Continuum International Publishing Group, London New York.

Starkey, K., Tempest, S., & McKinley, A. (Eds.) (2004). *How organisations learn. Managing the search for knowledge*. 2nd Edition. Thomson, UK.

Storksdieck, M., Werner, M., & Kaul. V. (2006). *Results from the Quality Field Trip Study: Assessing the LEAD program in Cleveland, Ohio*. Annapolis, MD: Institute for Learning Innovation.

Strgar, J. (2007). Increasing the interest of students in plants. *Journal of Biology Education*, 42(1), 1–5.

Strike, K. A., & Posner, G. J. (1985). A conceptual change view of learning and understanding. In L. H. T. West & A. L. Pines (Eds.), *Cognitive structure and conceptual change* (pp. 211–231). New York: Academic Press.

Taber, K. S. (2007). *Classroom-based Research and Evidence-based Practice*. Sage Publications, Los Angeles, London, New Delhi, Singapore.

Tal, R. T., Bamberger, Y., & Morag, O. (2005). Guided school visits to natural history museums in Israel: Teachers' roles. *Science Education*, 89, 920–935.

Timperley, H., Wilson, A., Barrar, H., & Fung, I. (2007). *Teacher Professional Learning and Development*. Wellington, New Zealand: New Zealand Ministry of Education.

Thomas, J. W. (2000). *A review of Project Based Learning*, report prepared for Autodesk Foundation, San Rafael, CA.

Tran, L. U. (2007). Teaching Science in Museums: The Pedagogy and Goals of Museum Educators. *Science Education,* 91, 278–297.

Tran, L. U. (2008). The work of science museum educators. *Museum Management and Curatorship*, 23(2), 135–153.

Tran, L. U., & King, H. (2011). Teaching Science in Informal Environments: Pedagogical Knowledge for Informal Educators. In D. Corrigan, J. Dillon & R. Gunstone (Eds.).*The Professional Knowledge Base of Science Teaching*. Springer Dordrecht Heidelberg London New York, 279–293.

Thorlindsson, T., & Vilhjalmsson, R. (2003). Introduction to the Special Issue: Science Knowledge and Society. *Acta Sociologica*, 46(2), 99–105.

Tunnicliffe, S. D. (1996). A comparison of conversations of primary school groups at animated, preserved and live animal specimens. *Journal of Biological Education*, 30, 195–206.

Tunnicliffe, S. D., & Reiss, M. J. (2000). Building a model of the environment: how do children see plants? *Journal of Biological Education*, 34, 172–177.

UNCED (1992). Agenda 21: Chapter 36. Rio de Janeiro: United Nations Conference on Environment and Development. http://www.iisd.org/rio+5/agenda/chp36.htm Accessed 5 August 2013.

Van Aalst, H. F. (2003). Networking in Society, Organisations and Education. In OECD (Eds.) (2003). Networks of Innovation, Towards New Models for Managing Schools and Systems. https://www1.oecd.org/site/schoolingfortomorrowknowledgebase/themes/innovation/4128351.pdf Accessed 6 April 2014.

VanDriel, J. (2010). Professional Learning of Science Teachers. In C. Bruguiére, A. Tiberghien & P. Clément (eds). *Topics and Trends in Current Science Education* (pp. 139–159), Springer.

Van Oers, B. (1998). From context to contextualizing. In E. Forman & B. van Oers (eds.), *Mathematics learning in sociocultural contexts. Special issue of Learning and Instruction* (pp. 473–488), 8(6).

Venville, G. & Dawson, V. (Eds.) (2012). *The art of teaching science: for middle and secondary school.* Second Edition, Allen & Unwin, Sidney, Melbourne, Auckland, London.

Vergou, A. (2010). *An Exploration of Botanic Garden – School Collaborations and Student Environmental Learning Experiences.* Thesis (Doctor of Philosophy (PhD)). University of Bath.

Vieluf, S., Kaplan, D., Klieme, E., & Bayer, S. (2012). Teaching Practices and Pedagogical Innovation, Evidence from TALIS, OECD Publishing, Http://dx.doi.org/10.1787/9789264123540-en Accessed 6 April 2014

Vygotsky, L. S. (1978). *Mind in Society: the development of higher psychological processes.* Cambridge, Harvard University Press.

Vygotsky, L. S. (1966). Development of higher mental functions. In A. N. Leontyev, A. R. Luria and A. Smirnov (Eds.) *Psychological Research in the USSR.* Moscow: Progress Publishers.

Vygotsky, L. (1981). The instrumental method in psychology. In J. Wertsch (Ed.), *The concept of activity in Soviet psychology* (pp. 134–143). Armonk, NY: Sharpe. Wade, R. (1984–1985). What makes a difference in in-service teacher education? A meta-analysis of research. *Educational Leadership*, 42(4), 48–54.

Wandersee, J. H., & Schussler, E. E. (2001). Towards a theory of plant blindness. *Plant Sciene Bulletin*, 47(1), pp 2–9.

Wandersee, J. & Clary, R. (2006). Advances in research towards a theory of plant blindness. *Proceedings of the 6th International Congress on Education in Botanic Gardens*, Oxford, England, 10–14 September 2006.

Weber, S. (2008). Intercultural learning in business and human resource education. In Nijhof, W. J., & Nieuwenhuis, L. F. M. (Eds.), *The Learning Potential of the Workplace* (pp. 47–69), Rotterdam, Netherlands: Senge.

Weibell, C. J. (2011). Principles of learning: 7 principles to guide student-centered, personalized learning in the technology-enhanced, blended learning environment. http://principlesoflearning.wordpress.com. Accessed 29 November 2013.

Wellington, J. (Ed.) (1998). *Practical Work in School Science. Which Way Now?* London: Routledge.

Wenger, E. (1998). *Communities of Practice: Learning, Meaning and Identity.* Cambridge University Press. Cambridge.

Wenger, E. (2000) Communities of practice and social learning systems. *Organisations*, 7(2), 225–246.

Wenger, E., McDermott, R., & Snyder, W. M. (2002). *Cultivating Communities of Practice*, New York: HBS Press.

Wertsch, J. V. (1998). *Mind as Action.* New York, Oxford University Press.

Wichmann, A., & Leutner, D. (2009). Inquiry learning. Multilevel support with respect to inquiry, explanations and regulation during an inquiry cycle. *Zeitschrift für Pädagogische Psychologie*, 23(2), 117–127.

Wilde, M. & Urhahne, D. (2008). Museum learning: A study of motivation and learning achievement. *Journal of Biological Education*, 42, 78–83.

Yakhelf, A. (2010). The three facets of knowledge: A critique of the practice-based learning theory. *Research Policy*, 39, 39–46.

Zint, M. (2012). Advancing environmental education programs: Insights from a review of behavioral outcome evaluations. In Brody, M, Dillon, J., Stephenson, B., and Wals, A. (Eds.), *International Handbook of Research in Environmental Education*. Routledge, New York, NY.

6. Lists of Figures and Tables

Figure 1	Common reformulation of Vygotsky's mediated act	25
Figure 2	The structure of a human activity system	25
Figure 3	Two interacting activity systems as minimal model for the third generation of activity theory	26
Figure 4	The expansive learning cycle	28
Figure 5	STEM related training offers at the Pedagogical College in Tirol	89
Figure 6	Dewey's model of reflective thought and action	93
Figure 7	Reflection took place on 3 levels	106
Figure 8	Project progress	114
Figure 9	Project countries	130
Figure 10	Mediating activity in INQUIRE	136
Figure 11	The INQUIRE project activity system	137
Figure 12	The Spanish partner activity system	143

Table 1	Aspects of teacher competence (EU Expert Group, 2013, p. 45)	81–82
Table 2	Science teacher pedagogical content knowledge (PCK), aspects and categories	84
Table 3	Summary table of project objectives	112
Table 4	Work package summary	117
Table 5	Data source	139–140

www.ingramcontent.com/pod-product-compliance
Lightning Source LLC
Chambersburg PA
CBHW042142160426
43201CB00022B/2377